Compquest Volume 2

Compquest Volume 2

In Search of Computer Literacy

Jay S. Lurie

Writers Club Press

San Jose New York Lincoln Shanghai

Compquest Volume 2
In Search of Computer Literacy

All Rights Reserved © 2001 by Jay S. Lurie

Writers Club Press
an imprint of iUniverse.com, Inc.

For information address:
iUniverse.com, Inc.
5220 S 16th, Ste. 200
Lincoln, NE 68512
www.iuniverse.com

This publication contains the opinions and ideas of its author. It is intended to provide helpful and informative material on the subject matter covered. If the reader requires personal assistance or advice, a competent professional should be sought.

The author and publisher specifically disclaim any responsibility for any liability, loss or risk, personal or otherwise, which is incurred as a consequence, directly or indirectly, of the use and application of any of the contents of this book.

ISBN: 0-595-17588-0

Printed in the United States of America

I dedicate this book to my daughter, Haley.

Contents

List of Illustrations

Acknowledgements

I want to thank my wife Angie for her patience during all the time that it took me to write this book when I seemingly may have ignored her. I also thank her for helping me at times do some of the more menial tasks required in bringing this book to print.

Introduction

Compquest Volume 2 is geared towards an intermediate computer user—at least someone that knows the basics. It is certainly not a prerequisite to read volume 1 to understand this one, but it would be advisable to read it if you don't know anything about computers. Although the 2nd volume is a natural sequel to the 1st, they are written as separate entities for the most part. Therefore, someone that knows computer fundamentals may want to dive right into volume 2. It can be read as a standalone book, but the 2 volumes do share some resources and have other obvious affiliations of a 2-volume set. For example, volume 2 starts at chapter 16 instead of chapter 1.

Whether you are new to computers or an old timer, you are probably aware that computers can be very frustrating. Just keep in mind that when you endure a frustrating problem on a computer, you will come out a little bit wiser at the end when you finally figure it out. And you will figure it out. Don't give up and keep on trying.

One main difference between a novice computer user and an intermediate or expert user is the level of acceptance with computer quirks. A novice will get frustrated with any little error message that they run across on a computer; a savvy user may get frustrated from certain illegal operations and the like, but they know in the back of their mind that that's the nature of computers. Of course, the level of difficulty will differ between a novice and an expert. A brand new computer user may get frustrated because they can't tell when to single-click or when to double-click the mouse. An intermediate or expert computer user may get frustrated at some sort of hardware conflict or something of that nature.

Remember that not only should you not give up, but most computer problems have a fairly easy solution. Notice that I said most and not all. If you know basically how a computer works and have an understanding of your hardware, you will usually be able to methodically figure out problems that you encounter. I have run into many problems that I couldn't figure out right away. I figured them out either by trial and error, asking my colleagues, calling tech support, or by just figuring them out on my own. If I am stumped, I find it helpful to walk away for a while and do something else; sometimes, I even need to sleep on it. In many cases, the solution will dawn on me out of the blue.

Just a couple of months ago I was networking 2 systems and I was running into all sorts of small hurdles along the way. Although some strange unanticipated things were happening with the hardware, I managed to jump all of the hurdles that the pesky peripherals placed in my path. At the same time, I was installing a large hard drive, moving a small hard drive to another machine, and generally playing musical hard drives.

I finally got everything installed—2 network cards in one machine and 1 in the other—and I was pretty satisfied that everything was properly configured and yet I could not get the computers to communicate with each other. I checked all the settings, checked them again, reinstalled software, hardware, and racked my brain. Finally, I tried a new cable and guess what? It worked! I was glad to find out that the problem was so simple, and yet I felt a little foolish. I could have been up and running about 2 hours sooner if I had just tried a different cable. The thing about it was that a crossover cable, that will directly connect 2 computers, looked similar to another cable called a CAT 5. The CAT 5 cable is just slightly thicker, and I accidentally bought a CAT 5 and a crossover cable when I meant to buy 2 crossover cables. The point I am trying to make is that what appeared to be a complex problem turned out to be simple. When you are troubleshooting a computer, start with the easiest or most likely fix first.

If that doesn't work, go to the 2nd most likely thing and so on. Don't try too many things at once because you may have a hard time identifying what actually fixed a problem; don't overlook the obvious!

There is a lot of information that is in store for you in this book squeezed into only 10 chapters. The first 2 chapters of this book, Chapter 16 and 16.5, together really comprise 1 monster of a chapter. They probably could be a small book in themselves. After those 2 chapters, it is all downhill—until Chapter 25 anyway, but that is the last chapter and it mainly encompasses hardware and it's the epilogue rolled into one.

I believe that you will learn a lot from reading this book unless you are a proclaimed computer expert already. I enjoyed writing it and I hope you enjoy reading it. At any rate, I want to personally thank you for taking your time to read this book amongst all of the other books in this genre.

—Jay Lurie

Chapter #16

What is up with all the Folders in the Windows Explorer?

Let's explore your computer a little bit. You should not be ashamed to learn or ashamed that you have to learn. We are all learning. It seems like a lot of people set out thinking that they can't learn to operate a computer. If you have that mindset, you will not learn and you will continue to struggle doing routine tasks like sending e-mail or moving a file. This is not DOS commands or mapping a network drive here folks. So wake up and smell the 21st century. Computers are amongst us, and they are not going away. They will just increase in reliability from here, but they will be more complex and yet more user-friendly. There is one thing for sure that is another irony: Computers will enable many jobs to be eliminated and yet create more computer jobs; it will be more and more of a requirement for jobs in today's market and to get through life. Okay, I just wanted to get that off of my chest. And if that offends you, lighten up a little bit would ya?

AND WHAT'S WITH ALL THE ICONS ON THE DESKTOP?

Let's start on the Desktop. You already know what a few of the icons are. The Recycle bin is the garbage can (It's called that on a Mac computer); My Computer shows all of your drives, Printer, Dial-up networking, and Control panel. The icons on your Desktop will vary widely depending on what programs are installed on a particular system. You will typically have at least one icon that represents your ISP such as AOL, CompuServe,

Prodigy, etc. Also, on the Desktop may be seen AOL Instant Messenger, that looks like a little yellow man, Realplayer, games, Network Neighborhood, WinZip, My Briefcase, Outlook Express, and numerous others. You will typically have the Internet Explorer, which is your Web browser. Explorer enables you to view Web pages. It is NOT a connection. Most of the time there will be a bar that runs along the bottom of the Desktop. This could be on the side or even at the top of the screen. It consists of the Start button, *Taskbar*, *Systray*, and the ***Quick Launch Toolbar***. You will only have the Quick Launch Toolbar if you have Windows 98 or later. It is just what it sounds like; it provides a quick way to launch certain programs such as Internet Explorer.

TIP Recreate the Show Desktop shortcut from the Quick Launch toolbar:

If you accidentally delete the Show Desktop shortcut from the taskbar's Quick Launch toolbar, you can restore it by going to C:\WINDOWS\ Application Data\Microsoft \Internet Explorer\Quick Launch. Create a new text file with the following contents:

[Shell] Command= IconFile=explorer.exe,3 [Taskbar] Command=Toggle Desktop Save the file as SHOWDESKTOP.SCF. This will restore the shortcut. You can create a text file using Notepad. Click

Start>Programs>Accessories>Notepad. Type the contents above.

Click File>Save As on the toolbar. Where is says Save In, navigate

To the Quick Launch folder as stated. For File Name, type

SHOWDESKTOP.SCF.

TIP Add programs to the Quick Launch to make them one click away:

Presumably, you've got your favorite applications on the Start menu, so they're just two clicks away. Here's how to make them only one click away: Right-click on the Start button and select Open from the Context menu. Select all the shortcuts you want, and drag and drop all of them onto the Quick Launch Toolbar. There are 2 little arrows on the right of the Quick Launch Toolbar. If you click on the arrows, it will pop up a menu showing all of the programs that you may have added.

TIP Start Menu tricks:

Add a folder to the Start menu that holds all the documents you use frequently. Right-click on the Start button and choose Open. Then right-click on the folder background, choose New/Folder and give the new folder a name, like My Files. For permanent documents in other folders, drag and drop shortcuts into the new folder. Or just copy or create new documents right in the My Files folder. Either way, all you'll have to do is click on Start and open the My Files folder to access your most important files.

TIP Start Menu items:

Here's a tip that lets you put Start menu items in the order you want and also launch them with keystrokes. In Win95, Right-click on the Start button, then select Open. Rename each item by placing a number in front of it. Now you can open the Start menu by pressing Ctrl+Esc. Launch the program of your choice by simply pressing the associated number. For Win98, simply drag and drop items to place them in the order you want. Launch items by pressing Ctrl+Esc, then the letter of the item you want to launch, followed by the Enter key.

TIP Selectively delete items from the Documents menu:

The Documents menu lists the last 15 files that have been accessed. Normally, to delete things from the Documents menu on Windows 98, You click Start>Settings>Taskbar & Start Menu>Start Menu Programs>Clear under the Documents heading at the bottom of the window. On Windows Me, click Start>Settings>Taskbar and Start Menu>Advanced>Clear where it says *To remove records of recently accessed documents, programs, and Websites, click Clear.* (Why they did away with the and sign {&} and replaced it with the word *and* on Win Me I really don't know). The aforementioned methods are all or nothing at all when It comes to deleting the items on the Docs menu. If you

Want to selectively delete things, read on—The items on your Documents menu (Start/Documents) are really just shortcuts in your C:\WINDOWS\RECENT folder. You can selectively delete items there by opening the folder and deleting the shortcuts you don't want.

Internet Explorer and Internet Connections:

If you are an AOL or a CompuServe 2000 member, you need to sign on and minimize the program to launch Internet Explorer. Just sign on as usual, then minimize the program by clicking the minus (-) sign in the upper-right corner next to the square and the (**X**). This connection resembles a direct connection to the Internet and that's why you want to choose that option when configuring software that requires a connection to the 'Net if you have either of those services. Programs such as Outlook or Outlook Express, Quicken, Norton's update, Windows update, Turbo Tax, Camera software, and games often require an Internet connection. The other option that these programs requiring an Internet connection may have as a choice is something like "Connect using a modem" or "Always dial my default connection." You want to select the option that says "Connect using a LAN (Local Area Network)," "I have a direct Internet connection," or something similar, when configuring any program that requires an Internet connection and you are using AOL or CompuServe 2000.

The reason why you do not choose the modem option that may be something like "Always dial my connection," "Connect using a modem," or "I have a dial-up connection," is because that is the setting that you would choose to set up Internet software if your ISP uses ***Dial-up networking***. Dial-up networking is the Microsoft Windows dialer. Some programs have a proprietary dialer, meaning that they have one built in, and they do not rely on the one that comes packaged with Windows. However, some other programs, and most general purpose ISPs (A connection and maybe a mail client), use DUN (Dial-up networking). You can configure DUN so that when you click on a browser, or another program that requires an Internet connection, it will bring up a sign-on screen. You'll be prompted for your user ID and your password. Then it will log you onto your ISP and launch the Web browser.

In My Computer, there is usually an A drive which is your 3 ½" floppy and a C drive which is the main drive or hard drive inside of your computer (the tower unit). The hard drive is usually a box that's about 1¼" thick 4" wide and 7" long (**fig. 51**). It contains metal plates or disks called platters that magnetically hold information. These disks spin at a high rate of speed. A fast drive will turn at 7200 rpm, and a lightning fast one these days will spin at 10,000 rpm. You are going to pay about

$600-$1000 but if you want speed, go for something like the Seagate Cheetah ***SCSI*** (Small Computer System Interface pronounced "scuzzy"), and you will scream at just over 10,000 rpms (revolutions per minute).

Fig. 51 20 GB Western Digital hard drive shown.

IS IT FIXED OR IS IT MEMOREX?

Other than the floppy drive and hard drive, you will usually have a CD-ROM drive or a CD Rewriteable drive. A CD-ROM can only play CDs, and a Rewriteable can play CDs and copy files to a Rewriteable CD. You may have some other form of **removable media**. Removable media refers to anything that isn't a **fixed disk**. A fixed disk is your C drive-it is the main drive that holds the majority of your information. You may have a 2nd fixed disk or more. Fixed means that you can't just eject a disk out of the drive and take it to another location such as with a CD-ROM or floppy drive; it is more or less a permanent fixture on your computer.

A possible configuration might be a 2nd physical hard drive, with those 2 drives partitioned. If 2 drives were each partitioned in half, you would have 4 pieces. That would be C, D, E, and F drives, respectively. Therefore, it would push your CD-ROM drive up to G. You can partition a drive in all kinds of configurations, but it is common to partition a drive in half to make 2 virtual drives of the same size out of one drive. If your 1st hard drive has filled up, you can get a 2nd physical drive which will become drive D. This would push the CD-ROM up to drive E. This letter-switching will usually occur automatically; it is part of plug & play. Windows is usually pretty good about these things, but sometimes it is necessary to set these drive letters manually.

Dial-up networking provides you a way to dial up to remote servers such as your ISPs. It also is capable of *VPN* (Virtual Private Networking) which will connect you directly to another computer. So if you want to share files on 2 different computers, this may be an option. For more information about VPN, see Windows HELP. Click **Start>Help** and search for VPN.

TIP Ways to share files between computers:

Besides networking systems and Virtual Private Networking, you can share files between computers by using some software programs that are available on the market. Two of the well-known ones are Laplink and PC Anywhere. These programs allow you to directly dial into a computer from another computer using a modem. You can then view the contents of the drives of both computers in a Windows-Explorer-type-view. You can then drag and drop files from computer to computer just like you can manipulate files in the Windows Explorer. These programs are excellent easy solutions to copy large files from one computer to another if your files are too large to fit on a floppy disk and you don't have any larger form of removable media such as a CD burner.

The printer icon is pretty obvious, and the control panel we will talk about after the Windows Explorer. There is a lot in there, and it is where you can make many configuration changes and adjustments to your computer. Usually the only other thing that will be in My Computer is a Scheduled Task icon that allows you to schedule certain maintenance programs on your computer to make them occur at a specified time without you being there. You can set any program to launch automatically from the scheduled tasks folder. You will only have this feature if you have Windows version 98 or above.

TIP Computer maintenance:

You can keep your hard drive running smoothly by running scandisk and disk defragmenter on a regular basis. These should be done about 4 times a year, and if you install and uninstall a lot of programs, you should probably do them monthly. Click Start>Run. On the Run line type scandisk and click Ok. Make sure that the C drive is selected, click inside the circle to select Thorough, and make sure that the Automatically Fix Errors box is checked. Then just click Start. After that is done, close the scandisk window and Click Start>Run again. Erase scandisk from the line and type in defrag and click Ok. Again, make sure that the C drive is selected and click on Start. Windows 95 has a bad habit of always saying that you don't have to run a Defrag, but run it anyway because it won't hurt even if you don't really need to run one. After running both of these, shut down the computer all the way and wait at least 10 seconds and boot back up. You can keep your hard drive fit & trim by running Disk Cleanup if you have Windows 98 or above. Click Start> Programs>Accessories>System Tools>Disk Cleanup. Make Sure that C Drive is selected (it should be already) and click Ok. Put a check in every checkbox, unless you have a good reason to leave some of the files on the system, and click Ok. This will remove files that just take up space that you don't really need such as your temporary files and the files in the recycle bin.

TIP Advanced Computer maintenance:

When you're done with programs and uninstall them, the uninstall routine will not always remove them completely. These fragments left behind may cause problems down the line. Here are tips to cleaning up after a program is uninstalled. The programs I refer to are only available in Windows 98, 98SE, and Me.

A) Check the file folder that contained the original program. Often saved games or character files remain on the computer even after uninstalling them. Delete the lingering folder and regain some disk space.

B) Check your startup folder using msconfig.exe. Many programs will leave "stubs" in this folder, even after they're removed. Unchecking the startup program in msconfig will regain system resources and you may find all manner of useless stuff that can be easily shutoff without having to resort to editing your registry. See the tip at the end of Chapter 25, *Using MSConfig*, for details about using this utility.

C) Use System File Checker (sfc.exe) and Version Checker (vcmui.exe) to assure that your system files have not been corrupted, deleted or changed by an install/uninstall routine. Games are notorious for installing old versions of DirectX over a newer one. This can cause video, sound and joystick problems that can be easily cured by checking for and restoring the files with the most recent file version number and or date. Don't pay too much attention to file dates as they sometimes are erroneously saved as the date they were installed, not the create date.

D) Run dxdiag.exe if you have problems that you know are related to DirectX. You can see if your drivers are up to date, check to see if they are working properly and change some default DX settings for compatibilty. If DXDiag says the driver is uncertified, don't worry too much unless you know the driver is the problem, "certified drivers" are not usually the most recent or best for your games. These utilities will improve the performance of Windows and help overcome problems that stem from incomplete uninstallers.

EXPLORING WINDOWS EXPLORER

The Windows Explorer is intended to give you a birds-eye view of all of the files on your hard drive. You can view files on any drive in the Explorer as well. There are a few different ways to get to the Explorer: Click on **Start>Programs>Windows Explorer.** You can click on **Start>Run.** On the Run line type in **explorer** and click **Ok**, or you can hold down the Windows key (If you have a modern keyboard it will be in between **Ctrl** and **Alt** in the lower left corner of your keyboard) and hit the letter **E** at the same time. See **Appendix A**, *Shortcut Keys for Windows*, for more of these Windows-key shortcuts.

You can choose between several options of how to view the icons in Explorer. Do you want large icons or small icons? Just click the **View** button on the toolbar and select the different options such as **List**, **Details**, **Thumbnails**, **Large Icons**, or **Small Icons** and see which one you like the best.

Basically, the Explorer is a hierarchical view of the file structure. When you see a + sign next to a directory, it means that it can be expanded; it means that there are some contents inside of that directory. When you open up Explorer, look for the + sign next to My Computer and click on it. Remember that My Computer shows all of your drives, so it will drop down a list of all of your drives and there will then be a – sign next to My Computer, meaning that it is expanded to show all of the contents. Click on the + sign next to the C drive or Hard Drive. Now you will see all of the files on your main drive where Windows is installed.

Windows Explorer is a two-pane view, meaning that there is a left and a right side divided by a vertical scrollbar that scrolls the left-hand side; there is another scrollbar at the far right that controls the right side. When you click on a folder on the left, it will show all of the contents of that folder on the right-hand side. Notice that if you click on a folder on the left, it will not only show the contents on the right, but it will automatically turn the sign into a – on the left next to the folder that you clicked on, thus showing the contents on the left as well. This is provided that the folder you clicked on had a + sign next to it to begin with. Also, notice that if a folder doesn't have a + sign next to it, it will be necessary to click on it on the left to show the contents on the right window pane, but nothing will drop down underneath that file on the left. The reason why is that the + sign symbolizes that the folder is actually a directory that has some contents inside of it. If a folder doesn't have a +, it means that it is a folder and not a directory. A folder may have some other files in it even though it does not have a + sign next to it. You can find out by just single-clicking on a file on the left and see what comes up on the right. If the window is blank, then the folder is empty.

If you scroll down the left windowpane a little bit, you will eventually run into your Windows directory. Windows is usually a gigantic directory because this is where the actual Windows operating system is installed and all of its associated files. Another big one is the System directory that is located inside the Windows directory. System comprises a lot of the disk space that Windows takes up, but Windows itself is still much bigger than the System directory. A lot of the files that you will see in here are operating system files and they won't mean a whole lot to most people; most of them aren't like a program that will actually do anything or a text document that you can read. Some of them may open up in Notepad, or another text editor, but it will show what looks like gibberish because it is in programming language. Feel free to experiment here and open up some files. You won't harm the computer—just don't delete anything!

TIP Internet Explorer Setup Files:

When you install Internet Explorer 5.x on Win9x, a new folder will be created in your root directory called WINDOWS UPDATE SETUP FILES. The folder is filled with setup files that take up between 10MB and 20MB of space on your hard disk. It's a good idea to save them for a while after installing IE5 to make sure it's running properly. That way you won't have to download the program again if you need to reinstall. After using IE5 for a while without any problems, you can delete these files to regain the disk space.

Some items of interest in the Windows directory are the Temporary Internet Files, History, and Cookies. These 3 folders store various things that pertain to all of the Web sites that you have visited. The History folder contains a list of all of the WWW addresses that you have been to. These will usually be broken down into subfolders such as Today, Last Week, Monday, Tuesday, etc. You will need to open up those subfolders to actually see the Web addresses. The Temporary Internet Files folder contains HTML documents and graphics from the Web sites that you have visited. The Cookies folder contains cookies that Web sites plant on your computer. Sometimes, these are used for authentication when entering a secure Web site, and sometimes cookies are used for personalization. It is safe to delete the contents of any of these 3 directories that the Microsoft Internet Explorer uses to cache information from the Web sites that you visit. As a matter of fact, if you want to cover your tracks, you definitely want to delete the contents of the History, Cookies, and Temporary Internet Files directories. If you are trying to track down where someone has been on the Web, you should look in these directories—particularly the History.

A good article that will give you more insight into the subject matter discussed in Chapter 16 is **5***Windows File Management—Organizing Your Files & Folders Into A Logical Sequence*, noted in **Appendix S**, *Resources*.

Chapter 16.5

The Control panel

TIP Make Windows Me bare all:

Keep in mind that by default Windows Me will not show you all of Your Control Panel items, so it may appear to you as if things are missing when you open the Control Panel for the first time. Once you open Control Panel, just click the link over to the left that says *view all Control Panel options*.

Fig. 52 Control Panel

TIP Control Panel on the Start Menu:

Control Panel is one of the more frequently used folders in Windows, but it's not always easy to access. You can, however, make the Control Panel applets available directly from the Start menu. First, right-click on the Start button and choose Open. Then, right-click on the background area in the Start menu folder and choose New/Folder. Rename the folder with this string: Control Panel.{21EC2020-3AEA-1069-A2DD-08002B 30309D}

(Windows 95 users can copy and paste this filename from the TIPS.TXT file found in the Windows folder.) Press Enter. This will place Control Panel directly on the Start menu, with the applets appearing on a cascading menu that opens when you move the cursor over Control Panel. For frequently used Control Panel applets, make shortcuts to the applets and add them to the Start menu or the desktop.

You can create a cascading folder for Printers (and for Dial-Up Networking under Win95) as well. Right-click on Start and select Open, right-click on the folder background and choose New/Folder and then enter one of the following lines:

Printers.{2227A280-3AEA-1069-A2DE-08002B30309D}

Dial-Up Net.{992CFFA0-F557-101A-88EC-00DD010CCC48}

We will break down the control panel into sections since it is broken down into separate icons in Windows—perhaps 25 icons in Windows 98. I have 23 on this machine I am sitting at now. I have 31 control panel items on a machine with Windows Me on it. Each subsection of the control panel is called an *applet*. Are you ready for this?

Accessibility Options-Includes tools to change keyboard, sound, display, and mouse behavior for people with mobility, hearing, or visual impairments. This icon may not appear in the control panel if it has not been installed.

Add New Hardware-place where you can add new hardware if Windows doesn't detect it with it's plug & play interface. If you install a piece of hardware, like a sound card, Windows will usually detect the device and prompt you to put in the driver disk that came with it. It copies some files, namely the device drivers, and you are on your way. If you add new hardware to the computer and it does not detect any hardware upon boot up, you will need to open up Add New Hardware and click **Next**. Windows will then search for all new hardware. If you installed a modem and Windows does not detect it, you can use the Modems icon in the control panel to add the modem.

Add/Remove Programs-Usually you can just install a program from the CD, and it will even autorun a lot of times so you don't even have to click on the CD-ROM icon or type a command line like D:\setup to kick off the CD installer. However, if a program won't install any other way, you may want to try it here. If it won't install in Add/Remove Programs, you may have hardware difficulties or other software/hardware conflicts or complications such as a bad CD.

Add/Remove Programs also offers the option to uninstall programs safely. If a program is listed in there, and you want to remove it, it should be done through Add/Remove Programs. If a program isn't listed in Add/Remove, look for an uninstaller in the Programs directory. Sometimes, if the application is listed on the Programs menu (**Start>Programs**), you can hover your mouse over the application listing, and on the cascading menu to the right you may see an uninstall option.

Add/Remove has a Windows Setup tab at the top. Through Windows Setup, you can add components that may not have been installed with the original installation of Windows. One example is Accessibility Options mentioned before. You can add Games, Online Services, Virtual Private Networking, and numerous other things.

TIP Accessibility Options options:

Windows comes with a few options designed to make it more accessible to handicapped or injured users. One of these options is MouseKeys, which lets you move your mouse pointer with the numeric keypad on your keyboard. This is useful if you're recovering from a repetitive strain injury caused by overly vigorous use of your mouse, or you have a notebook on which you don't want to install a mouse. Turn on MouseKeys by double-clicking on the Accessibility Options icon in the Control Panel; then click on the Mouse tab and select Use MouseKeys.

TIP Make keys beep when hitting Caps Lock:

If you frequently hit the Caps Lock key by accident, open Control Panel's Accessibility Options applet and put a check in the Use ToggleKeys box on the Keyboard tab. Then select the General tab and clear the check box next to "Turn off accessibility features." From now on your computer will beep if you press the Caps Lock, Num Lock or Scroll Lock keys.

One other thing to mention about Add/Remove Programs: There is a Startup Disk button at the top next to Windows Setup. The Startup Disk allows you to create a boot floppy disk that can help you to boot the computer if it will not start normally. You may need this to reinstall Windows, and the disk will give you the option of Real Mode CD-ROM support if you boot the computer from the floppy. In layman's terms, you shut the computer down, put the floppy in the drive and turn it back on. Choose the option to boot with CD-ROM support and you will have access to your CD-ROM in DOS mode; Real Mode support means DOS support or that you will have access to your CD-ROM in DOS mode which is ordinarily not the case. It will bring you to an A prompt (**A:\>**) and all you would typically need to do to reinstall Windows is put your Windows CD in the CD-ROM drive and type D:\setup (where D= your CD-ROM drive letter). It would be advisable to make one of these startup disks before you find yourself locked out of your computer. It will require 1 blank floppy disk.

Date/Time-Give ya 3 guesses on this one. This is your clock. If your system clock in the lower-right corner of your Desktop has the wrong time this is where you go to set it. Don't forget to select the right time zone on the time zone tab and check the box at the bottom that says automatically adjust for daylights savings time.

Desktop Themes-This is a neat feature that was an add-on in Windows 98. In other words, this did not exist in Windows 95. Basically, you can choose from myriad themes including 60s USA which will put some psychedelic wallpaper on the Desktop, and Jungle will put a jungle scene on the Desktop and play sounds like a monkey screaming or a tiger growling in place of the sounds that Windows plays ordinarily. Or, you could try the Under Water theme, a personal favorite of mine. It kind of makes the Desktop look like a fish tank, and you will hear all sorts of underwater sounds. You can also preview the current Windows settings here and preview the screen saver.

Fig. 53 Display applet in Control Panel.

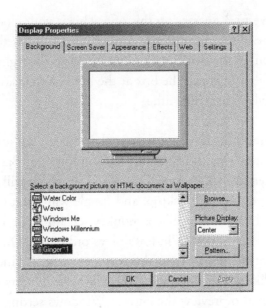

Display-You can make a lot of configuration changes to your video settings here.

Everything too big? Make all your icons smaller here. Or, if everything is too small for you to see, make your icons bigger here. Here's how to adjust your video settings:

To change the resolution on your screen, navigate to the control panel. **Start>Settings>Control Panel**. Double-click on the **Display** icon as shown in **fig. 53**. Click on the **Settings** tab at the top right. You will see a Desktop area setting. It will be something like 640x480. Slide the slide bar to the right to adjust this to say 800x600 then click **Apply** then **Ok**.

Restart the computer if asked or select "Apply this setting without restarting" if that option is offered. The larger the numbers, the smaller everything will be on your screen; 1024x768 will make everything very small. If the desired setting does not stick, then your video card will not support the resolution. You would need to contact your computer manufacturer in this case to update your video driver.

I like my Desktop area or resolution set at 800x600, but that's just me. However, most Web graphics are tailor made for the 800x600 resolution. But there's nothing wrong with running the 1024x768 option or whatever. You will just see more of the screen that way, but everything is going to be small. Also, you can select your color palette on the Settings tab. The lowest depth is usually 16 colors, then 256, High Color 16 bit, True color 24, and True color 32 bit, which is the most true-to-life setting; true color will render the on screen graphics using 16 million colors. Incidentally, when the video card needs an updated driver or there are other configuration problems, we often need to change to 256 colors because there may be times when the computer freezes up when it is set on True Color 24 or 32-bit. You really won't notice that much of a difference a lot of times at 256 colors unless you play high-end computer games or use AutoCAD. AutoCAD is a very sophisticated engineering and architectural tool. If you do notice a very grainy screen on 256 colors, that is another clue that you need an updated driver. One last note is if you don't have the correct driver installed for the video card in the first place, it may only have the choices of 2 colors and 8 colors in the Display control panel. This is because the video card is installed with the generic Windows driver, and it will only display on a very low color depth.

You may have various tabs at the top of the Display window depending on what type of video card that you have. If it is very sophisticated, there may be 16 tabs or even more. I have one on a computer that has 16 tabs in the Display applet. The video card on that computer is an 8MB Matrox

Millennium G200 AGP. I will only describe the tabs that most people will have in the Display control panel and like I have on this computer I am working on now. To adjust the video settings that we talked about so far, you would need to be on the Settings tab in the upper-right corner of the Display window. From here on out I will break the rest of the Display tabs down reading from right to left and elaborate on them:

Web-You can view your Active Desktop as a Web page; it is just what it sounds like. The Desktop will present the presence of a Web page. You can also put the Microsoft Internet Explorer channel bar on the Desktop. I find this sort of annoying, and it is really not that advantageous. Although if it works for you, go for it! The channel bar is a vertical bar that sits by default on the right-hand side of your Desktop. See fig. 54 for a peek at the channel bar. It is something that doesn't make much sense unless you are on a network or have a direct connection to the Internet. The channel bar promised to be pretty popular at one time as part of Microsoft's push technology. I don't think that it got off the ground like Microsoft expected, however. You can click on Folder Options at the bottom of the channel bar, and you will see 3 tabs at the top: 1) General 2) View 3) File Types. There are many options here, but they are beyond the scope of this chapter. You usually want to stay with the defaults anyway unless you have a good reason for changing something. If you do experiment here, just make 1 or 2 changes at a time and see what it does. The description there will basically tell you what it does, but at least if you just make 1 or 2 changes, it won't be that difficult to remember how to change things back if need be.

Fig. 54 Channel bar

Effects-This tab is where you can change the thumbnail picture for your icons. You also have various settings that you can adjust that are related to your icons. One thing to note is at the bottom under the **Visual Effects** heading is *Animate Windows, menus and lists*. If you have Windows Me, it will be *Use transition effects for menus and tooltips*. There are rare conditions where it might be necessary to disable this if you have certain display problems. Or you may not like the feel of animated Windows. In Windows 95, when the cascading menus come up, like when you click on **Start>Programs>Accessories**, they are rigid. On Windows 98, menus sort of glide because of the animated windows. The Windows kind of just "Snap to" in Windows 95 we would say. Gliding windows in Windows 98 might make you nauseous, however, and you will want to uncheck the animated windows checkbox.

Appearance-This is where you can actually change the way that windows appear. You can change things so that the title bar that runs across the top of every window is green instead of blue, for example. There is a **Scheme** drop-down list where you can choose from many different preset Windows colors such as High Contrast #1 that will make your background black and the title bar electric blue. Be careful of some of these schemes. If you make your background black, you may not be able to see black text on the screen in certain situations. It is a good idea to remember what the settings were, as it is when you make any changes to your computer, so you can change back if something that worked before suddenly stops working. Another important thing to note about this tab is that you can change the font that is used to label icons as well as myriad other tweaks you can make under the **Item** drop-down list. I have seen the standard font that Windows uses to label the icons get corrupted and either no text will appear beneath the icons or the text will be broken up or splotchy. All you generally need to do to fix this problem is to switch the font. Select **Icon** in the Item drop-down menu, and it will make the **Font** drop-down menu active. If you choose something in the Item drop-down that doesn't require a font, the font drop-down will be inactive (grayed out). In the Font drop-down, choose any other font, and if the text under the icons is still broken or faded, try Ariel Black {Western}; that will usually work every time.

Screen saver- This one is pretty obvious. You will have quite a few if you have at least Windows 98. You can tweak the options on a screen saver by clicking on **Settings** or click on **Preview** for a sneak peek. Also of interest may be the Power Saving features for your monitor. If your monitor shuts down after so many minutes, this is where you want to go to adjust it. Click on **Advanced** and check the box to show power meter on taskbar; you will then see a little plug with a wire attached to it down by the system clock in the lower-right corner. One thing to point out is how to add a screensaver to your system—a subject that came up a lot when I did tech support. As you know by now, all Windows files have a 3-letter extension. A screensaver has the extension .scr. See **Appendix E**, *File Extensions*, if you want to see more Windows file extensions. These will be located in **C:\Windows\System**, so you need to download a screensaver in that directory in order to be able to see it in the **Display>Screen saver** window. You can download the screensaver and move or copy it into the **C:\Windows\System** directory if you don't download it into there directly. Most of the time when you download something from the Web, like a screensaver, there will be instructions that accompany it. If things don't work as I have described, check those instructions because sometimes there are specific things that you need to do with a particular program to make it work.

TIP Get more info about your programs:

If you can't find info any other way on a program, most if not all, computer programs have a Readme.txt or Readme.1st file or something similar that is geared toward giving you basic setup instructions. It will also outline any major compatibility problems that have been noted with their particular program—such as this program will turn your screen black if you have a Voodoo Banshi video card. You need to update the driver for the card or it will not work properly with this program. You can find these types of text files in the programs root directory. A lot of times this is located in the Program Files folder. Just open up My Computer then the C drive and look for a folder called Program Files. Open that up and look in there for a folder that represents your program. When you open that up, you should be able to find at least one text file that will tell you a bit more about the program—it will tell you who the manufacturer is and how to contact them if your lucky. A text file can be denoted by what looks like a little pad of paper with what appears as written lines of text on it. Text files will open automatically in a program called Notepad that will already be installed on your computer.

Background is just the Desktop wallpaper, so I won't elaborate on that one too much. However, you may download backgrounds from the Web and want to incorporate them into your system just like a screen saver. All you need to do here is click on the **Browse** button and navigate to wherever you downloaded the background file. I should mention that you can gain quick access to the Display applet by right-clicking on your **Desktop** wallpaper and then left-click on **Properties**. Now on to the next control panel applet.

Fonts and Game Controllers-are the next 2 icons. You can download strange fonts from the Web that are stored in the Fonts applet. That way you could type e-mail in calligraphy or some other fancy font. Certain games might tell you to go to Game Controllers to configure settings that are needed for games. This applet may be called Gaming Options. There really isn't a whole lot more to say about these two.

Internet or Internet Options-This is where you can change the settings of your Internet Explorer. If it is labeled Internet, you have IE 4.x or earlier, and if the icon is named Internet Options you have IE 5.0 or above. The latest version of IE as of this writing is 5.5. **Appendix B**, *How to Set Internet Properties in the Control Panel,* outlines how to purge the cache and check other settings here. It outlines what settings you need for America Online or CompuServe 2000 or even a standard ISP. If you used to be able to get on the Web and now you can't, you need to follow the instructions to check your Internet settings.

The browser cache is a folder where your browser stores graphics and text from Web sites that you have previously visited. Storing visited Web sites this way makes future visits faster when you access that site again because some of the graphics are already stored on your hard drive. Graphics can load faster from your hard drive then they can from your modem—especially if you have an analog modem and not a cable modem or equivalent. The cache folder where these files are stored is **C:\Windows\Temporary Internet Files**. There are 2 other folders associated with the cache: History and Cookies. They both reside in the **C:\Windows** directory also. The History folder stores the history of all the WWW sites that you have been to, and the Cookies folder stores cookies that are distributed by some Web sites for personalization. **Appendix B** includes instructions to delete the files using Internet Options as well as deleting the files manually in the Windows Explorer as we talked about earlier in this chapter.

The next Control panel applet to note is Multimedia.

Multimedia-On the Audio tab you might want to select the box that says "Show volume control on the taskbar" if you have lost your sound and you know that your speakers are hooked up correctly. Right-click the little speaker in the lower-right corner next to the system clock. The speaker will present itself when you select the show volume control option. If the volume control is all the way down or on mute, you won't be able to hear anything even if you have your speakers turned on and hooked up correctly. Double-click on the speaker or right-click it and left-click on **Open Volume Controls**. This opens up a whole new window; you want to make sure that none of the mute boxes are checked at the bottom here either unless you want them to be.

Network-The only reason that you might want to go in here is if you can no longer get on the Internet or it loads a certain percentage of a Web site and then stops. The settings for the adapters in the Network control panel are outlined in **Appendix C**, *How to Set Up the Network Control Panel*. The only other thing this applet is good for is if you are actually configuring a network. A ***network*** is where 2 or more computers are physically hooked together as opposed to a ***standalone machine***.

*See instructions in **Appendix B**, *How to Set Internet Properties in the Control Panel*, for information concerning Internet settings for certain ISPs. The settings in the Internet control panel work hand in hand with the Network settings.

*Some ISPs require that you specify an IP address or they require other settings than the ones that I describe for a standard ISP in **Appendix C**. You may want to check with your particular ISP because it may be necessary to enter IP address numbers for the TCP/IP adapter, for example.

Passwords-this one allows you to set a password for Windows. The main purpose of this is so that several users can retain their Desktop settings. In other words, several people may each have their own password; logging on with each password would result in using that user's individual Desktop settings. So if Mary likes the screen resolution at 1024x768 but Lou is far-sighted and needs it large at 640x480, they can each log on with their individual passwords and won't have to keep changing the settings back and forth. Another applet called **Users** is kind of like a mirror or even an extension of the Passwords applet; basically these 2 applets work hand in hand. Compare the 2 applets in **fig. 55** & **fig. 56**.

Fig. 55 Passwords applet

Fig. 56 Users applet

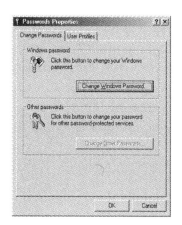

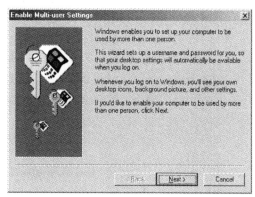

Power Management-A mirror image of what you get when you click on Settings on the Screen Saver tab in the Display properties. Again, this is where to set how long your monitor stays on before it automatically shuts down or where to set the time before the hard disk spins down.

Regional Settings-You can change the language to something other than English here. Also you can adjust the way the computer displays numbers, currency, time and date. Set the date for instance to display like dddd, MMMM dd yyyy like Monday, February 07, 2000 or MMMM dd, yyyy like February 07, 2000.

Sounds-You can change the sounds associated with certain events here. The Desktop themes will change your sound associations also. Have fun here. Be creative, but be careful.

System-This is a big one here. This is where you can make system-level changes to your computer. You can tweak nearly anything you want that relates to your computers hardware and overall performance. There are four tabs here that will be denoted in the ensuing paragraphs.

General-This tab shows the Windows version such as 4.00.950B, which is common for a Windows 95 version. One machine that I have is running Win 98 (Not 2nd Edition), and it is version 4.10.1998. Windows Me will typically be version 4.90.3000 (see **fig. 57**). This page also tells you the processor type. This can be Pentium (r) if it's a Pentium. It will say Pentium (r) II if it's a Pentium II; it can say other various things for the processor such as GenuineIntel.

Fig. 57 System applet General tab.

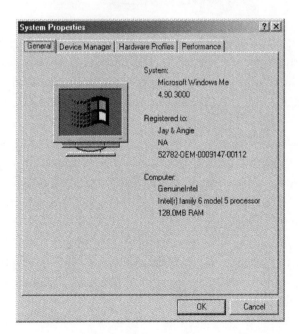

Device Manager-This tab lists all of your hardware. You really don't want to make changes here unless you are computer savvy. To go into great detail here is beyond the scope of this book. But one thing to note is that this is where you would usually go to update the driver for a component. Click on the little plus (+) sign in a little box to the left of one of the components. This will drop down everything in that list. For example, click the (+) sign next to modems or display adapter, which is your video card. Click on the individual device to highlight it and click **Properties** at the bottom. Click on the **Driver** tab at the top and then click on **update driver**.

You can also disable hardware in the Device Manager. You may need to do this at some point if you have a device (hardware) conflict. Instructions are covered in **Appendix Q**, *Instructions for Disabling Hardware*.

TIP Create a shortcut to Device Manager:

Here's a secret tip for creating a shortcut to the Device Manager: Right-click on the Desktop and choose New>Shortcut. Type C:\WINDOWS\CONTROL.EXE SYSDM.CPL,,1 in the Command Line box and click on Next. Name it Device Manager (or another name of your choice), then click on the Finish button. Assign a new icon to the shortcut as you would any other.

TIP How to create an icon:

Take any .BMP file, rename it to give it an .ICO extension, and voila! Instant icon. You access the file in the normal way: Right-click on the current icon for a shortcut, select Properties from the Context menu, select the Shortcut tab and click on the Change Icon button. Now use the Browse button to find your new one.

Hardware Profiles-You probably won't need to go here, but what you might use this for is to boot the same computer with a network configuration and boot as a standalone computer. Sometimes network software conflicts with certain other software, so you may want to boot with a standalone configuration when you plan to use software that conflicts with your network instead of disabling the network card. You could use hardware profiles to select which modem you wanted to use by default if you had 2 separate modems in the computer.

Performance-This page tells you the system resources expressed as a percentage like 83%. You generally want this to be at least 80%, and 85-90% is even better. You can gain access to the *virtual memory* settings from here. The Virtual Memory button will be at the bottom left on this screen, but you really don't want to specify your own virtual memory unless you are pretty familiar with computers. This can cause problems, but if you do specify your own virtual memory, you generally set the minimum and maximum at 2-3 times the amount of RAM. You will see the RAM at the top of the Performance tab. If it says MEMORY 64.0MB, you have 64 Megs of RAM. If it says 32.0MB RAM, you have 32 Megs of RAM, and if it says 128.0MB RAM, you have 128 Megs of RAM Memory. If you have 64 Megabytes of RAM, you would set the minimum and maximum to 2.5—3 times the RAM. 64 x 3 =192. You would want to set the min and max for the Virtual Memory to 192.

If you click on the **File System** tab at the bottom of the Performance window (next to the Virtual Memory button) you can change the typical role of the computer from Desktop to Network Server; you can do this even if your computer isn't on a network at all, and in some cases it will make the machine run a lot faster. The only other one that I want to point out in this area is the **CD-ROM** tab at the top of the screen (after you click on the File System button). This should be set to Quad speed or higher unless you know otherwise—even if you don't have a 4X CD-ROM drive. The rest of the buttons up there should normally not be tinkered with such as the Troubleshooting tab. It even tells you at the top of the Troubleshooting window that **It is recommended that only advanced users and system administrators change these settings**.

The other important thing on the Performance tab is the Graphics button that is located at the bottom in between the Virtual Memory and the File System tab. The Graphics tab will take you to a screen where you can adjust your hardware acceleration. There is a slide bar there that goes from NONE to FULL, and it will normally be on FULL by default (see **fig. 58**). If your computer locks up or freezes a lot, you may want to slide the slide bar so that it is one increment to the right of NONE. If it still freezes up, go back in there and slide it to NONE. If this solves your problem, you have video card issues, and the permanent fix will be to update or reinstall your video card driver. If you adjust the hardware acceleration, you will need to click **Ok** twice, and it will prompt you to restart the computer.

Fig. 58 Graphics button in the System/Performance applet.

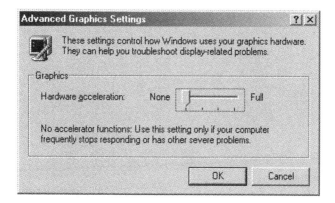

You probably won't notice a difference with the hardware acceleration on low unless you play a lot of computer games or use high-end graphics programs like AutoCAD. Contact your computer manufacturer to obtain the latest video card driver if turning the hardware acceleration to NONE solves your freezing problem. With the new driver, you could turn the acceleration back to FULL and it should not cause your system to freeze anymore. Like I said though, you may not even notice a difference with the acceleration set all the way down. In that case, you may not even want to worry about updating the driver unless you have other related problems.

One more thing to mention about the System applet. You can access it by 2 little-known shortcuts: Right-click on **My Computer** and left-click on **Properties**. You can also press the **Windows** key and **Pause Break** simultaneously. You will have a Windows key in the lower left corner of your keyboard if you have a modern 101-key keyboard. If you have a Windows key, it will be located between the **CTRL** and the **ALT** keys. The **Pause Break** key can be found in the upper right corner of your keyboard.

TIP Cleaning up the Control Panel:

If your Control Panel is cluttered with icons you don't need, delete some of them. In the C:\WINDOWS\SYSTEM directory, you'll find a corresponding CPL file for each Control Panel item.

Move the ones you don't want to a safe place on your hard disk. When you open Control Panel, those icons won't appear.

Chapter #17

All about the Internet

IS THAT AN E-MAIL ADDRESS OR A WEB ADDRESS?

Let's talk about the Internet: http://www.favoritesite.com or http://www.disney.com are Web addresses. johnsmith@compuserve.com, royhigg1245@bellsouth.net, janet1234@aol.com, gagglygirl@cs.com, or tina@yahoo.com or even johnsmith@edu.net are all e-mail addresses. To go to the Web on America Online or CompuServe 2000, you can type a Web address on the Keyword line or Go word line. Or, you can type a Web address on the address line that spans across the top of the screen on both services. On a standard ISP, you may need to type in the **http://** before a Web address. It is important not to mix up an e-mail address with a WWW address. A Web address is like http://www.microsoft.com or https://www.bankomexico.com. The extra s on the end of the http stands for a secure site. This is a bank, and they would have 128-bit encryption technology which is a very strong security measure, and it is only allowed in the United States and Canada which would be contradictory with Bank of Mexico, but that is only an example. Outside of these domains, the maximum security a browser can have is 40 bit—at least with the Microsoft Internet Explorer. To read a little further into this subject, check out the piece at the end of this book **Appendix D**, *128-bit Browser Encryption.*

BEING ONLINE vs. BEING ON THE INTERNET

The Internet and being online are not exactly the same thing. If you have America Online or CompuServe for instance, you generally make a dial-up connection with your modem to the Internet. Remember that your modem is like a telephone, and it dials up over your phone line to connect to your ISP. At this point you are online, but you are not on the Internet. To be on the Internet (The WWW—World Wide Web) you need to fire up your Web browser. In other words, type in a Web address on your address bar such as http://www.disney.com. Press the **Enter** key on your keyboard or click **GO** to the right of the address bar and away you go! You will now be catapulted onto the World Wide Web. So if you call technical support and say "I can't get to the Internet," they might think that you can sign online but you can't get to a Web address when maybe the modem isn't even connecting and you should say "I can't sign online in the first place much less get to the Internet."

A LOT IS SPENT ON THE INTERNET

There is a lot happening on the Web these days in case you didn't notice. I think it was evident in Super Bowl XXXIV, in January of 2000, where more than half of the commercials were for dot com companies; they were the most expensive commercials all year even. Some of these dot com companies paid $2 million for these 30-second spots. I hope it was worth it! This is the epitome of how the Internet is shaping not only our personal lives but also the entire economical structure. The Internet is also putting a lot of traditional bricks & mortar businesses under, or at the very least, the Internet is drastically changing the way people need to do business.

6"*Oh don't look so gloomy. The Web isn't going to dismantle the entire economy brick by brick. But it's forcing all companies to rethink the way they do* *business—-to rethink the very industries they're in. amidst this rethinking, opportunity knocks. Many businesses, for example, treat their Web sites as medieval science projects: Hang a shingle on the Net, try this, try that. Needless to say, such endeavors are doomed. Companies that integrate the Internet into their core businesses are more likely to cheat the grave than digital moon-lighters. Wily entrepreneurs that can help with this integration stand to make a bundle."*

Many companies have gone online and ditched their physical store. One example is http://www.egghead.com. The owner of Egghead realized that he had no future in selling software from a downtown boutique. With all of the files available for download on the Internet, it just didn't pay for the company to keep a physical store with the high overhead.

7 "Will the company survive? It's too early to tell. Eventually businesses and consumers alike will stop buying applications of any kind. Instead they'll click to a Web site, use a program from the site's server, then save the file on their system's hard drive. In other words, Egghead. com's meanest bout still lies ahead. Investors believe the company can measure up. It certainly won't be caught short on guts. And it's merger with Onsale.com can't hurt."

YOU CAN BET YOU CAN FIND IT ON THE 'NET

You can find nearly anything on the Internet if you know where to look. The WWW is equalizing the world a little bit more. Knowledge is power and it was not too long ago when you had to be rich or at least know some influential people to get certain privy information like stock quotes. The Internet has allowed the average person to get such information as real-time stock quotes, or you can even visit the Library of Congress from the comfort of your own home with the touch of a button. This evens things out a little bit, and it doesn't limit this kind of information to the rich and famous. The rich still get richer and it still takes money to really have a lot of mobility, but the Internet has made it so that the average Joe/Jane can make a name for himself/herself. With a bit of luck and a lot of determination, the average person can be wealthy by taking advantage of the privy information that can be had on the Internet. There are people that are making thousands of dollars per week playing the stock market. There are probably some people that are making more than that day-trading on the Internet; in some cases, they quit their daytime jobs and play the market full time. The Internet has probably had one of the most profound (some brokers might have another word for it) effect on stockbrokers. It hasn't put everyone out of business and it may not put the strong companies under. The large investment houses can usually be found on the Web also, but it has definitely reshaped the way that they have to do business.

It wasn't too long ago when you would find hundreds upon hundreds of stockbrokers on the trading floor moving millions if not billions of dollars a day. Nowadays, the Internet is definitely pushing a lot of people out of this sector. There are brokers that I have heard about that have been doing the same thing since the '70s that are now seeking other opportunities. You see these people used to be able to make a point or two from every transaction in addition to their commission. With stock sites like E-trade or Schwab, an average person can complete a trade for half (and maybe a lot less) of what it would cost with a conventional broker. In addition, people can conduct trades in real-time and have access to real-time quotes. These are things that used to only be available to a stockbroker, so now the average person can really make money in the stock market. Since it is so convenient to buy and sell stock, often times these people will make a dozen or so trades a day. They do not go for the big money on one stock usually, rather they make their money from shaving ¼ point here and ¼ point there.

8 *"not only do investors get cheaper commissions, faster trades, and longer playing hours by trading online, says Mark Thompson, senior vice president of* *online brokerage (Schwab.com). They also get a world of late-breaking financial information virtually unavailable five years ago. Schwab.com's leap to the Net was more than an endorsement of online stock trading. It was a ringing brass bell to individual investors everywhere that they're paying too much for a piece of the action."*

9 *"In fact, the economy promises to become so service-happy that you may never have to get out of your pajamas again. Only months ago, the United Parcel Service enjoyed one of the largest initial public offering in the history of the stock market. Investors can thank the prospects for mail-order sales via the Web. Meanwhile, billions of dollars are flowing into Web-based home delivery services as fleets of trucks take to city streets across the country. The massage is clear. A company that truly wants to sell you something will ring your doorbell with it in hand: lawnmower parts, ready-to-cook gourmet meals, batteries for your TV remote, bug spray, you name it. Web businesses that shorten the time between mouse click and delivery will win big. So will those that manage to do it cheaper than local merchants. This is not exactly news."*

Fig. 59 Interconnect points

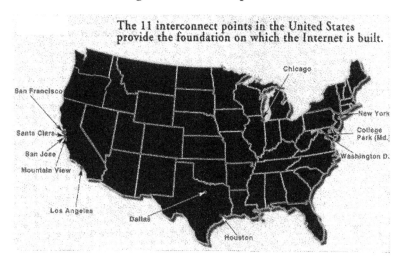

The 11 interconnect points in the United States provide the foundation on which the Internet is built.

THE STRUCTURE OF THE INTERNET

The Internet is built on 11 interconnect points in the United States as illustrated in **fig. 59**. The cable that connects these points is referred to as the ***Backbone***. The more directly you are connected to the Backbone, the faster your access will be depending on exactly how you connect to the Internet (via modem, network, cable modem, etc). All connections and personal computers that have Internet access eventually get routed back to the Backbone, but there is an extensive web of connections that blanket the United States (And a lot of the world for that matter since it is the World Wide Web) much like the World Wide Web itself. The main difference between the two is that on the World Wide Web the connections are via hyperlinks so they are virtual. The Internet itself is connected by thousands of miles of cable, and it is physically hooked together.

Chapter #18

E-mail

```
Subj: E-mail Tutorial #18
Date: 2/20/00 12:51:18 PM Eastern Standard Time
From: Orion2400
To: Orion2400
Sent on: AOL 5.0 for Windows sub 66
```

There's a whole chapter devoted to e-mail because this is the number one reason why people get on the Web right? E-mail and the WWW are the primary reasons why people get a computer these days. I know that people ask me more questions about those 2 things than anything else. That's why you will find that the majority of this book focuses on these subjects.

NO STAMP OR RETURN ADDRESS REQUIRED

E-mail is free as of this writing, and it can be sent to the far ends of the earth. You should ordinarily be able to send mail and receive mail to and from any mail system. There are system problems and sometimes addresses are misspelled, however. Also, there are many mail programs that allow some sort of filtering capabilities or 'controls.' People may not realize that they have mail controls blocking mail or that they have controls at all for that matter. Mail blocking could possibly be the reason why someone would not be able to receive mail, so it is worth a look if nothing else makes sense. Sometimes they are set automatically to block all mail, and you have to turn that filtering off. So if you think that is the case, check with your ISP and make sure that you can receive all mail. If a friend is not getting any of your e-mail, make sure you have the correct address and have them check with their ISP.

In most mail programs click on **Send Mail** (or something similar) to send your e-mail. Click on **Create Mail** (or something similar) to bring up an e-mail window. Where it says 'Send to' or maybe 'address' or just 'to,' or something very similar, you type the person's e-mail address that you are sending to. It isn't necessary to put your address in e-mail. Mail programs fill that in for you! So it's not like traditional mail (snail mail) where you fill in a return address. The mail will come over with what's called a mail header as shown at the beginning of this chapter. The mail header shows whom the mail was sent from and whom it was sent to, and every mail server that it may have passed through in between. In this case, I sent the mail to myself (Orion2400) from myself (Orion2400) using AOL version 5.0 on February 20th, 2000. The next paragraph is an example of a more complex mail header. Don't worry if you can't make heads or tails out of it. I just wanted to show you what one looks like, but you will never have to decipher one of these unless you become an Internet Postmaster.

Headers

Return-Path: <owner-iunews@INFO.IUNIVERSE.COM>

Received: from rly-za04.mx.aol.com (rly-za04.mail.aol.com [172.31.36.100]) by air-za02.mail.aol.com (v76_r1.8) with ESMTP; Fri, 29 Sep 2000 18:19:43 -0400

Received: from info.iuniverse.com ([64.41.150.94]) by rly-za04.mx.aol.com (v75_b3.9) with ESMTP; Fri, 29 Sep 2000 18:18:58 -0400

Received: from info (64.41.150.94) by info.iuniverse.com (LSMTP for Windows NT v1.1b) with SMTP id <0.0004BB3D@info.iuniverse.com>; Fri, 29 Sep 2000 15:13:53 +0100

Received: from INFO.IUNIVERSE.COM by INFO.IUNIVERSE.COM (LISTSERV-TCP/IP
  release 1.8d) with spool id 149507 for IUNEWS@INFO.IUNIVERSE.COM; Fri, 29
  Sep 2000 15:13:03 +0100

Received: from toexcel (38.26.93.125) by info.iuniverse.com (LSMTP for Windows NT v1.1b)
  with SMTP id <0.0004BB3C@info.iuniverse.com>; Fri, 29 Sep 2000 15: 13:02 +0100
  X-Sender: iunews@iuniverse.com (Unverified)

X-Mailer: QUALCOMM Windows Eudora Pro Version 3.0.3 (32)
Mime-Version: 1.0
Content-Type: text/plain; charset="us-ascii"
Approved-By: "iUniverse.com Newsletter" <iunews@IUNIVERSE.COM>
Message-ID: <3.0.3.32.20000929181839.0293ecc8@iuniverse.com>
Date: Fri, 29 Sep 2000 18:18:39 -0400
Reply-To: "iUniverse.com Newsletter" <iunews@iuniverse.com>
From: "iUniverse.com Newsletter" <iunews@iuniverse.com>
Subject: iUniverse.com Newsletter, 10-2-00
To: IUNEWS@INFO.IUNIVERSE.COM

You also don't have to click a stamp on e-mail. To recap how to do this:
Click **Create mail** (on CompuServe 2000), **Write** (on AOL), **Compose
a message** (on Outlook Express), or **Create** (on CompuServe Classic
version 4.0.2 or less shown in **fig. 60**). Fill in the address box that might
be labeled 'Send to' or 'To' or something along these lines with not your
address but the person or persons you are sending e-mail to. You can
usually send mail to multiple people by separating the addresses by a
comma and a space. For example: johnsmith@bellsouth.net, georgeban-
ter123@aol.com, *sidneypointer@cs.com.*

Fig. 60 CompuServe Classic version 4.0.2 e-mail form

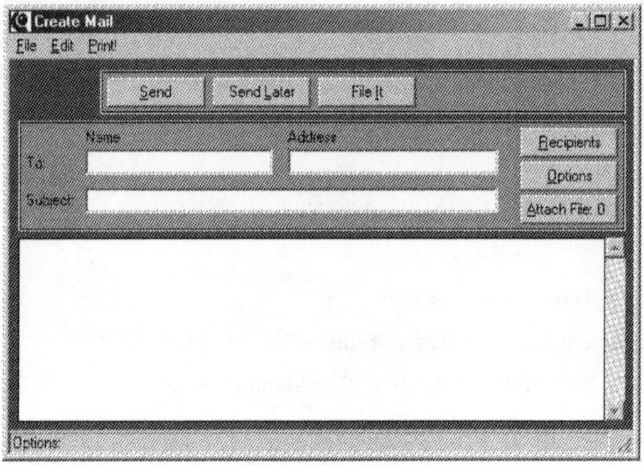

You see how that works? 2 addresses on the same line separated by a comma and a space will send mail to both the intended recipients. However, if you send to multiple addresses and just one address is wrong, it will prevent the entire e-mail from being delivered. Therefore, if you are sending e-mail to 10 people and are unsure of one address, but you know that 9 addresses are valid because you have sent mail to them before, send to the 9 people and copy and paste your message into a new mail window so you don't have to retype it and send it to that one address you are unsure of individually. That way if the one address is wrong, it will be the only e-mail that wasn't delivered, but the other 9 people will receive the e-mail.

HOW TO ACTUALLY SEND E-MAIL

After you have entered the e-mail address of the person or persons that you want to send to, enter some kind of a subject and fill in the body of your letter with your message then click SEND or SEND NOW or something similar. There are many variations of e-mail programs, but they really all work on the same principles that happen to be pretty similar to traditional mail. You put whom

you are sending it to, the subject and the main message. The main differences between snail mail and e-mail, besides the obvious, are that you don't need a stamp and you don't have to put a return address on e-mail. There are different ways to attach files to e-mail and read attachments that you receive although we will cover that in the next chapter. America Online and CompuServe 2000 have the most user-friendly e-mail of any ISP; some others are pretty difficult to configure if you are new to computers. They all work on the same principle though—even attaching files is basically the same idea. Really, if you've worked one e-mail program, you've worked them all. For the most part, if you are proficient at using any e-mail program, you can use any others because you can just apply the same principles to another e-mail program.

RAIN, SLEET, OR SNOW YOUR E-MAIL WILL BE THERE

E-mail can usually be composed offline. This is advantageous because if you just plan on writing mail for an hour why sign on and clog up the network and risk losing the mail if you get disconnected? On AOL or CompuServe 2000 just click SEND LATER. You compose mail just like you would if you signed online, but just click **SEND LATER** when you are done. See **fig. 61.** is grayed out and the Send Later button is active because this shows the sign-on screen but is not actually signed online.

Fig. 61 AOL e-mail form. Notice how the Send Now button

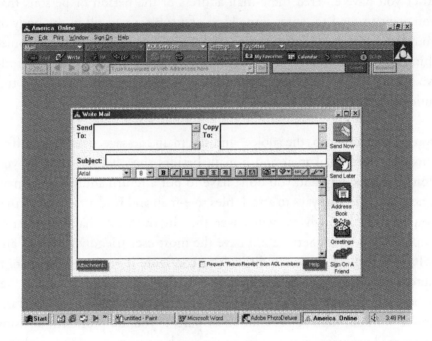

To repeat this, you compose mail just like you would if you signed online, but click SEND LATER when you are done. The next time you happen to sign online, you will get a message "You have mail waiting to be sent, do you want to send it now?" You say Yes to this, and all of your mail will be sent. It doesn't matter whether you sign on tomorrow, next week, or next month. It will send all the mail that you have accumulated offline. It won't work exactly like this, or it will work in a different manner if you don't use AOL or CompuServe 2000. Remember that you can have your ISP software onscreen and talk on the phone with only 1 phone line; the computer won't require the phone line until you click on whatever it is that makes your modem start to dial. When the modem dials, you will normally hear the modem **handshake** that sounds like loud squelch from a radio when it is not tuned into a station. Therefore, when you have your sign on screen up, you will not actually be online until you click the sign on button and your modem dials. On this offline sign on screen you can write e-mail—at least on America Online or CompuServe 2000.

Another fallacy is that you can't receive e-mail unless you are signed online. This is not true at all. You don't even have to have your ISP's software installed on your computer to receive e-mail. You see if you have e-mail, your e-mail account resides on the host computer, meaning your Internet companies computers or servers as they are called on a grand scale. The only reason you need to install your ISP's software is to draw a connection between you and your online account.

So as long as you have paid your ISP bill, you will have an account and you will continue to get e-mail—even if you don't have a computer for a period of time. However, sometimes e-mail is deleted off of an ISP's mail server after several weeks or so. If you receive important e-mail and you expect not to be able to check your e-mail for more than a couple of weeks, you should check with your ISP and make sure that the mail will be there when you sign on the next time. If your ISP deletes mail automatically from their mail servers, once it's gone, it's gone. It would be like if you deleted a file from your computer and then emptied the recycle bin; there is probably no way that they can get it back for you. I talked to people who claimed that they had this really important e-mail that they wanted to get back, but it had been 5 weeks or so since they had checked their e-mail. They were angry because they were not informed that the ISP would delete e-mail automatically after about a month. I would ponder why they wouldn't check their e-mail for 5 weeks if it was so all-fire important.

Chapter #19

E-mail Attachments

The above is MAIL ATTACHMENTS typed in the Wingdings font. Fonts will be discussed in the next chapter, but it is pertinent to e-mail attachments. You will no doubt be receiving different fonts in your attachments and you will be able to send attachments with all sorts of wacky fonts when you are done with this book. This text is written in Times New Roman 12-point font. The symbols above represent the Wingdings font in 22 point. I thought this would be a good introduction into the Fonts chapter because you may get some mail that looks like all Wingdings.

Let's get down to the lesson at hand. Strange fonts may come over as an attachment or they may come directly in e-mail. What you do in a case like this is highlight all of the text that may look like symbols or gibberish, and if your mail program allows you to change the font, just select a more standard one like Arial, Courier New, or Times New Roman. If you did get an attachment rather than text directly in e-mail, the attachment will open in an application that you have installed on your computer. If the attachment is a text file (.txt), it may open in Notepad or Wordpad. At any rate, if the application supports different fonts, you can change the font there. You will know what the current font is by what is displayed on the font drop-down menu. In most word processors, there is a font drop-down menu and there will be another drop-down list right next to it where you can select the size of the font called the *pitch*. Pitch is just a unit of measurement for fonts. A pitch of 72 means that the letter would be 1 inch tall.

An e-mail attachment is something that is frequently sent across the Internet so that the document retains it's original formatting. For example, if you make a document in Microsoft Publisher, you may be able to copy and paste that into e-mail, but all of the color will be stripped off, and any kind of customization, such as fancy fonts or paragraph formatting, will be lost. Normally everything will revert to plain black text in a case like this. Therefore, for uniformity, many documents are sent as attachments. Also, sometimes a text message may be too long to fit into your e-mail program, so it would be necessary to attach a file that the recipient can download and open on their computer using an application that they have.

ALL FILES ARE NOT CREATED EQUALLY

Sometimes, the recipient has to have a particular program to open up your file. This will probably be the same application as you used to create the file. If you received a Microsoft Publisher file, you would need to have Microsoft Publisher on your computer or else you would not be able to read that attachment. You could download it and open it up, but if you don't have the correct program to read the file, something else will try to open it such as Windows Notepad. If that happens, it is likely that your attachment will look like gibberish. **Don't get this confused with what may appear as gibberish but is really a strange font like Wingdings**. Like I said, When text is pasted or opened in a text editor, it will tell you what the font is in the font drop-down list.

Also, don't forget that you could receive an e-mail with strange looking characters or symbols in it that were created using ALT commands as shown in **Appendix L**, *Alt Commands*, or you could be looking at Emoticons as shown in **Appendix O**, *Emoticons*.

If you change the font to something standard, like Times New Roman, and you still can't read the attachment or your word processor won't let you change the font, you probably have a ***Mime*** or ***Zip*** file that opened in the text editor. You will need a more specialized application to properly read these types of files.

All files in Windows have a 3-letter extension. This extension provides a clue as to just what program is needed to open it. A Microsoft Publisher file has the extension .pub. If you received an attachment with that extension, you would know that you need Publisher to read the file. The bottom line is that sometimes you actually need the program installed on your computer that was used to make a file that was sent to you in order to view it properly. **Appendix E**, *File Extensions*, will show you a rather large list of file extensions. There are so many types of files, that it is likely that you will run across one in your e-mail attachments that isn't even covered on the list in the Appendix. In addition, new file extensions are created all the time as new applications are written for Windows.

FILE ENCRYPTION, COMPRESSION, AND RESTRICTIONS

When you download a file, it is usually not up to your online service or ISP to help you open it. They will usually help you find the file, but your Internet connection provides a medium to download files and that is it. Once they are on your computer they are your responsibility. That's why you have to be careful what you download these days. There are viruses floating around in e-mail attachments. Anything else that your ISP does for you relating to e-mail attachments is out of courtesy if they are downloaded on your computer. You see there is more than meets the eye with

Internet e-mail. First of all, there is no Internet standard yet, so files might be encoded in a format called MIME. The file will usually have a file name ending in .mim. Such as mydocument.mim. A Mime file is a kind of compressed file like a .zip (zipped) file. For more information about Mime, look at **Appendix T**, *Mime—Attaching Files to Internet Messages*, at the end of the book. The Mime article is an excerpt from *The America Online Tour Guide* by Tom Lichty.

Also, a document or file may be encoded with another format besides Mime. Two formats that I know of besides MIME are Binhex and UUencoding. If you get a Mime file and you need to decode it, you can use many programs. One popular program that can decode a Mime file is Winzip. Winzip can actually perform many functions like zipping and unzipping files. If you want to get Winzip, visit the Web site *www.winzip.com*. I mentioned that Winzip can zip and unzip files. Sometimes you might get a file in e-mail that has been zipped, and it will usually have a file extension of .zip such as myfile.zip. The purpose of zipping files is to facilitate sending them over the Internet. Zipping a file will take a very large file and make it maybe half the size or less. This can not only make it quicker to upload and download, but most mail programs have a file size limit. Lets say that you want to send a file that is 20 Megabytes in size, but your e-mail program doesn't support files any larger than 15 Megabytes. You can zip the file and make it say 12 Megabytes in size, and it will make it possible for you to send. Another reason why people will zip a file is to take many files and zip them into one file. When you receive a file like this, it is necessary to unzip the file to break it down into all of its individual components instead of just one .zip file. Sometimes, the Internet mail system will automatically zip multiple files like this and it will turn an e-mail attachment into a .mim file. Mime stands for MULTI-PART INTERNET MAIL EXTENSIONS and means that there are multiple parts or many files zipped into one file. **Fig. 62** illustrates how a .zip file will appear. **Fig. 63** is showing Winzip opening a .zip file.

Fig. 62 This is how a zip file will appear.

**Fig. 63 Winzip application that is able to open zipped files.
You would just click Next on the screen shown.**

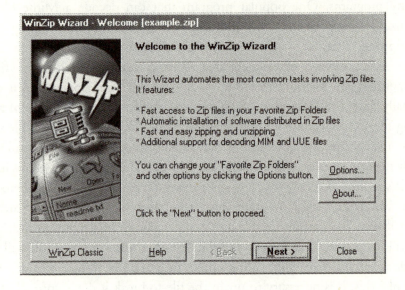

Some files are not cross-platform compatible. For example, you may get a file that was made on a Macintosh with the extension of .sit. If you try to open this file on your PC, it will not work. Some files just cannot be read on an IBM PC that were made on a Macintosh; sometimes files cannot be read on a Macintosh that were made on a PC. To combat this problem there are certain formats that are cross-platform compatible such as TIFF (Tagged Image File Format), a graphics file format that is cross-platform compatible unlike GIF files that are PC-specific. A very popular cross-platform file format is PDF—files that can be made by Adobe Acrobat available at *www.adobe.com*. The main appeal of Adobe is that any file that is put into this format can not only be read cross-platform, but it will keep its look and feel no matter what. The 3-letter extension on an Adobe Acrobat file is .pdf, so if you receive a file in this format, you know that you will need Adobe Acrobat to open it. If Adobe is installed on your computer, it will normally open a PDF file if you just double-click on the file. You will see a lot of help files on the Web in this format because of its versatility. Usually a Web site that offers a help file in Adobe format will also offer the program free for download or at least have a link to the Adobe Acrobat Web site. Adobe makes many sophisticated programs that can do all sorts of fancy formatting and Web publishing or publishing in general. These types of programs are not free, but they are very good. However, the basic Adobe reader that can open up .pdf files is free for download.

As you can see, there is more to it than meets the eye with file attachments. Downloading a simple file and opening it may seem like a daunting task. This is not your ISP's or even Microsoft's fault.

That is just the nature of the Internet. Because there is no standard protocol yet to transfer files across the Internet, what seems as if it should be simple can turn into an experience fraught with hardship. Remember that computers haven't been around all that long in the over-all scheme of things and the Internet is still under development. Keeping those things in mind may alleviate some of your frustration when dealing with file attachments.

Chapter #20

The Internet part II

What are those Search Engines for anyway?

There are lots of Search Engines out there; their sole purpose is to help you find things on the Internet. America Online has a good one at *www.aol.com*. Yahoo is a formidable engine at *www.yahoo.com*. You also have *www.lycos.com*, *www.hotbot.com*, *www.37.com*, *www.metacrawler.com*, *www.altavista.com*, *www.google.com*, and *www.dogpile.com*. Check this one out at *http://searchenginewatch.com*. There is an international search engine at *http://www.twics.com/~takakuwa/search/search.html*. There are many more search engines, but this is enough to keep you busy for a while. However, check out **fig. 64** for a good list of these search engines.

Fig. 64 Search engine table from www.compquest.org/searchengines.htm

Alta Vista	AOL Search	Lycos	Hot Bot	Finland.com
Infoseek.com	Excite.com	Google	Earthlink.co	AllTheWeb.com
Direct Hit	7Search.com	IOPort.com	Snap	Dog Pile
Open Directory	One2Seek.com	Meta Gopher	Netscape	ICQit.com
Meta Crawler	Starting Point	The Net One	MicrosoftNet	Profusion.com
Yahoo	Web Data	SearchingWeb.com	SalukiSearch	USWest.net
Oingo search	Jayde search	InfoHiway	100hot.com	Compuserve.com
StoreSearch.com	Family FriendlySearch	MAMMA.COM	Mega Web search	Rocket Links search
Search A Lot	IWon.com	SeekAmerica.com	What U Seek	Fat Head Search
C4.com	MonsterCrawler	News-4-U.com	ShopNow.com	AllOneSearch
Ask Jeeves.com	CentraPoint.com	Find Link.com	WhatsNewToo	Infoseek.com
Titan Search	BellSouthMyWav	MyGo.com	ByteSearch.com	NetTaxi
GoToWorld.com	FindWhat.com	FrodoSearch	Go2Net.com	GoHipsearch
HotRate.com	Goto.com	TheInfoDepot	Debriefing.com	Go.com
Surffast.com	Clickey.com	Powersearch.com	MetaLocate.com	Search.com

I generally lean towards MetaCrawler, 37.com, W3, or Alta Vista, but I use or have used them all. One of my favorite Engines off all time is W3 at *http://cui.unige.ch/meta-index.html.* You can click on *Other interesting things* (Jargon, Acronyms, WIRED ...) and on the next page click on *Acronym Search* then scroll down the page a bit and click on *Search for an acronym* and see it's expansion. Then simply type in whatever acronym you are looking for at the top of the page and hit the Enter key on your keyboard. This acronym database is good for computer lingo like VESA or BIOS, but I have found that there are many acronyms in there that don't pertain to computers such as I searched for ASAP and it yielded the results **As Soon As Possible**. This Engine is very deep, and when you find a word, it is generally a hyperlink that you can click on to get a more in-depth meaning or you can even submit a new meaning for a word, or you can coin (make up) an acronym and submit it for publication into the W3 Acronym database.

Different search engines are better for different kinds of subjects and there are different methods that you can use for your searches. This is beyond the scope of this chapter, but to find out more about how to use search engines check out **Appendix F**, *How to use Search Engines*, in the back of this book.

HOW DO I GET TO THEM THEN?

To get to one of these search engines without a hyperlink, you simply type in the address, like **www.lycos.com**, into your Web browser's address bar and hit the **Enter** key and away you go. Once you get there, type in something that describes what you are looking for. If you collect coins, type in coins or rare coins, for example. Most search engines allow for a Boolean search. What this means is that you can use words like **and, or, not**, or **but** in your search. These are good distinguishing words that will help narrow down your search. For example, type cats **not** dogs, songs **not** music or poems. If you are searching for local maps and it brings up 1000 maps from all over the world, you could use a ***Boolean*** search and narrow it down. On the line where you type your search words on the search engine, type in State maps **or** US maps, and if that doesn't yield the results that you want, try using state maps **not** world maps. Well, you probably get the idea, and you can apply it to your own search. On some search engines you can use + or—in front of a word like +maps-worldmaps or +tulip bulbs-light bulbs or even +hotels +Paris -"bed and breakfast." The search engine appendix goes into some detail on this subject, but the last paragraph gives you the information in a nutshell that you really need to know about search engines. Furthermore, various search engines may or may not support some of the ways mentioned to narrow down your search. Consult the help files or FAQ on the search engine Web site to find out what kind of techniques can be used on a particular search engine.

Search engines these days serve as a portal to the Internet and frequently they will have other features besides just a search. A lot of these portals host Web space, have online shopping malls at least linked from their site, and they have unusual features like Alta Vista has an excellent language translator at *http://babelfish.altavista.com*. There are other language translators such as Foreign Language Translator at *http://www.freetranslation.com*. So if you type in Spanish you can convert it to English or vice versa.

I took 2 years of intensive College Spanish. One summer I took only Spanish but yet I went to college full time. Let me tell you that I studied my butt off! I was getting to the point where I could speak about as well as a Spanish kindergartner, and I could comprehend Spanish like a 1st grader. But it has been some years and with a foreign language if you don't use it you do lose it. I really can't speak much Spanish anymore, but I just know single words. I can pick out single words if I hear someone speaking Spanish, and I can sometimes put the meaning together (if the person isn't speaking too fast). I can carry on a decent conversation with a person that's fluent in Spanish with these language translators.

Fortunately, I can type fast and I have actually helped Spanish people fix their computer over the phone when they hardly spoke any English at all in some cases. You have to type in English what you want to say and then click on **Translate**. If you have the translator set to English to Spanish, it will tell you what to say. One problem is that the translation might be too literal and it really doesn't take colloquialisms into account. However, the Spanish person can usually figure out what you are trying to say. Also, if you know a little Spanish, it will really go a long way with this tool because you may be able to take what you know and add it to the translation appropriately.

SO HOW DO I GET TO THE WEB?

Well, a Web browser is what really reads Web pages. A Web browser is something like Internet Explorer or Netscape or Opera. There are some other browsers in existence, but Netscape and Internet Explorer are far and away the most popular. Web browsers are really computer programs like a computer game you play such as Solitaire or a word processing program. A Web browser is like a reader that can interpret Web pages. You connect with your Internet provider, such as America Online, and then you can crank up Internet Explorer and surf the Web. By the way, America Online uses Microsoft Internet Explorer as it's integrated Web browser. The Internet Explorer comes built into Windows 98, and if you had Windows 95, and didn't already have Internet Explorer, America Online would install it when you installed the AOL program. What this means is that when you go to the Web inside of AOL you are using the Microsoft Internet Explorer; it is the equivalent of clicking the Explorer icon on the Windows Desktop.

There are cosmetic differences between using the browser externally or internally, such as the AOL logo will be in the upper-right corner instead of the Microsoft logo when using AOL's integrated Web browser, but for all practical purposes they are the same browser. In order to use Explorer externally (outside of AOL), you would need to dial into your AOL account and minimize the AOL program. Then click on the Internet Explorer icon. The reason why you need to dial in first is that you need to establish an Internet connection in order to launch a Web browser because the browser is not an Internet connection in and of itself. You can use any Web browser with an ISP such as America Online, but with AOL you would need to use any other browser besides Internet Explorer externally since Internet Explorer is AOL's integrated browser. You can simply type in a Web address on the address line inside of AOL and hit the Enter key. You will go to the Web using Internet Explorer, so using that particular browser externally is kind of the long way around.

Nearly all ISPs will install a Web browser when you install their software. Some ISPs use Netscape and some use Internet Explorer. Most likely it will be either of the two on the ISP's CD-ROM. If you already have the browser that the ISP uses on your computer, it will only install it if you have an outdated version of the browser. For example, if you have Windows 95 and already have Internet Explorer 4.0, America Online will upgrade that to Internet Explorer 5.5 if you install the AOL 6.0 program from a CD-ROM. If you already had Internet Explorer 5.5, it will not install that part and it will only install the AOL program. Bellsouth.net, a good national-level ISP, uses Netscape as its internal browser. Therefore, if you installed that program and didn't have Netscape, or you had an outdated version, Bellsouth.net would either upgrade your old version of Netscape or install it in it's entirety.

WHAT'S THE SCOOP ON USENET & NEWSGROUPS?

(USEr NETwork) A public access network on the Internet that provides user news and group e-mail. It is a giant, dispersed bulletin board that is maintained by volunteers who provide news and mail feeds to other nodes. All the news that travels over the Internet is called "NetNews," and a running collection of messages about a particular subject is called a "newsgroup." Usenet began in 1979 as a bulletin board between two universities in North Carolina. Today, there are more than 50,000 newsgroups. News can be read with a Web browser or via newsreaders such as nn, rn, trn and tin.

Where did Usenet come from?

"Long before the Internet and e-mail became household terms — Usenet was actually started in 1979 by Steve Bellovin, Jim Ellis, Tom Truscott, and Steve Daniel at Duke University — electronic bulletin boards were used as a means for people with similar interests to communicate over computers. Nowadays, we call them discussion forums or newsgroups instead of bulletin boards, and there are thousands of them, hosted all over the world, covering every topic under the sun. So, Usenet became a thriving information sharing network. If you wanted to find a particular post in a high-traffic discussion forum, however, you had quite a job on your hands. The way that discussion forums work is a lot like the notes kids pass around in junior high school. Someone starts the note and passes it on, the next person adds their two cents and passes it back, the original author comments on the comment and passes it to someone new, and so on. In Usenet, the whole note is called a "discussion thread." There could be hundreds of threads about different topics within a discussion forum. Finding the one you need can be a little like the old needle in the haystack. To make it more complex, almost all newsservers expire messages after a few days or, at most, a few weeks. Expired messages are deleted from the live discussion forums and weren't viewable or searchable by users. And then Deja.com came along. In 1995, Deja News was created to provide a user-friendly interface to Usenet. Now, messages are archived, indexed, and can be searched, with an extensive array of searching and sorting options. This turns what was once an encyclopedic, but all too ephemeral and unmanageable, resource into a broad based reference tool that can provide maximum information for the investment of minimal time. The Usenet hierarchy Usenet is like a tree with thousands of branches. The large branches are top-level discussion categories, such as alt, which contain the smaller branches, such as alt.animals, which contain messages and / or divide into even more specific branches, such as alt.animals.dogs, which contain messages from people who are interested in that topic. The different parts of a discussion forum's name are always separated by a period, a traditional subcategorization symbol in the computer world. Each discussion forum contains threads which contain messages (also referred to as 'articles' or 'postings') — they look like e-mail between one user and another, but instead of just being sent between people, they're available for anyone in the world with access to read!"

Usenet resources: *http://www.usenet.com/ps.htm*   *http://www.alibis.com*
http://www.landfield.com/usenet

The following boasts **Uncensored** access to 80,000 newsgroups on 15 different servers: *www.usenet.com*

*Usenet definition from *http://www.techweb.com/encyclopedia*

**Where did Usenet come from?* from *www.deja.com*

What is a newsgroup?

Newsgroups are basically discussion groups. They differ from "chat rooms" in that they don't take place in "real-time." Rather, it works like this: Someone "posts" a message, (a letter, an essay, or a question) to the newsgroup. That message gets distributed all over the world. It'll be sent to thousands of different "news servers," basically archives of posts. Messages will be kept there for days, weeks, or months, depending on how the news server is set up. Other people can post replies to posted message if they want—or just read it, along with other people's replies. The largest newsgroups are international, have hundreds of regular participants ("posters"), and tens of thousands of regular readers.

3 basic types of newsgroups—

alt newsgroup (**ALT**ernative newsgroup) An Internet newsgroup that is devoted to a very specific topic, often one that is very controversial. Anybody can create an alt newsgroup without any formal voting from other users.

binaries newsgroups A newsgroup hierarchy designed to let people post graphics. Unlike Web sites, no one controls newsgroups, so people use the binaries newsgroups to "express" themselves, and you never know what you will find. Images are typically in .GIF or .JPG format, but because newsgroups can only handle text, images are stored in the text-based UUencoded format. Most browsers have built-in UUcode converters, so you can go to an **alt.binaries** newsgroup, download it in UUencoded format, look at it and save it to disk.

moderated newsgroup A newsgroup that is managed by a human referee who keeps the discussion focused and prevents it from getting out of hand.

*Newsgroup definitions from www.techweb.com (TechEncyclopedia)

How To Use Them

You can locate newsgroups at any search engine by typing newsgroups for your search criteria or by visiting *http://www.liszt.com/news*. You can either search or browse. Once you find one you like, just click on the name of the newsgroup, and it'll show you all the recent posts to the newsgroup.

Alternately, you can read the group with your newsreader, or your browser's built-in newsreader, if your ISP supports newsreaders. America Online doesn't support external newsreaders. In order to work, newsreaders need an NNTP (Network News Transfer Protocol) server, which AOL does not have. However, you can get to a good resource for newsgroups on AOL at Keyword newsgroups. Web browsers handle newsgroups differently, so it's hard to say exactly what'll happen next. But in Netscape and MSIE, for instance, a separate "news reader" browser will pop up and start filling with a list of messages you can read. Just click on the title of any message to start reading.

Or, maybe you'll get an error message: something like News Error!

News host responded: No such group

This means your Internet service provider (ISP) doesn't provide access to the group. (The group really does exist, though.) If you want the group badly enough, you need to write to your ISP and ask them to add the group: for example:

```
To: support
Subject: Please add newsgroup
Please add the newsgroup alt.radio.
```

Another primary resource for newsgroups is *www.deja.com*

Big Eight Top Level Newsgroups

comp   humanities   misc   news

rec   sci   soc   talk

Other Hierarchies

alt   aly   at   aus

austin   ba   bionet   bit

biz   ca   can   capdist

ch   chinese   davis   dc

de   demon   eunet   fido

fj   fr   gnu   info

it   k12   la   malta

maus   mn   ncf   no

ny   nyc   nz   ping

pl   sac   sat   teaser

toulouse   tue   tx   ucb

ucd   uiuc   uk   unet

usm   vmsnet   yolo   z-netz

zer

FAQs, Spam & Flame

"Did your mom ever tell you, "there's no such thing as a stupid question?" Mine did, and she was right. Except on Usenet. If you ask a question in a discussion forum that has already been asked and answered as part of a Frequently Asked Questions message, you could suffer a fate much worse than cod liver oil, a mouth washed out with soap or anything Mom had to offer. Most discussion forums have a FAQ, and most repost them regularly so they will be easy to find. From Deja.com's Power Search form, enter "faq" in the Keywords field and the name of the discussion forum in the Forum field and click the Search button.

You should get back a list of results containing the FAQ if one exists.

As you can probably tell by now, Usenet is full of its own terms (like FAQ) that it would be better not to be in the dark about. For definitions of words like spam — it's not just a lunch-meat anymore — flame, newbie and netiquette, check out Deja.com's Glossary."

WHY CAN'T I GET TO THE WEB ANYMORE?

Sometimes, the Web browser will work for a long time and all of a sudden you will stop getting to the Web for no apparent reason. This is not unusual and most of the time it can be easily fixed by changing the settings in the Network control panel and the Internet control panel to what they should have been all along. You may ask, "Well why did it work all along if things were set incorrectly?" A legitimate question, and the answer is that on a computer, or anything else for that matter, sometimes something will work on the wrong setting, but eventually it will break. Like if you leave your car tires too low on air they will wear out too quickly and eventually you will get a flat or they will fail on you. So maybe they worked for a year or whatever, but one day they just decided to go flat on you. Hopefully not on the way into work.

Read Appendix G, Computer Problems—*Why Am I Having So Many Computer Problems?* for more answers to the question "Why did it work and all of a sudden it doesn't when I didn't make any changes?"

If the problem is that the network adapters are corrupted, often the case, the only way it will work again is if you change everything to the correct settings and reboot the computer. When you do change the settings, the computer will build a driver information database, which basically means that it is refreshing those Network control panel files. Sometimes, it will ask for the Windows disk because it needs to get a file that has been damaged or just needs overwriting to change the network settings. The computer will then ask you to reboot so that the changes take effect. In some cases, if you don't have a Windows disk to refresh the files, you will not get back to the Web. You will need to buy or borrow a disk so that the computer can get the files that it needs in order for the Internet to work again. Check out Appendix B, *How to Set Internet Properties in the Control Panel*, and Appendix C, *How to Set up the Network Control Panel*, for detailed instructions on how to set the Network and Internet settings for certain ISPs.

I have seen computers that used to be on a network that were able to reach the Internet for a long time. Out of the blue they quit working, and sometimes they never worked again—at least without having a Windows CD-ROM. A lot of these cases were when someone would get an old computer from their company for free or really cheap. They got the computer as is with no Windows CD-ROM. They would sometimes be surfing the Web for months before it would just quit on them. Without the Windows CD, it is usually impossible to make it work again unless the Network Administrator copied the Windows CD to the hard drive somewhere.

Most people or even technicians will not know where these files may be because the Network Admin. could have put them anywhere. However, frequently you will find the Windows files in the C:\windows\options\cabs directory.

When a computer has been networked at one time, it is really best to format the drive and reinstall Windows in order to start fresh. The main reason why you want to reinstall Windows is that when a machine has been networked, the installation and use of applications can have strange and unpredictable results—especially if you are using programs that connect to the Internet. Often times, settings will need to be changed in the Network control panel; not only will it ask for the Windows CD, but it may very well ask for the networking disks, such as Novell, that you most likely won't have.

More reasons why you may not be able to access the Web

Sometimes you may stop being able to reach the Web because your Web browser has been damaged. There are a few things that can be tried to resolve this problem. In extreme cases, a complete browser removal may be necessary to make the Internet work again. These procedures are outlined in **Appendix M**, *Advanced Web Browser Removal.* What is so perplexing about Web problems are that the same symptoms can mean something is wrong in the Network control panel, a damaged browser, an issue in Windows, or even damaged ISP software. For example, without a file named wsock32.dll, called the Winsock, in the Windows\System directory, you will not be able to access the Internet. The file needs to be 65kb in Win 95, 40kb in Win 98, and 36kb in Win Me. Everything may work fine for a long time and suddenly you can't get to the Web one day. Although there are many reasons why that could happen, it may end up being a problem with the wsock32.dll file. Some reasons why the Winsock may fail all of a sudden, besides the file just corrupting on you, is that sometimes the installation of a program will overwrite, rename, or alter the wsock32.dll file in some way.

Furthermore, Windows 95 will likely have a Winsock file that is 21kb in size if it is an outdated or older version of Windows 95. The 21kb file will work for a while, but it seems as if it will definitely corrupt sooner or later. At that point, the only way to fix the problem is to extract a wsock32.dll file from the Windows CD. Of course, you could copy the wsock32.dll from another computer and then copy the file into the c:\windows\system directory on the computer that can no longer access the Web. Someone could even send you a Winsock via an e-mail attachment. Just be sure that you are dealing with the same version of Windows as the sender has. The wsock32.dll is different sizes on each version of Windows.

When extracting a Winsock, you don't have to delete or rename the current Winsock on your system. When you extract the file, it will overwrite your existing file. For example, the wsock32.dll from the Windows CD, that is 65kb for Windows 95, will just erase and replace the bad one that may be 21kb in size. The only reason why you may need to delete or rename a wsock32.dll is if you have 2 or more on the system. Although I have seen multiple Winsocks cause problems, usually it doesn't matter what other files that you have on the system named wsock32.dll as long as you have the correct one in the c:\windows\system directory. Following, you will find instructions to extract a Winsock from Windows 95/98. Windows 98 and Windows Me work basically the same way as far as extracting a wsock32.dll.

TIP Extracting Winsocks for Windows:

Windows 95

Open a Dos window cd\windows\command

type: EXTRACT /A /L C:\WINDOWS\SYSTEM D:\WIN95\WIN95_03.CAB
WSOCK32.DLL or

I would try the one below first. Most people have WIn 95 in the Win 95\System dir.

EXTRACT /A /L C:\WIN95\SYSTEM D:\WIN95\WIN95_03.CAB WSOCK32.DLL

The Winsock at this point may be in the C:\WIN95\System. You can verify. If so go to an

MS-DOS window. Start>Programs>MS-DOS Prompt: type cd.. and hit enter. You will be at

the C:\> then type cd\win95\system then at the c:\win95\system\>copy Wsock32.dll

c:\Windows\System and press enter.

a. Place the Windows 95 CD into the CD drive (ex. D: drive)

b. Click on the START button on the Windows 95 Taskbar.

c. Select RUN.

d. In the RUN field type the following command. This command will

search all the cabinet files on the Windows 95 CD and install

the WSOCK32.DLL into the WINDOWS\SYSTEM directory.

To reinstall the WSOCK32.DLL from the Windows 95 floppy disks.

a. Click START, select PROGRAMS, and then click MS-DOS Prompt.

b. Type "cd\" (without quotation marks), and then press ENTER.

c. Insert disk 12 of the Windows 95 disks into the floppy disk drive.

d. Type the following line at the command prompt, and then press
ENTER

EXTRACT /A /L C:\WINDOWS\SYSTEM\ A:\WIN95_12.CAB WSOCK32.DLL

e. Type "exit" (without quotation marks), and then press ENTER to
return to Windows.

Windows 98

To extract the WSOCK32.DLL, make sure that the Windows 98 CD is in the CD-ROM drive and then:

a. Click on START, then PROGRAMS, then ACCESSORIES, then SYSTEM TOOLS and finally select SYSTEM INFORMATION.

b. In the window that opens, click on TOOLS and select SYSTEM FILE CHECKER.

c. Click on "Extract one file from installation disk"

d. In the box labeled "Specify the system file that you would like to restore", type WSOCK32.DLL.

e. There are three buttons at the bottom of the window (Start, Close, Settings), click on START.

f. To the right of a box labeled "Restore From" is a BROWSE button. Click on it.

g. A window will appear with a list of the different drives. Locate the CD-ROM drive and double-click on it. This will show what is on the CD-ROM drive.

h. Locate on the CD-ROM drive a folder labeled WIN98 or Windows98. Double-click on it.

i. Click OK and then OK again.

j. After it has finished extracting the file, reboot the computer.

Chapter #21

The Internet Part III

All of the chapters in this book are filled with original content for the most part, but I did take the liberty of quoting a few publications here and there. This chapter is one of those times. For one thing, I pretty much mentioned everything I had to say in the other 2 Internet chapters, and I ran across some things that I just couldn't have said better myself and I thought they were worth putting in this 3rd tutorial specifically written about the 'Net.

ANARCHY ON THE INTERNET

I want to point out or reiterate that the Internet is a vast place that is primarily composed of many Web sites all linked together by a common thread. If you have an online service like AOL or CompuServe or MSN, they have their own specific content and they provide access to the Internet as well. If you go to the Internet and visit a general Web site, your ISP will have no control over it. The Internet is a nearly infinite space that no one entity has control over. In fact, there are very few controls are laws at all on the 'Net. There are groups that establish some general protocols for the Web such as the **W3** (World Wide Web Consortium), but they are not a governing body that makes or enforces laws. Some of this liberalism is bound to change in some areas anyway such as taxes. The government is still trying to figure out how get their piece of the pie, but for right now there is very little taxation on the Internet which is a good reason to purchase from the Web. It is also a motivating factor for Web businesses to set up shop.

If you purchase from one of the areas that are specific to your ISP, like a Keyword on AOL or a Go word on CompuServe, and you have a problem, they can do something about it at least to some extent. If you buy something on the general Internet, your ISP, like AOL, will not be able to help you if you have a problem because you are dealing with a separate company. They will probably tell you that you need to go to that particular Web site and seek help there whether it is technical in nature or whether you bought an inferior product and want your money back.

SHOPPING ON THE 'NET

In defense of Web sites, it is very safe to shop online in almost every case. Online stores normally use a secure Web server on the page where you enter your credit card information. If the site is secure, the address will start with https such as **https://www.merrilllynch.com**. Normally a non-secure site will start with http such as **http://www.somewebsite.com**. HTTP stands for *Hypertext Transfer Protocol* and the **s** on the end stands for secure. Also, on your browser window you may see a little picture of a closed lock on a secure site, but on a regular site the lock will be open. Nearly any online store will conduct financial transactions on a secure site, meaning it is extremely unlikely that your credit card or checking account information will get into the wrong hands.

It is at least as safe to shop on the Internet as it is in a traditional bricks & mortar store, and most of the companies are reputable, and you will get what you pay for. You might want to review the disclaimer before making a purchase, but like a traditional store they will usually offer some sort of money-back guarantee or at least stand behind their product in some way. The thing that always amazed me as an employee for a large ISP is that people were leery about entering their credit card information on their computer to start an account, but they probably would have no qualms about giving their credit card to a waiter in a restaurant who then takes the card and goes into an entirely different room! As safe as it is to enter your credit card information on the Web in general (as long as it is a secure site), it is even safer to enter this type of information on a large ISP's registration form. The reason why is that not only is it secure, but it is behind a *firewall*, meaning there is a double wall of security. A firewall is a system set up on a network, like on a corporate *local area network*, that keep unwanted people out of the network, and in some cases the *System Administrator* will configure the firewall to keep people at work from getting out. In other words, the company may not want employees surfing the Internet on the company dime or the firewall will be configured to keep employees from getting to certain places such as pornographic Web pages.

THE INTERNET IS RESHAPING OUR LIVES...

10 *"This is the Internet moment, and perhaps it was inevitable that it should come on the eve of the new millennium. Created more than a generation ago by a diverse assortment of academics, engineers, hackers, government scientists, digital hippies, and teenagers holed up in their bedrooms with primitive phone equipment, the Net has exploded. Day by day, the network becomes more mainstream, winding its wired way into millions of offices, schools, and homes. Nobody can calculate precisely how many Americans are using it, but more than 100 million people are believed to have Internet access..."*

"...It's hard to keep track of the evolutionary digital leaps. Consider just the past year or two: Former pro wrestler Jesse Ventura, of all people, became the first politician to win a major election via the Net. His JESSENET site raised money, organized volunteers, and disseminated messages for a fraction of what his opponents in the Minnesota gubernatorial race were spending on TV and newspaper ads. Come to the campaign rally tonight in suburban Minneapolis,

one JesseNet alert urged. And don't drink and drive—but if you do, and you get busted, make sure to tell the sheriff to vote for Jesse.

Politics will never be the same. At campaign's end, Ventura was the governor and a national figure, and he didn't owe a dime. No wonder Al Gore wants credit for the Net..."

"...It is clear that as individuals gain more influence, institutions and corporations will have less. They will still be more powerful than Harry and Martha, but Harry and Martha are a lot more powerful than they used to be...{Harry and Martha refer to the common person}"

"...Our own HolyCircle {People who hold all the power} takes a different form.

It includes media executives, publishing houses, and tony magazines; a handfull of powerful newspapers; producers, columnists, and pundits; academics and TV-show talking heads; key members of Congress and any given presidential administration. Its ideology isn't necessarily political or religious; it venerates cultural influence and marketing. And it excludes ordinary human beings.

The Internet, however, reconnects these ordinary folk.

From journalism to Wall Street, some of the world's most powerful institutions are reluctantly coming to grips with the Internet's inevitability. They still don't like it very much. They might ache for those recent but happier days when they could set their agendas unmolested, quietly selecting the books that would be big, the ideas Congress would debate, the candidates we would choose between, the hours when they'd rather sell stocks. But those days are gone, almost surely for good. And good riddance to them.

The Internet moment is a monumental one. It isn't about computers. It's about great and deep change—only just beginning—permeating almost every aspect of business, society, and culture.

The fact that this moment coincides so precisely with the arrival of the new millennium is not just a staggering coincidence but a great convergence, one historians will be sorting out for centuries.

Institutiones can sputter, fume, and strategize all they want, but this moment isn't just about start-ups, technology, or stock process. And it doesn't belong to them alone. It's Harry and Martha's moment too."

HOW DO I FIND SOMEBODY ON THE I0NTERNET?

I was asked time and time again how to find somebody using the Internet when I did technical support. There are many comprehensive Web sites that are good for finding people. Most of them can locate somebody based on just one bit of information, however you may run into a dead end if all you know is the e-mail address of the person that you are looking for. If the e-mail address is all that you know about the person that you are looking for, you may finally be tempted to call the Internet provider that the e-mail address comes from, but by law they will not be able to release any information. I have listed what I consider the best of the best as far as finding somebody using the Internet and their services are free for the most part. However, if you run into a stumbling block, it may be worth it for you to pay for these services. If you don't mind paying a nominal fee, check out *www.ussearch.com* or call **(800) 733 – 2243**. They are very good at what they do and you will probably find who you are looking for if you come up empty using other methods. They boast "Over 1 Million Successful Searches..." and "1000's of Databases..."

Lycos has a great search engine for finding people at *www.whowhere.lycos.com.*

These folks boast the most comprehensive search center in the world: *www.nedsite.nl/search/search.htm.* You can try *www.four11.com*, *www.411.com*,

www.switchboard.com, and *www.whitepages.com.* All of these sites offer a good means of finding a person based on just knowing some of their information.

A Little History of the Internet

The Internet started as a military project in the 1960s, and it was implemented in 1968-1971. The military then commissioned Advanced Research Projects Agency (ARPA) to configure fail-safe networks. The agency became the Defense Advanced Research Project Agency (DARPA), and the whole Internet was known as ARPANet at the time.

Computers were networked together during this time which means that they were connected to one another. These computers mostly ran on an operating system called *Unix*, a command line system similar to DOS. Nowadays, most computers run on a Windows operating system. A command line OS means that there are no pretty graphics and easy-to-use user interfaces, but it is necessary to type cryptic command lines to operate the computer. The networked computers were attached to servers which in turn connect to other servers called *Domain Name Service* servers. The DNS (Domain Name Service) servers allow computers to find each other, and in this type of configuration you can delete one or more computers without destroying the network.

Back in the early days there was low usage on the 'Net, and it was chiefly universities, large corporations, or research foundations that were online. Academic people decided they needed a similar type of arrangement in the 1980s, so they developed NSFNet (National Science Foundation Network). The educational network was structured like ARPANet. It wasn't too long before ARPANet and NSFNet established connections, and it was the beginning of the Internet as we know it today.

Both networks used TCP/IP as their protocol. TCP/IP stands for *Transmission Control Protocol/Internet Protocol*. Check the definitions in the Glossary for a further explanation of TCP/IP as well as some other common Internet terms. If you don't find your term in the Glossary, check **Appendix R**, *Internet Terms Glossary*.

11 *"The Internet took a leap forward in the 1980s, when the National Science Foundation (NSF) constructed a new, faster backbone network based upon Internet protocols to link colleges and research institutions to five new supercomputing centers located around the United States. As more computers joined the ranks, the value of the network increased, fueling an upward spiral that continues today on a worldwide level. Not every country is connected to the Internet, but the wired community takes all comers. The electronic village seemed to reach a critical mass in the early 1990s, when the easy-to-use World Wide Web sent the number of computers and people accessing it on an exponential curve that keeps climbing higher. In 1995, recognizing the increasingly commercial nature of the Internet, the NSF sold the last parts of its backbone still financed by the government. The present 'Net is a broad collection of large networks mostly run by big telecommunication companies such as Sprint and MCI. At several major access points, these top-level networks are connected to smaller and mid-level systems, and then to independent service providers.*

Today the Internet is a part of daily life. Even if you don't use it regularly, you hear about it through a growing onslaught of references and advertisements from all corners of popular culture. Solid numbers are impossible to come by, but an estimated 40 million computers are connected to the Internet in the US alone."

Pushing ahead...

Defining the 'Net

12 *"It isn't easy to pin down exactly what people mean when they talk about "going on the Internet." For some, it means sending E-mail; for others it's logging onto America Online or firing up a World Wide Web browser. Perhaps the language itself is the cause of some confusion. No one is ever "on" the Internet as you might be "on" a boat or airplane. The Internet is not a place we can visit and point out the main attractions. The 'Net simply waits in the background, ferrying information back and forth from your computer to computers around the world.*

The 'Net has a lot in common with our telephone system. if someone in New York City dials up a friend in San Francisco, a channel, consisting of copper wires, fiber optic lines, and perhaps something as exotic as a satellite is opened. Voices on each end are converted into an electonic protocol, or language, the phone system can manipulate. While all of this is going on, we don't think of telephone users as "jacking in" to the "Phone-net" or "surfing" through "phone-space." Instead, it is simply the mundane task of talking on the phone.

The differences between the way a telephone uses its network and a computer uses the Internet are important. Instead of transmitting point-to-point voice conversations, Internet pathways are used to exchange digitized computer data. Parts of a single E-mail message might travel through computers and lines owned by dozens of companies, schools, and government entities. This is why no one "owns" the Internet. In fact, the 'Net is owned in bits, small and large, by many someones, who all control their own part.

The reason computers can get along with each other is they all know the same lingo. This Internet language is called Transmission Control Protocol/Internet Protocol (TCP/IP). It might not be the best or prettiest language, but it is a standard any computer can use to communicate with any other computer with help from the right software. Though the way the Internet works might be different from telephones, the two tools have much in common simply because one is newer than the other does not mean it should be feared or shrouded in mystique. Anyone can use the Internet."

Chapter #22

More about E-mail and 3rd party mail clients

There are many mail clients available. The most popular of these include Outlook or Outlook express that are made by Microsoft. There is also Netscape mail that used to be called Messenger in their older versions of the browser. The advent of Netscape 6.0 brought Web Mail, a Web-based mail client that allows users to access their mail from any terminal with an Internet connection much like AOL's Netmail, called Mail on the Web. Web Mail is packaged with the Netscape browser much like Outlook comes with the Microsoft Internet Explorer. These two mail programs are the most popular, but there are several others in existence such as Eudora, Pegasus, and Juno. Juno has a free mail service; it's a little slow but it does the trick. Juno now offers a full-fledged Internet service that is fee-based, and the connections are slow but not as slow as their antiquated free mail system.

These mail programs mentioned so far use Internet standards. They use *pop3* and *smtp* protocols. These are Internet standard protocols and they stand for *Post Office Protocol version 3* (POP3) and *Simple Mail Transfer Protocol* (SMTP). Basically how it works is that there are computers called mail servers that process and handle the flow of e-mail. The servers that handle the incoming mail are called POP servers and the mail servers that handle the outgoing mail are called SMTP servers. Furthermore, there are networks of these mail servers all over the Internet; they move all of the e-mail.

O POSTMASTER, O POSTMASTER, WHERE FOR ART THOU?

If you send e-mail to an invalid address, you will receive an automated response from MAILER DAEMON. This is simply an address that the mail server spits out, and it is not from a human being. If you get one of these messages back, you should double-check your e-mail address that you are trying to send to. Maybe you can even contact your intended recipient some other way than e-mail like via telephone and verify the spelling of their e-mail address. If all of that checks out, it will do you no good to write to Mailer Daemon or to reply to a letter from Mailer Daemon. In a case such as this you would need to write to postmaster at whatever domain you are trying to send e-mail to. For example, if you are trying to send e-mail to johnsmith@communications.com, and your mail doesn't arrive, you would send an e-mail to postmaster@communications.com and ask why the mail didn't arrive.

If you are able to send e-mail to everybody but one person, then there is nothing your ISP is going to be able to do about it. Reason being is because the mail is not arriving at only one address. The fact that you can e-mail everyone else proves that your mail and your ISP's mail system are working. You can send an e-mail to yourself to test this if you don't know anyone but the one e-mail address that you are trying to send an e-mail to. Yes, you can send an e-mail to yourself. Just put your own e-mail address in the Send or Send To box. Once again, the following is an example e-mail address: Wynonajasper1@aol.com. The whole thing is the e-mail address; @aol.com is the domain. If you seem to have trouble sending e-mail to just one domain, try sending an e-mail to the postmaster of the domain. In the preceding example, you would write to postmaster@aol.com. The subject could be **mail problems** and you might write: *I try to send an e-mail to Wynonajasper1@aol.com and I get a Mailer Daemon* *message returned to me. Would you please look into this and tell me why the mail might not be going through?*

WE ARE EXPERIENCING TECHNICAL DIFFICULTIES

On the other hand, if none of your e-mail goes out or you can't send e-mail to anybody except people that use your same ISP, then this may be something that your online service can help you with. Don't expect tech support to be able to flip a switch and magically solve the mail problem, but sometimes there are system problems like when you have a snowy picture on your TV. You call the cable company, and chances are that they are fully aware that a cable has been cut in your area, and you can rest assured that they will have that HBO back on ASAP! In the event that the cable service didn't know about your TV outage, they would need to know so that they could dispatch some technicians to fix the problem. The representative at the cable company won't be able to flip some magic switch and make your cable come on immediately, but they will report it so that it can start being worked on. The same goes for your ISP. If you can't send mail to anybody, it is probably going to be a problem on the ISP's end and not a problem with your computer. It may be a system-wide problem where nobody can send mail, and they will usually be aware of these types of issues by the time you call. They will give you an estimated time of repair (ETR) if one is known.

Usually a system-wide problem like that would last an hour or two or perhaps a few hours. If the problem is more isolated, the representative that you talk to probably won't be able to do anything but file a system problem report that may take anywhere from an hour to a few days to fix depending on how severe the problem is. Usually with e-mail they will be able to get it up and running fairly quickly. If it is a bad access number, it could be down for a week or more. It is really up to the phone company to fix access number problems. Your ISP will coordinate with the phone company to fix the problem in the case of a bad access number, however.

Incidentally, AOL and CompuServe 2000 use the same mail server, so if you are an AOL member and send e-mail to a CompuServe 2000 member, all you need to put in the Send To box is the CompuServe member's member name. In other words, you do not have to include the domain **@cs.com**. If you are a CompuServe 2000 member and send mail to AOL, you can just use the person's screen name, and you don't need to include **@aol.com**. However, it will make it to its destination either way. Also, there are 2 CompuServes. CompuServe 2000 and CompuServe Classic. Classic is older, and if your friend has an old computer and CompuServe, you can bet that they are running Classic. Classic e-mail addresses are in the format personal address@compuserve.com, and CompuServe 2000 e-mail addresses are in the format member name@cs.com. America Online e-mail addresses are in the format screen name@aol.com.

To complicate things even more, there are proprietary mail systems that don't follow Internet standards. This means that they have their own protocols, and these systems don't use POP or SMTP mail servers. Some of these proprietary systems include America Online and CompuServe 2000 e-mail. These mail systems are easy to use, fully featured mail clients, and you can send and receive mail to and from anybody in the world for free just like with POP mail programs. Another example of a proprietary product might be a feature that exists on only certain makes of cars, but it doesn't exist on all cars, such as a rear windshield wiper.

Because of the nature of e-mail, usually 3rd party mail programs can't be used with proprietary mail systems. The main reason is that proprietary systems don't have a POP or SMTP mail server. Internet standard mail programs require the POP and SMTP information of your ISP in order to work. Since there is no POP or SMTP server with a proprietary system, then obviously mail programs like Outlook are not going to work since they need the POP and SMTP information in order to function. Interestingly, AOL and CompuServe 2000 use the same mail system, and now it is possible to use POP mail programs with CompuServe 2000. This is made possible by a new mail protocol called ***IMAP***. As of this writing, IMAP is not possible on AOL, but since it works with CompuServe 2000, I would think that AOL would be able to use IMAP in the future.

I have a scanner or a video camera now how do I send my pictures in e-mail?

I prefaced this section with the 3rd party (POP) mail information because you need to be aware of that to understand this piece. Some scanner or camera programs have e-mail buttons where you could ordinarily send e-mail automatically. However, these automatic e-mail buttons require that you have a POP mail client. So they will not work with AOL or CompuServe 2000 or another proprietary system. Since you can technically use POP mail with CompuServe 2000, there may be a way to configure these types of programs to work, but then again it may not be possible. Although you can use POP mail programs with CompuServe, there may be certain features that still won't work because it is really IMAP protocol instead of POP. IMAP is still new enough where everything that will work and won't work with certain ISPs and certain other software, such as camera or scanner software, is still unknown. And if there is a way to make it work, you can bet that your ISP won't help you with it. It does not fall within the realm of support that they are responsible for giving you, so it is the kind of thing that is not going to work unless you can make it work. Also, your mail client has to be IMAP compliant to work with CompuServe 2000, and AOL if they make their mail IMAP compliant, or it will not work anyway.

For assistance with attaching files using 3rd party mail programs, you would need to seek online help or contact the manufacturer of your mail client such as Microsoft for Outlook or Netscape for Netscape mail. There are so many different mail clients and so much scanner and camera software in the world that it would not be feasible for me to go into how to send e-mail attachments with every single one of them. Also, there is a plethora of help and FAQ already on the Internet that covers these subjects. Furthermore, there is **Appendix H**, *Attaching Files to e-mail using America Online or CompuServe 2000,* that will shed more light on the subject as far as how to do it with those 2 services.

I think the following is an interesting article and worthy of injecting into the e-mail chapter. Dr. Joe Burns is a well-known writer and professor that does tutorials on building Web pages and HTML language, the programming language that Web pages are written in. Dr. Burns' Web site is located at *http://www.htmlgoodies.com.* I thought it was time for a little fun to break up this monstrous chapter, and this letter will shed some light on e-mail etiquette so I decided to include it:

E-MAIL NETIQUETTE

by: Joe Burns, Ph.D.

13 *You know what I luv about email????? It allows people to express themselfs in a way that is cool and hip. IMHO, its a frm of speech that everybody should do cuz' its neet to read!!!!!!!!!!!!!! Your free to write what you want to should write and say. my friends and me have been emailin' for years. You know?!?!?!?!?!?! K? C-ya!!!!! ;->*

        *   *   *

Have you ever received an email that looked something like this? When I get an email that comes up as convoluted as this one, I like to take a moment and try to decipher what was a mistake and what was intentionally done incorrectly.

Let's see. If this were real, I would think that "luv", "cuz", "emailin'", "K", and "C-ya" were all done on purpose. "IMHO" are really initials that stand for "In My Humble Opinion". Another one I see a lot is "IIRC", "If I Remember Correctly".

Apparently the third sentence is very important. There are 15 exclamation points. I think the rule is that after seven exclamation points, the line can officially be called really important. After 20, it's really, really important. I remember when the big rule in email text was to not use all capital letters because it was equal to yelling. What's the difference between all caps and 15 exclamation points?

I think the rest of the grammar mistakes could then be chalked up to not paying attention in eighth grade English class.

So, have you ever received an email that looked something like this? I have. In fact, I receive them every day, and it's not just from students either. They come from business people, other professors, and my Dad.

I'd like to say it bugs me to the point where I would say something to the sender, but I rarely do. Don't get me wrong, I'm about as "Type A" as it gets, but email mistakes just don't bug me like I guess they should. Blatantly poor emails from students sometimes get under my skin, but past that, a mistake or two rarely bothers me enough to say anything.

I actually had to stop today and ask myself why I never thought about it before.

If I had to put my finger on a reason, it would be that I see email as a very informal kind of language. In my mind, it's equal to casual conversation, and casual conversation is nothing like the English you would use to write an academic paper (at least I hope it isn't).

Casual conversation is full of sentence fragments, sentences that don't contain proper subjects, and slang. Casual conversation between friends is fun. It's a good time. You make word shortcuts because you and your friend may only need to say a word or two to communicate a broad meaning about something or someone.

I would never talk to my boss like I would talk to my best friend. That's just not the way things work. When you're talking "up" in rank, you do clean up your English. You move closer to that academic English format.

Formal letters are one thing, email is another.

Right?

Wrong! So says Kenneth Brown, an assistant professor at the University of Iowa business school. He doesn't like that people don't take the same time in creating an email letter as speaking in person.

OK, I agree with that. I do not allow students to stand in front of me and use poor English. I'm a communications professor, for goodness sake. I would even think about correcting a student in an email, but my friends? My colleagues? My Dad?

Brown says he does.

Virginia Shea, who wrote the rules of Netiquette, says that you will be judged by the quality of your writing in your emails. She suggests we should all take the time to stop, read, and correct our emails before we send them out.

Would we have time? I can barely answer all I have now, let alone proof them all.

In a rebuttal to Dr. Brown's statements, an employee at an Internet start-up said that her poor emails are not grammatical mistakes, but rather typos.

There's a difference?

Apparently so. The Internet generation has taken casual Friday to a whole new level. I about fell over when I toured a new start-up and there were beds there in case any of the workers decided he or she needed a nap after lunch. They take things real easy, and their emails reflect that.

I'm the first to admit I don't carefully read over my emails before I send them, unless they are going to a person who is in a power position. If I'm sending an email to another professor in order to set up a quick meeting, I write it, sign it, and send it.

When I read about people requesting that emails be proofed, I decided to stop and read all of the emails I sent out this morning.

Wow. I'm a lousy typist.

So what's to be done? The battle is going to come down to the time factor versus good grammar. I'd like to say the grammar will win, but I don't know. People do not see email as a permanent item like a memo or a journal (even though it is), but rather as verbal communication. I did a survey a couple of years back that reported the same thing. Email was seen as far more verbal than written messages, even though it's fully text. People try to "talk" in their email. We've gone as far as to imply emotion through little smiley faces in the text.

But yet, typos still bother a lot of people. Let me tell you, when there's a typo on HTML Goodies, I get letters like crazy telling me what and where the problem is. I especially like the ones that seem to take pleasure in my having made a mistake, and then have misspellings in their own email. I've printed a couple of those to keep forever.

That got me thinking. I always make a point of looking at the emails I put together for my higher-ups. I wonder if others do the same. Professor Brown has made a broad, sweeping statement that may or may not have merit. I would like to see a study comparing emails people send to their equals (friends, colleagues) and emails they send to those in a position of power (bosses, managers). I would think that the emails sent to those in a position of power would have less typos.

I say that because if people consider email more verbal than written, then it would make sense that the pattern of using a more proper form of email would follow using a more proper form of verbal English. Anyone want to co-author? Shoot me an email...but make sure you don't misspell anything. ;->

(Smiley implying that was a tongue-in-cheek request.)

What other types of email might be prone to a higher level of attention? Just for fun, I went to my "favorite flames" directory to have a look at some of the flame emails I kept.

My favorite is the one where a woman gave me heck for being pompous due to my using "Ph.D." after my name. I kept it because she used her own title following her name when she signed the letter.

No typos. Hmmmm…

In fact, there weren't a lot of typos in any of these letters.

Of course, many of the words only contained four letters, so they were pretty easy to nail down. I'll bet these letters received a lot of attention to detail. I get mental pictures of someone ranting around the room speaking their e-mail out loud until they get just the right emotional punch out of the words. These things were well edited, no doubt.

I also keep nice letters. There were some typos, not too many, but still some. I guess when you're writing something nice, you're more concerned about the meaning than the grammar.

Could that be it? Does a friendly email get less attention to the English because it's an equal to "Attaboy!", "Way to go!", "You da man"?

I'll bet there's something to that. Either way, maybe it all comes down to the person sending and the person receiving.

We people are way too complicated to make a general statement that we're all bad emailers. I'll bet if we looked hard enough, the amount of grammatical mistakes in emails would bear out in some way.

But the question still remains…should I correct my Dad's emails?

Joe Burns is really an interesting individual, and if you want to check his Web site out, go to html goodies.com. Maybe you are interested in learning how to build Web pages. Dr. Burns' site is a great place to start.

There are a few Acronyms in Dr. Burns' article such as IMHO (In My Humble Opinion).

Read **Appendix I,** *Internet Acronyms,* to learn the most popular shorthand on the Internet. Shorthand on the Internet is acronyms that are frequently used in e-mail, chat rooms, forums, and newsgroups to abbreviate frequently used phrases.

The rest of this chapter consists of some excerpts from the *PC Novice Guide to Internet Basics* magazine. Check out one of these magazines if you get a chance—the following pieces illustrate how informative they are. If you want to read the full articles, check inside the front cover of their magazine. Magazines will usually give you instructions on how to order back issues inside the front cover somewhere. Or, you can visit their Web site. Most of the time you can find an archive of past articles on a Web site that represents a magazine.

The Life of E-mail

14"*Address. Subject. Message body. It's all there. Now just run a quick spelling check, and hit the Send button. From here on out, the E-mail message has left your hands. The forces of the Internet take over as the magical mystery tour begins.*

It can get somewhat complicated out there, but the basic steps are easy enough to understand…The first stage in the journey of an E-mail message is simply getting out of your computer. That might entail stuffing it through a modem on a dial-up 'Net connection or through a network adapter card on a local-area network (LAN). Either way, the message text must be converted into a form that can be stuffed through the available medium. For networks, that could be a variety of languages. With dial-up connections, the modem must transform your computer's digital code into the analog noises that can be transmitted over phone lines. Weaving its way through phone or network cables, our message arrives at computers run by the ISP or network administrator. What happens next depends upon, to an extent, which type of data is being sent. an E-mail message, for example, is sent to an outgoing mail server computer. The standard format for outgoing mail is Simple Mail Transport Protocol (SMTP), which is why many E-mail programs want to know the name of your "SMTP server."

The SMTP computer shoves the message, now encoded according to Transmission Control Protocol/Internet Protocol (TCP/IP) protocol, onto the 'Net with a push toward the first nearby router computer. At this point, our data is divided into numerous packets, each carrying a small fragment of the message along with the address of your recipient. Here, they bid adieu to one another, promising to meet again one day.

Routers are the traffic cops of the Internet, monitoring the flow of packets around the system. They read the destination information in each packet and send it scooting off toward the next router in the right direction. If the pre-ferred router happens to be malfunctioning or otherwise out of service, the packet will be sent on a more circuitous path. Other routers encountering the packet perform the same service.

Eventually, depending upon network traffic and luck, the packet reaches the destination ISP computer. There it meets with its brother and sister packets from back home and is reconstituted into the original message. The text is then stored until it is downloaded by your friend. For most people using ISPs, this step happens on a computer known as Post Office Protocol (POP) mail server. POP3 is the standard for receiving and storing Internet mail. When recipients check their mail, the POP3 server sends the messages on down to the E-mail client program through the modem/phone line or network card/network con-nection. A cute noise might play, indicating new mail in your friend's Inbox. So goes the life for Internet data."

No Stamp Required

Free E-mail Accounts

Abound On the 'Net

17 *"Some folks still remember the days when free E-mail service was a privilege, not a right. Several epochs ago in Internet time, or about two years ago on the calendar, it was a rare treat to have an E-mail account you didn't pay for. Academics and employees of forward-thinking companies were about the only people enjoying electronic messages at no charge. The public found the concept so novel that when a company called Juno made free accounts available to the masses in April 1996, it was snowed under with requests for the required software. Now finding a company offering free E-mail is about as tough as finding a corner shop willing to sell you a cup of gourmet coffee. Check out the The Free Email Address Directory (http://www.emailaddresses.com).*

The Free Email Address Directory *lists more than 250 sources of free E-mail addresses and says 100 of them arrived between January and June 1998 alone. These services have even achieved the ultimate stamp of joining the Internet mainstream: their own category listing in the Yahoo! Web directory (http://www.yahoo.com) with all of these options, if you're paying anything for basic E-mail service, you're paying too much..."*

How it works

"The "free" nature of most of these E-mail services deserves an asterisk. You'll pay nothing for the service, but you must pay someone else to help you get there in the first place. That's because most of these services are Web-based E-mail,

which means you access your Inbox like any other Web page. You won't have to learn any special E-mail software because you'll be using your regular Web browser to access the service. Controls for sending, reading, deleting, etc, are all in your browser window. Because you're working on the Web, you'll have to pay a monthly rate of about $19.95 to an Internet service provider (ISP) for Web access. Of course, along with access to the E-mail page, your ISP account gets you access to all kinds of information that is available on the Web. Some users, however, refuse to mess with the Web or pay a dime for E-mail. That's where Juno (http://www.juno.com) comes in. (By the way, your ISP fee probably includes an E-mail account.)…"

Even More E-mail

"Many users who already have an E-mail account through work, school, or an ISP still sign up for free E-mail because of several benefits it provides.

First, Web-based E-mail. is a great solution for people who need to stay in touch but are frequently away from their computer. Because you can visit your service's Web page and type in your Inbox's password from any computer with an Internet connection, it's easy to find a place to check your mail. Schools, libraries, clients' offices, airport 'Net kiosks, trade show booths, and many other locations can serve as your temporary post office.

The services also offer a welcome name change from your regular E-mail address.

When you sign up for an account with Hotmail (http://www.hotmail.com), for example, you can send and receive messages as Fowens@hotmail.com or Cheesehead@hotmail.com rather than Fowens@blancoindustries.com. This lets you send messages as a private individual rather than an employee of your company.

Many users set up a free account so they can handle personal E-mail at work without using the corporate E-mail system (though that still involves using corporate PCs for personal messages)…"

"…One drawback to a free account is the possible stigma of an address ending with something such as "@yahoo.com." In certain crowds, a tag from a free service labels you as something of an amateur, or at least someone with no built-in credibility. Some folks would sooner read a marketing proposal from steveclark@ibm.com than steveclark@yahoo.com. Many free services help you avoid the problem by offering vanity addresses ending in things such as occupations (@journalist.com or @lawyer.com, for example, at lycosMail) or even personal interests (@starwarsfan.com, for example, at My Own Email at http://www.myown email.com). My Own E-mail Services often charge around $14.95 per year for a vanity address."

Pick Your Service

"The sheer volume of services available today makes choosing one a big task. You can narrow the field by looking only at the services offered by companies with the best reputations. These include the following:"

AltaVista E-mail   **www.altavista.iname.com**

Hotmail   **www.hotmail.com**

Juno   **www.juno.com**

LycosMail   **www.lycosemail.com/member/loginpage**

MailExcite   **www.mailexcite.com**

Net@ddress   **http://netaddress.usa.net**

Yahoo! Mail   **www.mail.yahoo.com**

"...Visit each service's home page to check out the functionality its E-mail accounts offer. there are enough good services to let you be choosy and demand features such as the ability to filter messages, create multiple folders, attach files to messages, create address books listing frequent correspondents, and keep a healthy number of messages sitting in your Inbox..."

"...Check out the sign-up procedure and decide whether you're comfortable divulging the personal information requested. You even can go so far as signing up for and maintaining several accounts for a while to see which one you like best. The size of the free E-mail market means you're free to choose the service that suits you."

Chapter #23

Dial-up Networking & Ways to Connect to the Internet

This is a rather tough subject to approach, and we are entering into the intermediate computer user zone on this one. Don't worry though, we won't cross the line into the advanced zone since this is a novice computer user book. Some of the things in this chapter will be a reiteration of some information given in other chapters. The main reason for the repetition is just for review purposes. Also, the information should be fresh in your mind for you to understand this chapter, and if you set the book down some days ago, you may have forgotten some of the key points. I will be spewing out some computer terms, but just check the Glossary in the back of the book if you have any questions.

The way that we generally connect to the Internet is via a protocol called TCP/IP. This stands for *Transmission Control Protocol/Internet Protocol*. Remember in the last chapter how POP3 and SMTP are the Internet Standards for e-mail? Well, TCP/IP is the Internet standard for a connection to the Internet. In order to make a TCP/IP connection, you must have a file called Wsock32.dll in your C:\Windows\System directory. On Windows Me this file should be 36kb in size. On Windows 98 this file should be 40kb in size, and on Windows 95 the file should be 65kb. Sometimes, if you have trouble getting to the World Wide Web, the Winsock file is the wrong size, you may have too many Wsock32.dll files on the system, or the Wsock32.dll is in the wrong location. This is something that is easily overlooked, and if a lot of things have been tried and your Web browser still isn't working, it is a good idea to check that the Wsock32.dll is correct.

Sometimes, it is necessary to extract a new Winsock (wsock32.dll) from the Windows CD-ROM in order to fix a problem accessing the Internet. Instructions are outlined in Chapter 20, *The Internet Part II.*

Also, there must be certain adapters in the Network control panel in order to reach the Internet. These adapters and their settings will vary depending on what ISP you have. Keep in mind that we are talking about stand-alone computers here with Windows 95 or Windows 98/Windows Me using a straight dial-up connection opposed to computers that are on a network. A **network** is loosely defined as 2 or more computers that are joined together so that they can share resources. Resources could be files, printers, scanners, etc. The reason why we won't be discussing networks is that they are usually pretty complex, and there are really an infinite number of configurations that they can have. That's one reason why most Internet providers won't support their software on a network.

The ways in which networks can be set up is so vast that it would take an immense amount of knowledge for a tech support person to provide general support for networks. If you run a network, you should know what you are doing, and if you can't make it work, forget it. Furthermore, most ISPs are geared more towards families as a rule and not really the corporate LAN (Local Area Network) environment. However, there are more and more people that are experimenting with home networking these days in order to share resources or to gain other advantages of a network.

Windows uses a dialer called ***Dial-up Networking***. If you use DUN (Dial-up Networking), it doesn't mean that you're on a network necessarily. DUN got it's name primarily because it allows a user to dial into a LAN (Local Area Network) from a remote location using a modem. Traveling professionals that dial into their corporate LAN from the road such as in a hotel room usually use DUN.

A lot of ISPs use DUN and some use their own dialer called a ***proprietary dialer***. Remember proprietary e-mail from the last chapter? Two Internet services that use their own dialer are America Online and CompuServe 2000. Some examples of ISPs that use DUN are CompuServe

Classic, MSN (Microsoft Network), and Bellsouth.net. CompuServe 2000 and CompuServe Classic are owned by the same company, which is America Online Inc. H&R Block used to own CompuServe; at that time it was before CompuServe 2000, so it was just known as CompuServe. When CompuServe 2000 was introduced, the other CompuServe came to be known as CompuServe Classic to differentiate it from 2000: **fig. 65** shows the Connect screen of CompuServe 2000, and **fig. 66** shows the Connect screen of CompuServe Classic. If you don't find definitions for some terms used in this book in the Glossary, or particularly terms as used in this chapter that relate more to the Internet, check **Appendix R,** *Internet Terms Glossary.*

Fig. 65 CompuServe 2000 connect screen.

Fig. 66 CompuServe Classic connect screen.

At any rate, America Online took a lot of the features from AOL and some of the features of CompuServe and rolled them into a package called CompuServe 2000. When CompuServe 2000 came out, all of the versions that preceded it became known as CompuServe Classic. The latest version of Classic is 4.0.2, and it is completely different than CompuServe 2000. CompuServe has been around for years, since 1969 to be exact, and there were many version upgrades up to and including 4.0.2. As of this writing, there have been only two upgrades to CompuServe 2000—CompuServe version 5.0, or it could be called CompuServe 2000 version 5.0, and CompuServe version 6.0. CompuServe 2000 is not an upgrade from the Classic version 4.0.2. The two programs are completely different. That is why the e-mail addresses differ. Classic e-mail addresses are in the format personal*address@compuserve.com*, and CompuServe 2000 addresses look like member *name@cs.com*. Furthermore, one is not necessarily better than the other, but it really depends what you use your computer for and what features you want in an ISP; it is really just a matter of opinion.

CompuServe 2000 is a lot more similar to AOL than CompuServe Classic; this is evident because although there are many differences between the 2 programs, the dialer that AOL and CompuServe 2000 uses is nearly identical and they share the same dial-up network. Also, because they make the same kind of TCP/IP connection to the Internet, the Network settings are the same for both programs whereas CompuServe Classic requires different network settings because it makes a completely different kind of connection to the Internet as well as using a different set of access phone numbers than AOL or CompuServe 2000. Classic uses Dial-up Networking and AOL and CompuServe 2000 (CS2K) use a proprietary dialer. The end result is really the same. I mean you end up on the Internet either way. It is simply 2 different roads that end up in the same place. The DUN (Dial-up Networking) road may be a little more of a direct path, but it is a hard road to drive and it should only be attempted by a skilled driver; there are some profound problems that can arise with DUN. The proprietary dialer road may be a few miles out of the way, but it is a smooth paved flat road with clear directional signs and a scenic view. There really isn't a whole lot that can go wrong with a proprietary dialer like AOL uses. Not that nothing ever goes wrong, but the problems are usually easily fixed. At least there are only so many things that can really go wrong (or so many reasons why you can't connect). Most of the time, the modem can be tweaked to make it connect with a proprietary dialer. The worst case scenario is that you have to get an updated driver for your modem, or the ISP or modem software may need to be reinstalled. I have seen Dial-up Networking problems so profound and so frustrating that Windows needs to be reinstalled to make it work again—or at least that is probably the easiest path. See **fig. 67** for a peek at DUN.

Fig. 67 Dial-up Networking (DUN) connect screen.

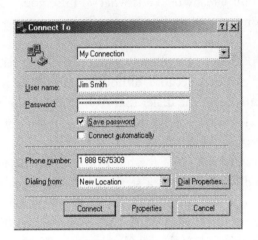

Because of the differences between DUN and the AOL dialer, programs that require an Internet connection will need to be configured differently for each type of connection in order to properly connect to the Web. In **Appendix B**, *How to Set Internet Properties in the Control Panel*, and **Appendix C**, *How to Set Up the Network Control Panel*, I will outline some differences that you may encounter, and I will compare and contrast the Network and Internet configurations between the 2 types of dialers.

I HAVE A BRAND NEW COMPUTER WHAT DO YOU MEAN MY RESOURCES ARE LOW?

First I feel like I need to lay a foundation before I go on to the next explanation. Some of this is going to be a review. But like I said before there is some intentional redundancy in this book just in case you missed it the first time or you just read some of the book or random chapters individually.

First of all, Dial-up Networking doesn't use as many system resources as a proprietary dialer. Don't be surprised if you can connect to a ***plain-vanilla ISP*** and stay connected but you constantly get disconnected from AOL. This is usually not due to network traffic or something on AOL's end. I have America Online and I never get disconnected. Don't you think if you were prone to get disconnected on AOL that everyone would disconnect? I have several computers in fact, and none of them disconnect when on AOL. So you ask why might someone disconnect on AOL or CompuServe 2000? The answer is simple: Resources! There are other more conventional reasons why you might disconnect such as phone line noise or an incorrect modem setup in the online software, but these days disconnecting while online is likely due to low system resources. The resources should be at least 85% to stay connected to AOL or CompuServe 2000 or any other ISP that uses a proprietary dialer. If your resources are low enough, you will likely disconnect from your ISP even if they use Dial-up Networking.

The way that you check the resources on a system is to double-click on the **My Computer** icon on your Desktop. Click on **Help** in the upper-right corner then click on **About Window 98**, or **Windows 95**, or **Windows**. The resources will be expressed as a percentage like 75% or 82%. If this percentage is not at least 85%, or say a minimum of 80%, the modem is likely to disconnect if you have an ISP with a proprietary dialer like AOL or CompuServe 2000. Certainly if these are lower than 70%, you will disconnect or not get connected in the first place unless you are lucky. The other number you will see there is the Physical Memory Available to Windows. This defines the amount of RAM memory on the computer. 130,384 kb would be 128 MB of RAM, for example. Resources aren't always going to be the cause of a modem disconnecting, and it isn't as big of a factor with Windows 95 as Windows 98, but it is certainly something to check if you get disconnected from your ISP a lot. Due to the way a lot of the later-model modems work, and the fact that Windows 98 seems to suck up more system resources than Windows 95, I have found that this is a major cause of modems disconnecting in recent months.

The most likely reason why the resources will be low is that there are too many programs in the **Startup group**. What this means is that the computer manufacturer loads a lot of programs on the computer, which is a good thing really. There are often hundreds of dollars in just software that is preloaded on your computer, and this doesn't even include Windows that costs $200 by itself. What's not so good is that sometimes the manufacturer puts every program on the computer in the Startup group, meaning that they all load every time you start the computer and then they run in the background usually without you even knowing it. That is why a brand new computer can have low resources. Each program that is running uses a little bit of your resources; 15-20 items in your startup group can easily suck up 30% of your resources. At the same time, a lot of modems these days require a lot of resources from your system in order to stay connected. If the resources are low, the modem signal will weaken, and it will likely disconnect. Sometimes, you may be able to connect and stay connected for the most part with low resources, but your modem may not live up to its full potential. For example, your 56k modem may connect at a lot less than 56,000 bps (bits per second). This is another issue that has many possible reasons, however. Some of these reasons are outlined in **Appendix N**, *Why Don't I Get 56K?*

Fortunately, low resources are easy to fix, but you should check with your computer manufacturer or else your warranty might be void if you try to fix this yourself or if someone else besides the manufacturer does it. In case you wonder how it is done, I will outline the instructions in the next section.

How to disable your startup group in one fail swoop

Click **Start** then **Run**. Make sure that everything is erased off of the Run line where it says *O*pen:

Type **MsConfig** (capitalization doesn't matter) and click **Ok**. Click the circle where it says **Selective startup** to put the little black dot in there; if it's in there already then leave it alone. Click on the checkbox at the bottom where it says **Load startup group items**. Make sure that it unchecked the checkbox there. Leave everything else alone on this page, and click **Apply** at the bottom and then **Ok**. Say Yes to restart the computer, and you are done. **fig. 68** shows the MsConfig screen that I am describing.

Fig. 68 Microsoft Configuration (MsConfig).

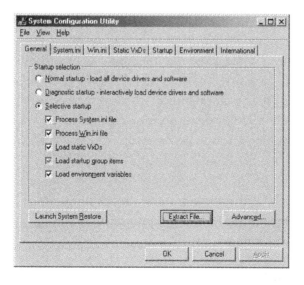

A SOFTMODEM IS HARD ON YOUR PROCESSOR

Low resources might not be an issue if you use Dial-up Networking because DUN uses totally different connection protocols than a proprietary dialer. Furthermore, the resources wouldn't be that much of a problem with certain kinds of modems even with a proprietary dialer. However, these days a lot of modems, called *soft modems*, use a lot of system resources.

One of the toughest questions to answer when I was a technical support representative was "why has it worked for all these months if the problem is my resources?" People would make the valid point that they didn't change anything on their end, so why did it work, in some cases for quite a few months, and just all of a sudden quit working. I mean the resources would have been about the same the entire time. I didn't just get this question about a modem disconnecting, but I was asked the same basic question about all kinds of problems.

The question quite honestly used to make me cringe. The reason why I didn't like this question is really two-fold: First or all, there is no definitive answer. Secondly, I could sense that the question was more profound than simply customer curiosity. Some people I think were just inquisitive, but the difficult people, that were argumentative, seemed to wish to prove me wrong—and take pride in doing so. The customers that wouldn't take no for an answer had some reason why they didn't want to call the system manufacturer I believe. Whether it be because they didn't have anyone to call (computer is out of warranty, manufacturer is out of business, or system was bought at a retail outlet or from a mail-order catalog) or because they would have to pay for tech support, I could understand their persistence.

However, some of these cases dealt with new brand name computers—those cases I didn't understand. I mean it may be inconvenient to call your computer manufacturer, but life is usually inconvenient. I mean the way I had to look at it was that it is not my problem if it is something to do with Windows and not my software. I'm sorry that you have to call the manufacturer, but go complain to them if you have to wait on hold for 3 hours or something like that. I am only referring to the huge manufacturers that net in the billions of dollars every year. If they are shorting their customers on tech support, then they need to hear some complaints so that they can revise their support system.

I have had some of our customers tell me that their computer manufacturer told them that the reason why they couldn't connect to us was that we had problems with our software; they were assured that nothing was wrong with their modem. I am not sure how they would come to that conclusion or what tests they had run, but I would usually see if they could connect in another program that uses that modem such as HyperTerminal. If they couldn't even connect in another communications program, then the problem clearly didn't lie with the Internet Provider but it is something to do with Windows, the modem, the telephone line, or the physical wiring of the connection—definitely not the ISP. While this is obvious to me, I couldn't blame a computer novice for being oblivious to the fact that if the modem doesn't even connect with another program then there is some other problem besides our software. Unfortunately, as a technician for an ISP, I was usually guilty until proven innocent, but people would take the word of the manufacturer as gold. I couldn't blame some of these poor people again because they often found themselves being bounced back and forth between the ISP's and the manufacturer's technical support departments, each telling the person that it is the other ones fault.

TIP How to conduct a modem Line Test in HyperTerminal:

HyperTerminal is a communications program that has many purposes, and it is good for testing a modem when there is some doubt as to whether the modem won't connect with certain software because the software is bad or because of a more general modem or connection issue. You get to HyperTerminal by clicking Start>Run. Type *hypertrm* on the Run line and click Ok. This is a program that can be added to Windows using Add/Remove Programs if your computer tells you that it cannot find hypertrm. If HyperTerminal is installed, you will get a screen that asks for a name and an icon. Ignore the icon and type in *Test* for a name and click Ok. On the next screen there will be a line where you can type in a phone number. Ignore the area code—in other words if it is there, leave it and if it isn't, leave it. Type the following number on the line where it is labeled Phone number: 1-847-262-6000 By the way, you don't have to use any spaces or dashes in the phone number, but it will connect either way.

If your modem is working properly, you will be connected to a Line Test that tests the integrity of your modem and your phone line. When you are asked for your first name, type *line* and when it asks for your last name, type *test*. It will then perform a series of diagnostics on your modem and telephone line and give you a synopsis at the end. If you cannot connect to this Line Test, chances are that you have modem or telephone line issues and you should probably consult your computer manufacturer and tell them that you cannot connect in HyperTerminal. If it tells you at the end that your phone line does not support 56k, you will never get above about a 28.8 kbps connection unless your phone company gives you a cleaner phone line. However, they are only obliged to give you a line that is cleanenough for a 9600 bps connection, so good luck!

The Web address for the line test is http://www.3com.com/ 56k/need4_56k/linetest.html

BUT IT'S WORKED ALL ALONG!

For the most part it really is a legitimate and good question why something would just stop working when there have been no changes. It is a question that I'm sure I would ask if I was a computer novice—certainly if I never took tech support phone calls. I think what bothered me the most about this question is that it was difficult to provide an answer without sounding sarcastic.

Although some of the reasons I am going to give you will sound condescending, I am really not trying to be. When I would answer the question over the phone, I'm sure that a lot of people thought that I was trying to be smug—In most cases, I was not trying to do anything but give the person a straight answer by drawing an analogy. I would say that I've had a lot of used cars, and many of them started up every morning and worked for months in some cases. Most of my used cars would refuse to start sooner or later for various reasons. After all I didn't change anything right?

If your computer doesn't meet the minimum system requirements it may explain why something quit working—even if it has been working for months. You have no right to complain or expect support if your system is outdated. System requirements are established for a reason and they are usually a lot more generous than they should be. If your computer doesn't meet requirements, something will probably quit working sooner or later—even if everything worked for a year or more. The analogy that I used a lot was that running a lot of the sophisticated software out nowadays with a slow processor, like a 486, is like pulling a semi trailer with a Volkswagen Beetle. It may chug down the road for a block or two, but it will probably blow up on you eventually.

The subject of a computer failing is usually a lot more profound than a used car analogy, however. The answer is actually based on the same principle as anything that may work for a long time and just quit one day out of the blue. The specific answers are going to be different of course because we are talking about a computer specifically and not a TV, car, toaster, or anything else.

The most logical answer that I can think of as to why a computer will stop working in one way or another is as follows: I will cite a specific example because the answer is obviously going to vary with each problem that may arise; the principle will be the same, however. Let's take the example that we were discussing before. You are getting disconnected from your ISP, and the tech rep tells you that your resources are low. They have been the same the whole time, so what gives? I pose the question to you that if nothing changed on your end, why and how could the computer be acting differently? Logic tells you that there must have been some change on your ISP's end; that assumption may be correct. Your ISP may have updated something on their system that rendered your resources insufficient—much like how the evolvement of the Internet has rendered a 2400-baud modem fairly useless. It may be that your telephone company has rerouted the analog signal so it takes a less direct path—I mean after all, the telephone company is definitely going to be a factor with a dial-up connection. The reason why you started disconnecting may be something other than resources. It may be that you have more line noise than you used to; it's possible that because of any one of the aforementioned reasons, and then some, you may need to get an updated driver for your modem if you suddenly start getting disconnected from your ISP or if you can't get connected anymore at all. It does not matter if you just got your computer today. You may still need to get an updated driver. A driver usually won't cost you anything, and it normally isn't something that you physically need to put in the computer. A driver is software that you install; it can be downloaded from the Internet sometimes (See **Appendix J** *Downloading Files from the Internet*), and your manufacturer may be able to send it to you on a disk for a nominal fee. If something did change and you are suddenly having connection problems, it is a safe bet that whatever the change, it is not going to revert back to the way it was. Therefore, you will need to correct whatever the problem is on your end of the connection (your computer) to make it work again. Check out Appendix G, **Computer Problems**—*Why am I Having so Many Computer Problems*, for a more in depth look into why things may not work in the first place or why things may work for a while and just quit.

HARDMODEM vs. SOFTMODEM

The modems of old usually had an onboard processor that powered the modem itself, so the modem was pretty much self-sufficient. Soft modems have no onboard chip, but they use the CPU (Central Processing Unit) on the computer. So the modem is driven directly from the power of the computer itself instead of having it's own power supply. Therefore, it requires a lot of computer resources for the modem to connect and stay connected. This is why we live in the world of the $20 56k modem because if it uses the computer's power, it is less expensive to produce. Don't get too upset though because we also live in the day of the 3-figure PC. As a matter of fact, it's not unusual to get a PC loaded with software and memory and a printer for less than $1000 these days. It wasn't more than a couple of years ago when the same package would have set you back several thousand bucks. So if worse comes to worst, and you've tried everything and the modem still disconnects, then maybe you will be better off just trying a new modem. You can get the top of the line 56k for about $100, so you will really still be coming out far ahead in the over all scheme of things. You might not even need the top of the line either; you can probably get a more decent modem then the one that you may find in your budget PC for somewhere in the $50-$80 range.

EXTERNAL vs. INTERNAL BROWSER LAUNCH

Now that we've gotten that out of the way let's talk about Dial-up Networking a bit more. Because DUN is built into Windows and Microsoft makes Windows and Microsoft Internet Explorer, it can be configured so you can click on the Internet Explorer icon and it will bring up a dialogue box of your ISP if they use DUN. You will be prompted for your user name and password and you're connected to the Internet. America Online and CompuServe 2000 does not work exactly in this manner, so if you click on the icon on your Windows Desktop that says Internet Explorer, it won't go anywhere right off the bat. If your ISP does not use Dial-up Networking, what you need to do to get that Internet Explorer icon to work (to launch the browser by clicking on the Explorer icon) is connect to your ISP, minimize it and click on the IE icon. Incidentally, if you have AOL or CompuServe 2000, you have Internet Explorer built into the program. If Internet Explorer wasn't built in already, you wouldn't be able to get to the Web inside of these programs. Specifically, AOL and CompuServe 2000 use the Internet Explorer that is already on your computer and the programs are constructed so that they can use the same browser inside of them. The Web browser may look a little different, but it is Internet Explorer. The only big difference is that the CompuServe or AOL logo is in the upper-right hand corner instead of the Microsoft logo.

If you have AOL or CompuServe 2000, you can take the long way around and sign on then minimize the program by clicking the minus (-) sign in the upper-right corner then double-click on the Internet Explorer icon. However, this would be the long way of doing it since you would be using the same browser by going to the Web inside of AOL or CompuServe 2000 instead of using the browser externally. The only reason why you might want to take this longer approach is if you like using another browser like Netscape instead of Microsoft Explorer. In that case, you would have to launch the browser externally since Netscape is not built into these programs.

You will need to use the same method of signing on and minimizing the AOL or CompuServe 2000 program with any program that requires an Internet connection. You will need to set any applications that needs an Internet connection to the setting that says, "I have a direct connection to the Internet" or something similar. The other choice will be something like "Connect using a Modem," or "I have a dialup connection," or something of that nature. The dialup setting is used if your ISP uses Dial-up Networking.

Like I said previously, read **Appendix B** and **Appendix C** for an in-depth look at specific settings for the Internet and Network control panels for various ISPs.

Chapter #24

Fonts and Little Tips and Tricks With Pictures and Text

Wingdings

♁✂■✵♎✂■✵◆

◆✂■✵♎✂■✵◆✵🖱⌨●🗀🖮🗁🗄⌛☎

Wingdings 2

♁✂■✵♎✂■✵◆   📄

◆✂■✵♎✂■✵◆   📄🗨   ◆♒✂◆   ✂◆   ♋   ■♏◆   ✗□■◆

Wingdings 3

♁✂■✵♎✂■✵◆   📄

♁✂■✵♎✂■✵   📄🗨   ❋♒♌✂◆   ✂◆   ♋   □□♏◆◆◻
♏□□●   ✗□■◆

♋●◆□✎

or maybe you want to make a statement with goudy stout.

There are many many fonts out there, and a lot of them are free for download. Below are some urls for fonts.

http://www.onlinebusiness.com/shops/_computers/BEST_Fonts.shtml

http://www.freesitetools.com/fonts.html

http://fonts.tom7.com

http://www.microsoft.com/typography/fontpack/default.htm

http://trashed.org/sassyfonts

http://members.aol.com/typograf/english/fonts.html

http://Web.mit.edu/rdinner/www/fonts.html

http://www.buyfonts.com

http://www.fonts.com

http://www.freefonts.org

The main text is written in Times New Roman in 12 point and the Large Text above that introduces the chapter is written in Times New Roman in 18 point. This is 8 point This is 9 point This is 10 point This is 11 point This is 12 point, 16 point , 24point, and 28 point all in the Times New Roman font.

The designs above represent several different versions of Wingdings and then there's the Goudy Stout font—a favorite in England, and it really does make a statement I must say. If these Wingdings symbols were converted to a readable font, they would appear in plain English. The ones above are more or less typed at random. The symbols could be copied & pasted into AOL or CompuServe 2000 e-mail, or a similar utility, in order to convert them to plain text. Once the symbols are pasted into the mail window, just highlight the symbols, and switch the font to an ASCII type like you are looking at now. See **Appendix K**, *Description of ASCII and Binary Files*, if these terms make no sense to you. In other words, with the mail used by AOL or CompuServe 2000, highlight the line of symbols once they are pasted into the window where the e-mail message is normally typed. Select an English font like Arial or Helvetica and it will convert the symbols into English letters or numbers as the case may be. There is a drop-down list where different fonts can be selected in these mail programs. This will work in any other program that has a font selection such as MSWord.

Fonts are just the style in which text appears: Sometimes, with certain fonts such as Wingdings, each letter and number on your keyboard will be represented by a symbol. Your text would appear like the cryptic-looking "hieroglyphics" at the beginning of this chapter if you were using one of these type of fonts.

Mail will normally be able to be sent with any font in it. However, the person on the receiving end will need to have the same font installed on their computer in order to see it. If you want to send a letter in GOUDY STOUT, the e-mail recipient will need to have GOUDY STOUT installed on their computer in order to see it. To install new fonts on your computer, you need to open up the Control Panel then the Fonts applet. Click on **File** at the top left then choose **Install New Fonts**. Most of the time when you download something from the Internet, like fonts, there will be instructions that will tell you how to install it. Look for these things because sometimes they may not reach out and bite you. There may be a little link to click on that says "Read Me" or "Read Description" or something like that, and it could be easily missed. If it's an actual program, and not just a font, the Read Me file (the file that gives you instructions on what to do with a program and how to install it) will usually present itself once you start installing the program. Be advised that a lot of fonts installed on your computer can really bog it down. If your computer is slow, and all the obvious causes have been explored such as a full hard drive, then it may be worth checking how many fonts are installed and delete the ones that you can live without.

TIP Fonts not to delete:

Before you start deleting all those font files that make your system boot slowly, make sure that Windows doesn't need them. For example, you should not delete the following fonts: Arial, Courier, Marlett, Modern, MS Sans Serif, MS Serif (or any font with a name beginning with "MS"), Small Fonts, Symbol and Times New Roman. Also, don't delete any fonts that start with 8514 or VGA.

You may also have some hidden fonts that some application installed and needs, so you don't want to delete them either. To identify hidden fonts, open a DOS window and type CD \Windows\Fonts to switch to the fonts directory. Type DIR /AH and press Enter to see a list of hidden font files.

EMOTICONS

Kind of a neat feature of the 'Net is emoticons, which are symbols that express emotions. These are made by using combinations of letters, numbers, and punctuation marks. They are commonly seen in e-mail, instant messages, and chat rooms. You can view a large list of emoticons in Appendix O, *Emoticons.*

Another neat trick for you are ALT commands. Look at **Appendix L,** *Alt Commands,* at the back of the book to see these. ALT commands are your answer if you need Spanish symbols or really anything that's not on a standard keyboard. To use these commands, the ALT key and a number combination like 6694 must be pressed. The key combination would be said to be in the format **ALT+6694** in that example. A lot of the ALT commands have a 2-digit number instead of 4. It is necessary to hold the ALT key down and press the number combination while pressing the ALT key the whole time. After the number combination is banged out, let up off of all the keys, and the appropriate symbol will be typed.

Furthermore, there is a Character Map that resides in your Accessories or System Tools menu. Click **Start>Programs>Accessories>Character Map** in Windows 95 or **Start>Programs>Accessories>System Tools> Character Map** in Windows 98 or Me. You can easily view all of the characters available with any one font with this tool. Just choose the font that you want in the drop down list in the Character Map window. If Character Map isn't installed, you can add it using Control Panel's Add/Remove Programs applet. In the drop-down list under Font, select the font you're using in your document. Find the character you need, double-click it to add it to the Characters To Copy field, then click on Copy. Return to your document, place your cursor where you'd like the character to appear (or select a letter to replace) and press Ctrl+V to paste the new character.

A PICTURE REQUIRES 1000 WORDS

Pictures are going to be in a certain file format. Pictures made on one computer may not be able to be read on another computer. Some common picture formats are GIF, JPG, and BMP. On a computer a picture is not simply just a picture, but it can be in various file formats. Some are better at reducing file size and some are better at displaying a true-to-life detailed picture. In other words, photo quality is usually sacrificed for a smaller file size. If a picture looks very good, chances are that the file is large—but not necessarily.

There may be situations when you will want to save a picture in a certain format to fit a certain situation. For instance, if you are creating a Web page, generally bitmap images (.bmps) are not the best choice because they are large and they load very slowly. Programs can be used to convert bitmaps to **Graphics Interchange Format** (.gifs) that are much smaller files, and generally it doesn't compromise that much picture quality by converting files to GIFs. I already mentioned what GIF stands for: JPEG, sometimes seen as JPG, stands for **Joint Photographers Expert Group**. BMP stands for **Bitmap**.

To achieve a small file size, you should save or convert your images to GIF or JPG format. The reason why it is desirable to save the file in a small format is that it will expedite its transfer in e-mail across the Internet. You don't want your friend to get mad at you because it took 2 hours for him to download a picture of your dog. If you are sending a picture to someone with a Macintosh computer, you should save or convert your graphic into TIFF (Tagged Image File Format) format because that is cross-platform compatible. This seems a little complex, and it can be, but all you need to know for now is that every computer file has an extension. An extension is a 3-letter abbreviation. A text file might be something.txt, or something.doc. A picture file may be .bmp, .gif, or .jpg. There are all kinds of file formats, and some only can be read on a Macintosh computer and some can only be read on an IBM PC. Check out the URLs below for more info about file formats: There is a list of file formats in **Appendix E**, *File Extensions*, as well.

http://www.matisse.net/files/formats.html

http://www.whatis.com/ff.htm

TIP How to change file associations:

When you open up a file, it is supposed to automatically open up in an application that will be able to properly translate that file. If it doesn't open up properly, there are several things that you can do. Right-click on your file and left-click on Open With. You may get a cascading menu where you can select Choose Program... This selection will open up a whole list of programs from which you can choose one that will open up the file. If you don't get the cascading menu with Choose Program on it, just right-click on the file and left-click on Open With straight away; it will give you the same list of programs to choose from that you would get if you clicked Choose Program. If your program isn't on the list, you can choose Other... at the bottom of the list window. On older versions of Windows, you may not have the Open With option when you right-click on a file. All you need to do in this case is hold down your Shift key and right-click on your file. It will produce a different right-click menu that will give you the Open With option. You may need to left-click once to select the file then right-click on it in order to get the Open with option.

In some cases, you can rename a file to an extension that will make it open up with a standard Windows application. For example, rename a file called mouse.mme to mouse.txt and see if it opens up properly in Notepad. A lot of these methods are trial and error, but the more you experiment the more you will know. It helps to know what extension your file has, what it is supposed to open it, and other applications that may be akin to the one that is really supposed to open the file. If you don't have the necessary application to open a certain file type, you may be able to choose a similar application that will also be able to handle that file type. Remember though that in some cases, you will need to download a viewer to read your file or you will actually have to have the application installed on your computer that a file was created in or you will not be able to make it work.

TIP Associate programs with more than one file extension:

It's possible to associate multiple applications with a single file extension. For example, to associate the .DOC extension with Word for Windows and also WordPad, open any folder window. Choose View > Folder Options > File Types. In the Registered File Types box, find and select the Microsoft Word Document entry. Click the Edit button, and then the New button. In the Action box, type Open with WordPad. In the "Application Used to Perform Action" box, type the following line including the quotation marks and click OK:

"c:\program files\accessories\wordpad.exe" "%1"

(If you run into trouble, use Find Files and Folders to locate the path of WordPad on your PC and adjust this line.) From now on, when you double click any .DOC file, it will launch Microsoft Word. But you can also right-click it and choose "Open with WordPad" on the context. You can use the same steps to associate many other file extensions with two or more programs. Try it with .ZIP or .TXT, for instance.

A PICTURE BY ANY OTHER NAME WOULD SMELL AS SWEET

Files have formats so that the computer knows what kind of file it is. From that information it knows how to run that program or display the picture if it is a graphics file. The extension indicates to the computer what application is needed to open a certain file type. For example, there is a .bat file that stands for a batch file; this is a series of commands that tell the computer to do something directly. There is an autoexec.bat file that the computer looks at when it starts to see if there is anything that it needs to load whenever the computer starts. Therefore, Windows itself is the application that is needed to run a batch (.bat) file. Below is the Autoexec.bat file from the computer I am on now. The computer follows these instructions at startup. The line PATH C:\MOUSE; MOUSE tells the computer to load the software for the mouse so that it works when Windows starts up. Windows knows that a batch file is a series of instructions that it must carry out. If you open up a text file, that has the extension .txt, Windows will open it in Notepad by default because that is the program that is associated with a text file. It will remain that way unless the user changes the file associations on the computer.

AutoExec.bat

@if exist C:\WININST0.400\SuWarn.Bat call C:\WININST0.400\SuWarn.Bat

@if exist C:\WININST0.400\SuWarn.Bat del C:\WININST0.400\SuWarn.Bat

PATH C:\MOUSE;

MOUSE

File formats were mentioned in Chapter 19, *File Attachments*, and I have mentioned .zip files as well, so I'm not going to go into it again. Just realize that files can be saved in different formats, and sometimes, a specific program is needed to read a certain file type. For example, Scanner software called Visioneer Paperport, that is usually packaged with Hewlett Packard Scanners, will save a file in a format called .max. If no steps are taken to save the file any differently, it will typically save your scanned picture as a MAX file. If a file attachment recipient of a MAX file doesn't have a Hewlett Packard scanner, then chances are they don't have the Visioneer Paperport software on their computer. And without the Paperport software, they will not be able to read a file in that format. This example illustrates what is called a proprietary file format because it is not an Internet standard, computer standard, or cross-platform. In other words, it takes a particular program to read the file, and usually the program will not be installed on the computer when it comes from the factory. The application would need to be installed on your computer that a proprietary file was created in or else you will not be able to read the file when it is downloaded from e-mail onto your computer.

The best thing do in this case, as the sender of a file attachment, is to save the file in a format that is compatible with most computers such as GIF or JPG. In the case of a scanned picture, click on **File** in the upper-left corner and choose **Save As...** in your scanner software. There is a Save As Type drop-down list at the bottom of the window that will come up. All of the choices of the file formats will be presented there. In the Visioneer Paperport example, .gif or .jpg would be the best bet in most cases. These are Internet standard formats for pictures, meaning that usually there will be a program built into Windows that will be able to open these files properly. Another choice to Save As with a scanner might be a TIFF (.tif) file that will generally be very large, and it might take an hour or more to upload a simple picture in this format. The same picture saved as a GIF might take about 8 minutes or less to upload. Although as I mentioned, a TIFF file can be viewed on a Mac or a PC. And if the picture is saved as a .max, the recipient of the file will probably not be able to read it if they don't have a Hewlett Packard scanner. A file cannot necessarily be saved in any format desired. The choices are really set forth in the Save As...Save As Type drop-down window. If you want to save the file as another format than is offered by your scanner or camera software, it would be necessary to get a file converter (a program that is capable of converting files from one format to another) such as Adobe Photoshop, Paint Shop Pro, etc.

SAVINGS PICS FROM WEB PAGES

On the Internet, a picture can be saved right off of a Web site. Yes it can!! Just right-click on any graphic and left-click on **Save Picture As...** Usually the Save As Type choice will be whatever format the picture will be best saved as. Usually it's best to leave this alone and then just type in a file name. Let's say that you choose the name flower for the file and at the bottom it says .gif for the Save Picture As... choice. The entire file name would be flower.gif. Then, all you would need to worry about is where to save the file. It will go somewhere on your hard drive, but it will be up to you to find the file. I recommend saving a file to the Desktop until you are familiar with navigating your computer. When saving a file on the Desktop, the file will be right there with all of the other icons on the screen that come up when the computer is started. Right-click on a picture on a Web site. Left-click on **Save Picture As...** There will be another drop-down list at the top of the page that says Save In: Click the little arrow to the right of that and choose **Desktop** there. Then just click **Save** in the lower-right portion of that window. The file will be on the Desktop if done correctly. Furthermore, each icon on a computer will appear a certain way. A bitmap usually looks like a jar with three paint brushes in it and a piece of paper in the background. A JPEG appears as a painting that is primarily red, and a GIF appears as a painting that is primarily green. Thus, these types of files will be easily identifiable on the Desktop.

TIP How to change the Appearance of your icons:

You can change the associations of your icons just like you can with your file associations. In other words, you are changing the actual icon that is associated with a certain type of file. Open up My Computer and click on View>Options>File Types in Windows 95, View>Folder Options>File Types in Windows 98, or Tools>Folder Options>File Types in Windows Me. The screen you will be on is where you can change file associations—What application will open up what type of file automatically. However, to change the icon you want to click on Advanced at the bottom of that window. Then just click on Change Icon… at the top of the next window and you will get a whole list of icons from which you can choose. If you don't like any of the ones on that list, click on Browse… on the next window and you can point to any icon that you have on the computer. Like fonts, icons are abundantly available for download on the Internet; they usually have an extension of .ico.

EMBEDDED GRAPHICS

Another neat trick is that any graphic or picture from a Web page can be copied and pasted from one location to another location. With AOL version 4.0 or above or CompuServe 2000, a picture can be copied & pasted directly into e-mail. However, only someone with these programs will be able to see the picture in e-mail when they receive it. If your intended recipient has another service, besides AOL or CompuServe, the picture will need to be uploaded as a file attachment instead of just pasting the picture directly in e-mail. To insert a picture directly in e-mail, right-click on a picture that you want to save and left-click on **Copy**. Open up the e-mail on AOL or CompuServe 2000, and click on the window where you would ordinarily type your message. Right-click in that area and left-click on **Paste**, and the picture will be in there. When you insert pictures directly in e-mail, it is called an ***embedded graphic*** as opposed to sending the file as an attachment.

A picture can be pasted somewhere else as well such as Paint: Follow the instructions before for copying and pasting but instead of opening a new e-mail window, click on **Start>Programs>Accessories>Paint**. Click on **Edit** on the top menu in the Paint program and choose **Paste**. A message may appear that will ask if you would like the file resized. It depends on the circumstances whether you will want to click on Yes or No to this question. Try one of them, and if it doesn't look like it should, click **File** at the top and choose **New**. When asked if you want to save the file, say **No**. Then click **Edit** and choose **Paste** again. This time choose the other option. i.e. If you said Yes the first time, say No and see if your picture appears more like you wanted it.

Congratulations you have graduated this computer course!!

P.S. We were originally going to leave this book at 24 chapters. But in the effort to give our publisher (and our readers) their monies worth, we went one step further. Read on for Chapter 25 that could be construed as the Epilogue.

Chapter #25

(The Hidden Tutorial)

We were going to stop at 24 chapters, but we decided to make it an even 25. On our Web site, we have a link at the end of the 24th chapter that leads to Chapter 25. That is the only place that makes any reference at all to the 25th chapter, and that's why it is subtitled The Hidden Tutorial. You wouldn't know it was there unless you read all of the tutorials or at least you would have to read the entire 24th chapter to see the link (or scroll down to the bottom). There is a watered-down version of this book on our Web site, but there has been extra information crammed in the book that can't be found on the Web site. For example, none of the appendices can be found on the Web site per se. However, a lot of the information in the appendices are built directly into the chapters themselves or there are links that point to some of the information that are found in them. The book on our Web site is a rough draft, so readers can take it or leave it—bad grammar and all. The information is organized a lot better in the hard copy book. Our contact information can be found at the end of the book if you are interested in visiting our site to look at the electronic version of this book or to send us a comment/suggestion. See **fig. 69** for a glimpse at what our Web site looks like.

Fig. 69 Tutorial Web site www.compquest.org.

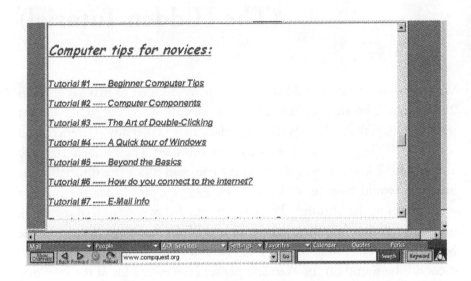

Hopefully, this chapter kind of sums everything up and answers some of the questions that you may still have after going through the 24 chapters. If you really want to learn computers, hang in there. You've probably learned a lot already, and maybe you've learned all that you care to and that's great; that would mean that this book was effective. We sincerely hope that you've learned enough to be content if you don't care about being an expert but you just want to know enough to be fairly comfortable on your PC. Whatever the case, remember that you will likely run into frustrating situations on your computer even if you are an expert. Remember that for each problem that you run into you will probably come out a bit wiser when you finally figure out the solution.

As a beginner you will probably have a lot of questions about why this doesn't work or why that doesn't work. Why does my modem disconnect? Why does this program conflict with that program? Why does something that seems like a simple concept not work on the computer or my ISP? The thing that you have to realize is that computer science is still far from perfect. Personal computers have really only been around for about 20 years, and they were very rudimentary until perhaps 10 years ago and really just about 5 years ago depending on how you look at it. Think of when the automobile was only 20 years old. It would have been circa 1920, and there were still a lot of kinks to work out with the car. Also, the parts and the way automobiles worked were not common knowledge. A call to tech support about your car might have gone something like this:

16 What if people bought cars like they buy computers?

General Motors doesn't have a "help line" for people who don't know how to drive, because people don't buy cars like they buy computers —but imagine if they did...

HELPLINE: "General Motors Helpline, how can I help you?"

CUSTOMER: "I got in my car and closed the door, and nothing happened!"

HELPLINE: "Did you put the key in the ignition and turn it?"

CUSTOMER: "What's an ignition?"

HELPLINE: "It's a starter motor that draws current from your battery and turns over the engine."

CUSTOMER: "Ignition? Motor? Battery? Engine? How come I have to know all of these technical terms just to use my car?"

HELPLINE: "General Motors Helpline, how can I help you?"

CUSTOMER: "My car ran fine for a week, and now it won't go anywhere!"

HELPLINE: "Is the gas tank empty?"

CUSTOMER: "Huh? How do I know?"

HELPLINE: "There's a little gauge on the front panel, with a needle, and markings from 'E' to 'F'. Where is the needle pointing?"

CUSTOMER: "I see an 'E' but no 'F'."

HELPLINE: "You see the 'E' and just to the right is the 'F'.

CUSTOMER: "No, just to the right of the first 'E' is a 'V'.

HELPLINE: "A 'V'?!?"

CUSTOMER: "Yeah, there's a 'C', an 'H', the first 'E', then a 'V', followed by 'R', 'O', 'L' ..."

HELPLINE: "No, no, no sir! That's the front of the car. When you sit behind the steering wheel, that's the panel I'm talking about."

CUSTOMER: "That steering wheel thingy— Is that the round thing that honks the horn?"

HELPLINE: "Yes, among other things."

CUSTOMER: "The needle's pointing to 'E'. What does that mean?"

HELPLINE: "It means that you have to visit a gasoline vendor and purchase some more gasoline. You can install it yourself, or pay the vendor to install it for you."

CUSTOMER: "What? I paid $12,000 for this car! Now you tell me that I have to keep buying more components? I want a car that comes with everything built in!"

HELPLINE: "General Motors Helpline, how can I help you?"

CUSTOMER: "Your cars suck!"

HELPLINE: "What's wrong?"

CUSTOMER: "It crashed, that's what went wrong!"

HELPLINE: "What were you doing?"

CUSTOMER: "I wanted to go faster, so I pushed the accelerator pedal all the way to the floor. It worked for a while, and then it crashed—and now it won't even start up!"

HELPLINE: "I'm sorry, sir, but it's your responsibility if you misuse the product."

CUSTOMER: "Misuse it? I was just following this damned manual of yours. It said to make the car go to put the transmission in 'D' and press the accelerator pedal. That's exactly what I did—now the damn thing's crashed."

HELPLINE: "Did you read the entire operator's manual before operating the car sir?"

CUSTOMER: "What? Of course I did! I told you I did EVERYTHING the manual said and it didn't work!"

HELPLINE: "Didn't you attempt to slow down so you wouldn't crash?"

CUSTOMER: "How do you do THAT?"

HELPLINE: "You said you read the entire manual, sir. It's on page 14. The pedal next to the accelerator."

CUSTOMER: "Well, I don't have all day to sit around and read this manual you know."

HELPLINE: "Of course not. What do you expect us to do about it?"

CUSTOMER: "I want you to send me one of the latest versions that goes fast and won't crash anymore!"

HELPLINE: "General Motors Helpline, how can I help you?"

CUSTOMER: "Hi! I just bought my first car, and I chose your car because it has automatic transmission, cruise control, power steering, power brakes, and power door locks."

HELPLINE: "Thanks for buying our car. How can I help you?"

CUSTOMER: "How do I work it?"

HELPLINE: "Do you know how to drive?"

CUSTOMER: "Do I know how to what?"

HELPLINE: "Do you know how to DRIVE?"

CUSTOMER: "I'm not a technical person! I just want to go places in my car!"

So be open-minded and remember that there are a lot of incompatibilities with computers. Not everything is really logical with computers, and something that might seem like it should be able to be done on your computer or with your ISP may be virtually impossible—at least at this point in time. See **Appendix G** *Computer Problems—Why Am I Having so Many Computer Problems?* for more insight on this subject.

There is so much software and hardware abound that the chance of incompatibility is great amongst computers. The same kind of conflicts as you may run into on a computer can arise if you try to put a Mazda transmission into a Chevy automobile, except software and even hardware isn't as clearly defined as auto parts. Software is software, and it is either made for a PC or a MAC or both and that's it. Computers have come a long way in a relatively short time, however. And believe me, they are a lot easier to use than they once were.

The Internet has grown exponentially in recent years, and it continues to do so on a daily basis to the tune of 100,000 words per day. It has grown almost to the point of utter saturation. You can find nearly any kind of information or product on the Web, and there is so much redundancy that I didn't even bother to go into a lot of Windows tips & advice. This kind of information is very bountiful on the Web and some computer magazines are solely devoted to discussing the different components of Windows and detailed tips & tricks that can be performed on the computer. Some of the better ones can be found in **Appendix S**, *Resources*.

The primary reason why I put this book together is because one thing I noticed is that while there are also a lot of beginner computer tips in the world, there is really not an over abundance of information that has no assumed computer knowledge. I tried to deliver this book from that perspective, and hopefully I explained things from a different angle than most books or articles of this nature. Also, I figured what's one more computer tips book ;-) It would seem that these days it's better to have too much information than not enough. The higher chapters in this book have some assumed knowledge, but just that of the previous chapters.

CHEAPSKATES RULE!

These are the days for the cheapskates because there is all sorts of free stuff and information around on the Internet. We have a decent freebies page on our Web site. There are links to the bulk of at least most of the major freebies sites on the Web. Check it out at *http://www.compquest.org/freebies.htm*.

At first glance it seems like the Internet would have posed a great hindrance for the average business. I mean all of a sudden a business finds itself behind the curve if they don't have Web presence. It obviously takes manpower and money to host a Web site and purchase a domain name, etc. While a lot of this might serve as an income tax write-off, it still isn't going to immediately spark any revenue in most cases. So how do companies manage to setup and run a virtual store in addition to a bricks & mortar store? Well, the fact is that being online has doubled the bottom line (or more) for many businesses so it's easy to justify an online store.

Another question that might be posed is how in the world do so many people offer freebies on the Internet? The answer is very simple: Advertising. Freebie sites typically acquire all of their revenue from companies that place *banners* on their Web sites. The banners will hopefully spark business for them. Obviously, the more attractive the freebie, the more traffic the site will generate. The more appealing the site, the more valuable it will be to companies wishing to advertise. Advertising takes many other forms such as direct mailings or forms that must be filled out that are sold to marketing companies that sell demographics statistics. The question is whether these freebies will continue, and the answer is likely they will. As long as companies feel like they are getting a lot of advertising bang for the buck, the freebies will continue. At any rate, this is a good time for a cheapskate!

DON'T FEAR YOUR COMPUTER AND BACKUP YOUR FILES

The most important thing that I think I could mention to a new computer user is just not to be afraid of the machine. No matter what you do to your computer, you are not going to blow it up unless you put a stick of dynamite inside the tower unit or something of that nature. If you totally screw up, you may need to reinstall Windows, but that's about the worst that can happen. If you run the restore disk that you normally get with a new computer, it will put everything back to the way the computer was when it came from the factory. You will have a clean slate (assuming that you bought the computer new or else a restore disk will put everything back to the original factory settings). Remember that if you deal in real estate, the 3 most important things are location, location, and location. When you are talking about computers, the 3 most important things are backup, backup, and backup. Take heed now. If there are any files on your computer that you can't live without, back them up as soon as you get a chance. These files might include tax or financial info, word or text documents, an address book, favorite places, or old e-mail that you have saved. Either contact your computer manufacturer for instructions for backing up your system, look in your computer manual, or check the computer's help files by clicking the **Start** button then **Help**. Or seek advice in another manner that you are familiar with. There are free tech support sites on the Web (links to these can be found on our Web home page) and some of them are listed in Chapter 6. You can find these sites by searching for technical support on a search engine. If you want to backup your address book, saved mail, or favorite places, your ISP can probably give you advice on backing these up. And, if you are unable to figure out how to back up your files or you are afraid that you might erase everything while trying to just back up the files, at least print everything out that is vitally important.

MY BACKUP STORY

When I was in the Army I was messing around with the computer that held all of the Battalion Supply department's vital information. I stumbled upon a way to partition the drive. At the time I had no idea what I did exactly, and I didn't even know that partitioning a drive would erase all of the information on it. Next thing I knew the computer wouldn't start up anymore, and I walked to the mess hall as calmly as I could to get someone I knew that worked in the Supply department and kept up the files on their computers. He also knew a great deal more than I did about computers at the time, and I figured he would know some way to get the computer to boot again. I told him that I really screwed up and that he had to come immediately. He had to tell the mess sergeant that he had an emergency because he was elbow deep in dishes at the time.

He sat down and typed in a few DOS commands, and after about 5 minutes he started shaking his head; he said something like "man you wiped the drive out." Well, there was a Major that was the head of the Operations department that happened to have a degree in Computer Science. We had seen this guy take a computer apart down to the individual microchips and put it back together. I mean he could disseminate a computer down into as many parts as you could possibly break it down to and piece it back together and make it work again without a manual or anything. I thought surely he would be able to restore this thing.

As we were waiting for the Major to arrive, a little crowd had gathered around the computer because the word got out fast as it usually does in the military. We stood there waiting for the Major to come and take a look at the computer, and I felt about 2 inches tall by that time. The tension built to a fevered pitch as we waited for him. It was about 10 minutes until he arrived, after the crowd had formed, but it seemed like 10 hours to me. The Major finally made his way down and I swear he wasn't sitting at the computer for more than a minute before he said, "it's gone."

It took a while before I lived that one down, but it turned out that a lot of people learned an important lesson that day. I learned the biggest lesson of course, but the Supply department learned to back up their information. They had a little bit of it backed up but not nearly everything.

That's probably why I didn't get court marshaled because they knew they were wrong not backing up all of their information. Also, all of us that worked on the Battalion computers learned how to partition drives which led to other advanced tricks. Some people actually thanked me a few months down the road for enabling them to learn new things. I submitted that story to *Reader's Digest* once for their *Humor in Uniform* piece, but they never printed it. In retrospect, I think it was ironically funny— although it was not the least bit funny at the time—how this fevered pitch built up only to be told in about 30 seconds by the resident computer guru that it was hopeless. Well, I guess you had to be there.

Computer Hardware

Now let's take a look at the inside of your computer's tower unit just in case you wonder just what makes it tick. First of all everything inside the computer is plugged into a ***motherboard*** which is really a large circuit board where cards plug into slots on the board. The motherboard is frequently referred to as the ***main board*** as shown in **fig. 70**. Sometimes smaller cards that plug into the motherboard are referred to as ***daughter cards***. On the main board there is a ***battery*** that's usually about the size of a quarter and maybe a ½" thick or so. The battery generally lasts 3-5 years, and it is doubtful that leaving the computer on all the time will save battery life. In fact, it might be the other way around. I turn my computer off when I am not using it. There are other good reasons why you should shut down your computer at least at night or when it's going to be several hours or more before the computer is going to be used again. Symptoms of a dying battery would include the system clock running slow. If you notice that your system clock is running slow, set the clock back to the correct time in the Time/Date section of the Control panel. If the clock continuously loses time, your battery probably needs replacing.

**Fig. 70 Motherboard—notice the fan to the right.
The CPU lies beneath the fan which keeps the chip cool.**

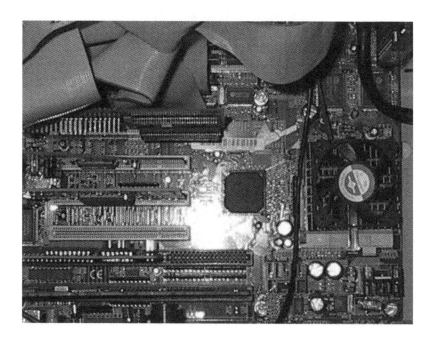

The *Central Processing Unit*, called the CPU or processor, sits on the Motherboard, and usually there is a fan directly over it because the CPU has a tendency to run hot **(fig. 71)**. The CPU is what you hear about that runs at a speed expressed in Megahertz (Mz) such as 400Mz, 550Mz, or 800Mz. The Central Processing Unit is basically the brain of the computer.

Fig. 71 Intel pentium 166Mz central processing unit.

Another device that plugs into the motherboard is the modem. We've talked about this one quite a bit in previous chapters. This is the device that dials out over your telephone line and enables you to connect to the Internet. There are 2 places to plug a regular telephone cord in the back of the computer that is really the edge of the modem that you can see without opening up the computer case. One of these ports is usually labeled **phone** and the other one may be labeled **line** or **telco**. The phone port is an optional convenience jack where you can plug a phone if you want to, but it is not necessary. If you have a laptop computer, your modem will probably be a PC card formally called a PCMCIA card (Personal Computer Memory Card International Association), and it will only have one place to plug the phone cord. The essential thing when connecting up to the Internet is to have one end of the phone line going into the line port (or the one that's not labeled phone), and the other end of your phone cord goes into a working phone jack in the wall. It is a good idea to run a direct line here especially if you can't connect to your ISP.

In other words, avoid running the wire through a fax machine, caller ID box, or even a surge protector if you are having connection problems of any sort. Once you can connect, you can try to integrate such devices. If you can't connect after adding such devices, you either have it hooked up incorrectly or there is something wrong with the device. Or, at least there is something wrong with the part of the device that you run a telephone cord through. I have seen surge protectors that had a bad circuit where the phone line goes. The other part might be fine, but the part that houses the electrical plugs works on a different circuit than the one that houses the phone cord. Therefore, one part of a surge protector can be perfectly fine when the other part may be faulty.

Next up would be the **sound card**. Fairly self-explanatory this one—no sound card no sound. Although CDs would still play because that goes straight through the speakers, and the signal doesn't have to pass through the sound card. You would be able to hear the modem dialing without a sound card because the modem has a speaker of its own in most cases. The sound card is where you could plug a microphone, headset, or MIDI. MIDI is a **Musical Instrument Digital Interface**, and it is a device that can bridge the gap between a musical instrument and your computer. If you have a MIDI and the proper software, you can play notes from a keyboard and they will be input into your computer. You could make sheet music from the notes that you played. Then, of course you could print out the sheet music with a printer. Look at **fig. 72** to see a sound card.

Fig. 72 Sound card

The ***video card*** is the next thing we'll look at as shown in **fig. 73**. The quality of the video card determines how good the graphics will look with a video game or a graphics intensive program like AutoCAD. CAD stands for Computer Aided Design, and many architects use this program as well as people with similar professions. The bottom line is without a video card of some sort on a computer, you would not see anything on the screen, but it would just appear black on the computer monitor. The video card controls how the graphics are rendered on your computer screen in general. You will usually only notice the difference between a mediocre video card and a good one if you are using a graphics-intensive program, however.

Fig. 73 Video card

The next item you might see inside your computer is RAM chips. RAM stands for ***Random Access Memory***, and it is the physical memory on the computer. Remember, RAM is different from hard drive space. If you think of a desk, hard drive space would be the space that you have available in the drawers, and the RAM would be the space that you have available on the surface of the desk. So regardless of how full or how much space you have in the drawers, if you have too little RAM,

it would be like if your desk only had a surface of say 1 square foot. If your desk had a surface area that was only 1 foot wide by 1 foot long, you couldn't put too much on that desktop at one time could you? RAM chips are usually 4-5 inches long and maybe an inch wide and ¼" inch thick more or less as shown in **fig. 74**. They slide down into a slot on the motherboard made to accommodate them just like all the other cards we are talking about.

Fig. 74   64 MB RAM chip

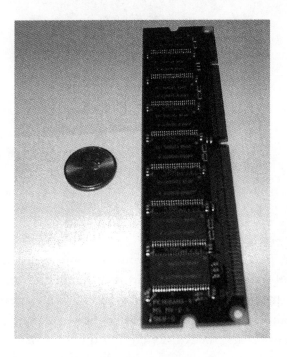

Most cards can be seen somewhat on the outside of the computer just to the point where you can see the end of the card. For example, you can only see the part where you plug the phone wire into the modem. RAM chips are completely encased in the computer's tower unit, and they will not be seen unless you look inside the tower unit on the motherboard. Other cards that you might see are a ***parallel port,*** where a parallel bi-directional printer cable (IEEE-1284 compliant) would plug into. There are ECP ports also that might be in your computer or you might install them in your computer to add extra ports. ECP stands for ***extended capability port.*** ECP ports can be used to add an extra parallel port or another type of port to your computer. You may already have a printer that is taking up your only parallel port. If you go out and get a scanner that requires a parallel port, it might be necessary to add an ECP port that would give you an extra parallel port for the scanner.

Fig. 75 CD-ROM drive

Fig. 75a Floppy drive

Some other things that you will see inside your computer are the drives. Like some of the cards, you will see the front of some of the drives on the outside of the tower. You will notice the CD-ROM drive **(fig. 75)** and the floppy drive **(fig. 75a)**. If you opened the computer case and you followed these drives to the back, you would see a ribbon cable that goes from the back of the drives to the motherboard. The hard drive is kind of like the RAM chips because you can't see it unless you open the tower unit. The hard drive is usually a silver box that is about 6 inches long, 4 inches wide, and 1 ½" thick. There will be a ribbon cable that runs from the hard drive to the motherboard like the CD-ROM and floppy drive **(fig. 76)**. The hard drive is the main drive on the computer, and it is what Windows is installed on as well as any other programs that might be on the computer. If your hard drive becomes full, you won't be able to install any more programs on the computer. If the hard drive gets really full, the computer will run very slowly, and it may even get to the point where it won't boot up anymore. If this happens, it will be necessary to either uninstall some programs to free some space, upgrade to a larger hard drive, or install a 2nd drive on the computer. If the computer gets so full that Windows won't start anymore, it can crash your computer, usually meaning that you will lose all data that you have on the system—further testimony that you should always backup important data.

Something that I think is worth mentioning is if you do lose information on your hard drive, and you didn't heed my advice about backing up your files, there are data recovery services that may be able to recover lost information. You usually would mail your hard drive to them, and they will mail your information back to you on backup disks if they are able to recover the data. The less disk activity done after deleting a file, the more of a chance you have of getting lost data back. That means if you delete a file accidentally, and want to recover it, do not install or delete any programs if you want there to be any chance at all of recovering your file. In many cases, these data recovery services are successful, but it will cost you a pretty penny. There are programs that you can install that can restore lost data in some cases. This is the one exception where you may want to alter the file structure by installing a program to recover data because it will be a much less expensive alternative to a data recovery service although the chances of recovery will be less.

**Fig. 76 Ribbon cable that hooks drives up to the motherboard.
Shown with a floppy disk for perspective.**

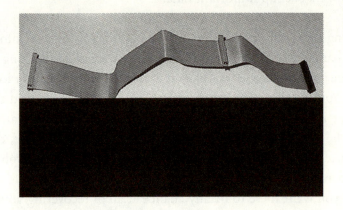

You can have up to 4 physical drives installed on a modern computer. A typical scenario for using all of these slots is a CD-ROM drive, a CD Rewriteable, and 2 physical hard drives. In such a configuration, the 1st drive is the master and the 2nd drive is known as the slave drive. The master drive is labeled letter C. All drives on a computer have a letter assigned to them. A slave drive is normally labeled letter D. And, if you have a CD-ROM in this configuration, it is labeled E and a CD-Rewriteable is the F drive. The CD-ROM drive (E drive) in this case is called the secondary master drive, and the Rewriteable CD-ROM (F drive) is called the secondary slave. The floppy drive is usually always labeled the A drive, and if you had any other drive, like a zip drive, it might be letter G in this scenario. While the main drive (primary master) is always assigned the letter C, the other drives can be changed around to reflect virtually any letter in the alphabet that you want. A lot of times the F drive will be skipped, and the CD-ROM might be drive E and the CD-Rewriteable would assume the G letter. In Summation, drives are called the **primary master, primary slave, secondary master,** and **secondary slave.** The majority of systems will not have any secondary drives, however.

In older computer systems, there was a protocol to describe how drives can be configured called *IDE* (Integrated Drive Electronics). In the IDE configuration, there can only be 2 drives on the IDE channel, meaning that you could only have a C drive and a CD-ROM drive at best. The floppy A drive works on its own channel and is different from IDE. Since you could only have 2 drives on the IDE channel, the only way that you could have a 2nd physical drive was not to have a CD-ROM drive, for all practical purposes. Of course, you could partition your C drive into many parts, so you could still end up with a C, D, E, and F drive if you partitioned your C drive into 4 parts; your CD-ROM drive would then be letter G. Modern systems use *EIDE* (Enhanced Integrated Drive Electronics), meaning that you can have up to 4 drives on the EIDE channel. This could include a primary master and slave, and a secondary master and slave. In short, Enhanced IDE added another channel that allows for 2 more drives. The 1st channel is the primary channel and the 2nd channel is the secondary; there can be 2 drives per channel. IDE only allowed 1 channel, and there could be 2 drives on that channel. You don't necessarily have to have hard drives on the primary channel and CD-ROM drives on the secondary channel either. However, drives run faster on the primary and that is why typically hard disks are installed on the primary channel. However, there wouldn't be anything wrong with installing a CD-ROM to your primary channel in the slave position. You may then install a 2nd physical hard disk on the 2nd IDE channel in the primary position and close it out by putting a CD-Rewriteable on the secondary IDE channel in the slave position. In that configuration, you would have hard drive (C), CD-ROM (D), second hard drive (E), and CD-Rewriteable (F), as the **primary master, primary slave, secondary master,** and **secondary slave,** respectively.

I want to stress that you can have more than 1 hard drive without having more than 1 physical drive. This can be achieved by partitioning your hard drive. In other words, you can have 1 actual hard drive and partition it into 2 parts and have a C and a D drive. Or, it can be partitioned into 4 sections and you will end up with C, D, E, and F, and then your CD-ROM would become letter G. A lot of computers come from the factory with the CD-ROM drive labeled letter G to leave room for 4 partitions or more physical drives.

A partition is just like a wall. So if your hard drive was a room, you could construct a wall to divide the room into 2 rooms or more, and you can place the partition or partitions anywhere you want. One purpose for this might be for organization. Maybe you want to keep all of your business programs on one partition and all of your games on another. Also, if a drive is very large, it makes it run more efficiently if it's partitioned in at least 2 halves. Just like in a room, you could construct a partition anywhere you like. You could make a tiny room that's 10% of the whole room and then have the other 90% on the other side of your wall or partition. The same principle applies with a hard drive: You can put the partition anywhere you want. Each partition would be assigned it's own drive letter as if they were different physical drives. The only real difference is that with 2 physical drives one is a master drive and one is a slave drive. With partitions, it is called a primary and a secondary partition even though they would each have their own drive letter as if they were 2 separate physical drives.

IRQs AND I/O ADDRESSING

Every piece of hardware on your computer has what is called an I/O (Input/Output) address and an IRQ (Interrupt Request). An I/O address is like a mailing address. Just like everyone that has a residence has a mailing address, every peripheral on your computer has an I/O address. That way the Central Processing Unit (CPU) knows where to find each piece of hardware just like the postman knows where to find your residence to deliver the mail. An Interrupt Request is so that hardware can request the attention of the CPU. If you have an IRQ conflict, the computer will usually freeze when any 2 devices having a conflict request to be used at the same time. You may have an IRQ conflict and not even be aware of it until you do something on your computer that involves the hardware that has a conflict. For example, if your modem and sound card are conflicting, you will probably never have a problem until you sign online and do something that requires the sound card. Since the majority of your applications probably don't use the modem and sound card at the same time, this may never pose a problem or it will take a while for you to run into difficulty. When 2 or more devices request the processor's attention at the same time, it is kind of like if you tried to write a letter and ride a bike at the same time. If 2 devices have the same I/O address, it is like if 2 cars tried to park in the same parking place simultaneously. A classic example of an IRQ conflict is when the mouse is installed on Com 1 that uses IRQ 4 and the modem is installed on Com 3 that also uses an IRQ of 4. When the modem is set in motion in this configuration guess what happens? The mouse will freeze. That one is not so common anymore, but it used to be a big issue with systems of a few years ago. See the following IRQ list that comes from one of my systems. Below the IRQs, I have listed detailed hardware information about my modem. Notice that the I/O address is 0x03E8, which would be said to be just 03E8. Also, the IRQ of Com 3 is 5 when I mentioned that Com 3 uses IRQ 4. This hardware information comes from a machine running Windows Me that has the ability to use it's resources much better than older operating systems and it assigned Com 3 the IRQ of 5 to avoid a resource conflict. More advanced operating systems are the reason why we don't see the modem/mouse conflict much anymore. Detailed information about your hardware can be found in the Device Manager as well as

System Information. **Start>Programs>Accessories>System Tools> System Information**. Look to the left and look under the Hardware Resources or the Components heading.

IRQs

IRQ 0 System timer
IRQ 1 Standard 101/102-Key or Microsoft Natural Keyboard
IRQ 2 Programmable interrupt controller
IRQ 3 Communications Port (COM2)
IRQ 4 Communications Port (COM1)
IRQ 5 U.S. Robotics 56K Voice INT PnP
IRQ 7 Printer Port (LPT1)
IRQ 8 System CMOS/real time clock
IRQ 9 IRQ Holder for PCI Steering
IRQ 9 IRQ Holder for PCI Steering
IRQ 9 IRQ Holder for PCI Steering
IRQ 9 Intel 82371AB/EB PCI to USB Universal Host Controller
IRQ 9 YAMAHA Native DS1 WDM Driver
IRQ 9 Creative AudioPCI (ES1371,ES1373) (WDM)
IRQ 9 3Com EtherLink XL 10/100 PCI TX NIC (3C905B-TX)
IRQ 10 Adaptec AHA-152X/AHA-1510 SCSI Host Adapter
IRQ 11 IRQ Holder for PCI Steering
IRQ 11 Matrox Millennium G200 AGP
IRQ 12 PS/2 Compatible Mouse Port
IRQ 13 Numeric data processor
IRQ 14 Intel 82371AB/EB PCI Bus Master IDE Controller
IRQ 14 Primary IDE controller (dual fifo)
IRQ 15 Intel 82371AB/EB PCI Bus Master IDE Controller
IRQ 15 Secondary IDE controller (dual fifo)

Hardware Resources

Name   U.S. Robotics 56K Voice INT PnP

Description   U.S. Robotics 56K Voice INT PnP

Device ID   ISAPNP\USR3090\B5D6D5AE

Device Type   Internal Modem

Attached To   COM3

Answer Mode   Not Available

Compression Off   &K0

Compression On   &K1

Error Control Forced   &M5

Error Control Off   &M0

Error Control On   &M4

Speaker Mode Dial   M1

Speaker Mode Off   M0

Speaker Mode On   M2

Speaker Mode Setup   M3

Speaker Volume High L3

Speaker Volume Low   L0

Speaker Volume Med   L2

I/O Port   0x03E8-0x03EF

IRQ Channel IRQ 5

Driver c:\windows\system\vmm32.vxd (, 1,008.76 KB (1,032,968 bytes), Not Available)

TIP Backup Tips:

It is a good idea to back up the following files on your computer

In case of a catastrophe. Create a folder to copy your files, such as D:\BACKUP.

It's better to do this on a different drive or partition, if possible, although it's not essential. Next, create a Notepad file called RESTORE.BAT and place it in your

C:\Windows directory. Copy and paste the following lines into this text file.

The d:\backup in each line must match the actual destination folder name you created on one of your hard drives or partitions, so change it accordingly.

copy c:\autoexec.bat d:\BACKUP

copy c:\autoexec.dos d:\BACKUP

```
copy c:\config.sys d:\BACKUP

copy c:\config.dos d:\BACKUP

copy c:\windows\control.ini d:\BACKUP

copy c:\windows\system.ini d:\BACKUP

copy c:\windows\win.ini d:\BACKUP

attrib -r -h -s c:\msdos.sys

attrib -r -h -s c:\windows\user.dat

attrib -r -h -s c:\windows\system.dat

copy c:\msdos.sys d:\BACKUP

copy c:\windows\system.dat d:\BACKUP

copy c:\windows\user.dat d:\BACKUP

attrib +r +h +s c:\msdos.sys

attrib +r +h +s c:\windows\user.dat

attrib +r +h +s c:\windows\system.dat
```

TIP Track Installation Changes:

You can use the System File Checker in Windows to find out exactly what effects a program has on your system when you install it. After installing a program, open the log by launching the System Information utility (Start>Programs>Accessories>System Tools>System Information).

Choose System File Checker from the Tools menu and click on the Settings button then click the View Log button. The log will tell you exactly what files were added to your computer during an installation and what files were updated with a newer version.

TIP Get rid of the Windows Password:

If you want to get rid of the annoying prompt that asks For your password when you start your computer, search **For a file in the C:\Windows directory with the extension of** .pwl. Delete this file. Actually you can search for *.pwl using the find files utility (Start>Find>Files or Folders or Start>Search >**For Files or Folder on Win Me) then click Edit on the menu bar and choose Select All. Click on File on the menu bar and click** Delete sending them all to the recycle bin.

This will reset the pop up User window to appear in a different format.

The window will now say, "If you don't enter a password, this window will not appear again." The one instruction this User window neglects to tell **you is to press the Enter key instead of pressing the OK button. When you reboot, the window will not reappear.**

TIP Using MsConfig:

Disable your startup programs to boost your system resouces.

With the MsConfig utility, you can do this all in one shot or selectively. Click on Start>Run. Type *msconfig* on the run line and click Ok. On the General Tab, there will probably be a dot in the circle next to Normal Startup. Click the circle next to Selective Startup and uncheck the box at the bottom that says Load Startup Group Items even if it looks grayed out.

If the dot is already next to Selective Startup then leave it there

And just uncheck the box, leaving all the other checkboxes alone.

If you want to selectively remove startup group items, click on the StartUp tab in the upper-right corner. All of the programs that are loading when your computer starts up will have a check mark next to them. Remove the ones that you want then click Apply then Ok. Restart the computer when it asks or your changes will not stick. If you have too many things that start up and run in the background it can really bog your computer down, cause the modem to disconnect, and cause program conflicts.

About the Author

Jay is an English major from the University of North Florida and he now resides in the suburbia of Jacksonville, FL. After a stint in the Army and attending college, Jay was the Vice President of an interior design company. He left that position to pursue a career in the high-tech sector; he has been working for a large Internet provider for several years now and took up writing as a part time hobby.

Appendix Index Volume 2

O *Emoticons*   (Chapter 19, 24)

P *Internet Explorer Keyboard Shortcuts*   (Appendix B)

Q *Instructions for Disabling Hardware*   (Appendix C, Chapter 16)

R *Internet Terms Glossary*   (Chapter 21, 23)

S *Resources*   (Chapter 16)

T *Mime—Attaching Files to Internet Messages*   (Chapter 19)

Appendix A
Shortcut keys for Windows

General Shortcuts

Operation	Key(s)
Bypass CD-ROM autoplay	Hold down Shift while inserting CD-ROM
Cancel dialog box	Esc
Cancel drag-and-drop	Esc
Capture screen to clipboard	Print Screen
Capture active window to Clipboard	Alt + Print Scrn
Choose command or option	Alt+*underlined letter*
Close program/window	Alt+F4
Command prompt bootup	Press F8 when Starting Windows 98 message appears
Copy	Ctrl+C
Cut	Ctrl+X
Delete	Delete or Del
Delete, no Recycle Bin	Shift+Del
Find files or folders	F3
Help	F1
Paste	Ctrl+V
Properties	Alt+Enter
Refresh	F5
Rename	F2
Shortcut menu	Shift+F10

Shut Down	Alt+F4 after all windows closed
Start menu	Ctrl+Esc or Windows key
Step-by-step startup Press	Shift+F8 at start up beep
Switch to another program	Alt+Tab
System menu	Alt+- (hyphen)
Undo	Ctrl+Z

Dialog Boxes

Operation	Key(s)
Cancel without saving	Esc
Checkbox on/off	Spacebar
Choose option	Alt+*underlined letter*
Click default (dark-rimmed) button	Enter
Click selected button	Spacebar
Cursor to end of line	End
Cursor to start of line	Home
Drop-down list (open)	Alt+down arrow
Next option	Tab
Parent folder (go to)	Backspace
Previous option	Shift+Tab
Scroll	up arrow, down arrow, Page Up, Page Down
Slider left/right	left arrow, right arrow
Spin box up/down	up arrow, down

arrow
Tab (next)   Ctrl+Tab
Tab (previous)   Ctrl+Shift+Tab

My Computer

Operation	Key(s)
Back	Alt+left arrow
Close	Alt+F4
Close active and parent windows	Hold Shift while clicking Close (X) button
Copy selected item(s)	Ctrl+C
Cut selected item(s)	Ctrl+X
Delete, no Recycle Bin	Shift+ Delete
Find Files and Folders	F3
Forward	Alt+right arrow
Paste	Ctrl+V
Properties	Shift+Enter
Refresh	F5
Rename	F2
Select all	Ctrl+A
Up to parent folder	Backspace

Windows Explorer

Operation	Key(s)
Collapse expanded folder	left arrow
Parent folder	left arrow
Expand folder	right arrow

Collapse selected folder	Num Lock +— (minus sign)
Select first subfolder	right arrow
Expand all folder below current folder	Num Lock + *
Switch between left/right panes	F6

Program Shortcuts

Operation	Key(s)
Cancel	Esc
Close document	Ctrl+F4
Close program	Alt+F4
Copy	Ctrl+C
Cut	Ctrl+X
Delete	Delete or Del
End of document	Ctrl+End
End of line	End
Find	Ctrl+F
Help	F1
Menu	F10
New document	Ctrl+N
Open document	Ctrl+O
Paste	Ctrl+V
Print	Ctrl+P
Pull down menu	Alt + underlined letter
Replace	Ctrl+H
Save	Ctrl+S
Select All	Ctrl+A
Select item from open menu	*underlined letter*
Start of line	Home

Top of document	Ctrl+Home
Undo	Ctrl+Z
What's this?	Shift+F1

Drag-And-Drop

Operation	Key(s)
Cancel	Esc
Copy file(s) being dragged	Ctrl+drag
Create shortcut(s) to dragged item(s)	Ctrl+Shift+drag
Move file(s) being dragged	Alt+drag

Accessibility

Filterkeys on/off	Hold down right Shift key for 8 seconds
High Contrast on/off	Left Alt+Left Shift+Print Scrn
Mousekeys on/off	Left Alt+Left Shift+Num Lock
Stickykeys on/off	Press Shift 5 times
Togglekeys on/off	Hold down Num Lock for 5 seconds

WinKey

Here's what you can use the Windows key for. It's key that's on newer keyboards in between Ctrl and Alt

* WinKey + E = *Opens Windows Explorer*
* WinKey + F = *Opens Find*
* WinKey + R = *Opens Run*
* WinKey + Pause = *Opens System Properties*
* WinKey + D = *Maximize / Minimize all windows*
* WinKey + M = *Minimize all windows*
* WinKey + Shift + M = *Undo minimized windows*
* WinKey + Tab = *Flip between open apps in the taskbar*
*WinKey+F1=*Help*

Additional Keyboard & Shortcut Tips:

Utilize those numeric keys

You can use the number keys on the numeric keypad as single-click keyboard shortcuts for launching your 10 favorite programs. Start by pressing the Num Lock key if it isn't already on. Next, right-click on an existing program shortcut and choose Properties. Open the Shortcut tab. Click once inside the Shortcut Key field, press the number key that you want to associate with the program, then click on OK. Repeat the steps for each application. For Internet Explorer, you'll have to make a shortcut to the Desktop icon first, then follow the same steps using the new shortcut. If your Num Lock key isn't turned on by default, check your system's BIOS setup for a Num Lock default setting.

Shortcuts at your fingertips

Your applications on the Start menu are just two clicks away. Here's how to make them only one click away: Right-click on the Start button and select Open from the Context menu. Select all the shortcuts you want, and drag and drop all of them onto the Links toolbar.

Resize windows using the keyboard

You can move or resize open Windows applications by using only your keyboard. First, press Alt+Spacebar to bring up a menu. Press S, then use the arrow keys to resize the window. Press M and move the window using the arrow keys. Press Enter to keep the window change or Esc to return the window to its previous state.

View all drives at once

You can view the properties of a drive by right-clicking on the drive icon in My Computer and then left-clicking on Properties. This will tell you the free drive space for one thing.

Here's a way to view the properties for multiple hard drives all at once. Open My Computer and select all your hard drives by holding down the Ctrl key and clicking on each drive. Next, right-click on any one of the drives and choose Properties from the drop-down menu that appears; Windows will create a single dialog with tabs for each drive. It also works for floppy, removable and mapped network drives.

Rapid Restart

Restarting Win9x is normally a four-step process (click on the Start button, select Shut Down, click on the "Restart the computer?" button and then click on OK). You can make it a one-step process by creating an icon on your desktop that restarts Win9x. Open Notepad and type @exit. Close the document and give it a name with a .BAT extension. Now save the file somewhere on your hard disk. Create a shortcut to the file by using the right mouse button to drag it to the

Desktop and then selecting Create Shortcut(s) Here. Right-click on the shortcut and select Properties. Click on the Program tab and select the Close on Exit box. Now click on the Advanced button and make sure "MS-DOS mode" is selected and "Warn before entering MS-DOS mode" is not selected. Click on the OK button twice. Give your new shortcut a unique icon and name. From now on, whenever you double-click on the icon, Win9x will restart, no questions asked.

Another restart

You can create a shortcut icon that will automatically reboot Windows. In the Command line, or Target field, type: C:\WINDOWS \RUNDLL.EXE user.exe,exitwindowsexec Name the new shortcut Restart Windows. Warning: This shortcut restarts your system without confirmation, so only double-click on it when you're sure that's what you want to do.

Eject a CD with your mouse

Right-click on the CD-ROM icon in My Computer and select Eject from the Context menu to eject the CD from the drive.

Disable Auto Run on your CD-ROM drive

Hold down the shift key while inserting the CD-ROM disk. Keep holding down the shift key for several seconds. The CD disk will not play. You can also disable the CD-ROM so when you place a CD in the drive it won't automatically play. Double-click on My Computer and then on Control Panel. Open the System Icon, then click on the Device Manager tab. Make sure there is a dot to the left of "view device by type." Click on the plus sign next to the CD-ROM drive. Right click on your CD-ROM drive and select properties. Click on the settings tab and click on the check mark that appears to the left of "Auto insert notification." This removes that check mark. Click on OK and then again on OK. When you restart the computer, it will no longer start any CD-ROM disk you insert.

Assigning Shortcut Keys

You can assign a Shortcut Key Combination to any shortcut icon, program, or file. The key combo will open your program even if you can't see it, like from inside another program, with a couple of keystrokes. Right click on any shortcut icon, including the ones on the Start Menu, and choose Properties. Type **Ctrl+ (any letter)** to assign the key combination. In Windows Me, type a letter where it says Shortcut Key; it will automatically fill in Ctrl+Alt+whatever letter you used. Then just click **Apply** then **Ok** at the bottom. Don't make 2 shortcuts with the same key combination and make sure the key combo is something you can remember.

Appendix B

How to set Internet Properties in the Control Panel

First, open the control panel (**Start>Settings>Control Panel**) or double-click on My Computer and Double-click on Control Panel. Double-click on the Internet icon (these icons in the control panel are in alphabetical order so look where the **I** should be here). The icon might be named Internet Options, which means that you have Internet Explorer version 5.0 or above. If this icon is named Internet Options (see **fig. 77**), I will cover the directions in the next section because the screens will be different than if your icon just says Internet.

Fig. 77 Internet Options in the control panel.

Remember, if your icon is labeled Internet, you have Internet Explorer 4.0 or below, and if it says Internet Options, you have Internet Explorer 5.0 or above. If you have IE 4.0 or below, click on the **Connections** button at the top of the screen.

You will see 2 connection options.

1) Connect to the Internet using a modem

2) Connect to the Internet using a LAN

For CompuServe 2000 and America Online, choose the option "Connect to the Internet using a LAN." For any other Internet service provider choose "Connect to the Internet using a modem." If you run AOL or CompuServe 2000 and another ISP, or dial into a network at work, then choose the option "Connect using a LAN (Local Area Network)." If something seems not to work correctly about your connections, switch to "Connect to the Internet using a modem" and see if it solves your problem. Click **Apply** then **Ok** at the bottom. If there is no APPLY, just click OK. With IE 4.x.x, you might have to switch these settings back and forth with multiple ISPs or if you are on a network or dial into an Intranet at work. The best solution here is to upgrade to Internet Explorer 5.x.x.

If you have Internet Explorer 5.0 or above, click on the **Connections** button at the top of the screen after you open the Internet Properties as shown in **fig. 78**. With America Online or CompuServe 2000, make sure there is a dot where it says, "Never dial a connection" even if it is grayed out. Click on the **LAN Settings** button at the bottom of that page and uncheck anything here that may be checked like "use a proxy server." If something is checked but grayed out, don't worry about it. Click **Ok** and then click on **Programs** at the top as shown in **fig. 80**. Click on **Reset Web Settings**. Leave the check mark in the "Also reset my home page"

box and say **Yes** to follow through with this. Also, make sure that there is
a check in the lower left corner where it says, "Internet Explorer should
check to see whether it is the default browser." Click **Apply** at the bottom
and then **Ok**. If APPLY is grayed out, just click OK to close the Internet
Properties.

Fig. 78 Connections button in the Internet Options applet

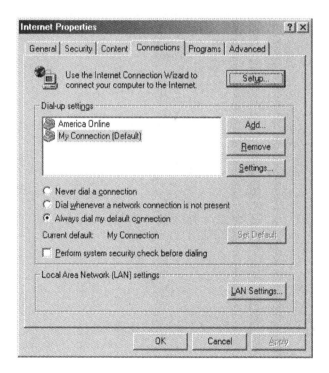

Fig. 80 Programs button in the Internet Options applet.

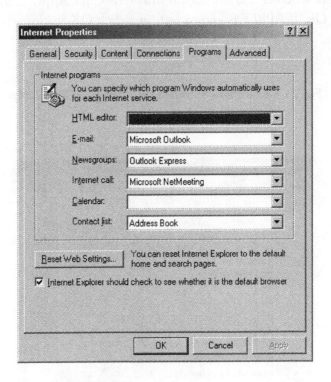

If you have another ISP besides AOL or CompuServe 2000, choose "Always dial my default connection" on the Connections tab. If you have AOL or CompuServe 2000 and another ISP, or you are on a laptop and dial into your corporate LAN, choose "Dial whenever a network connection is not present" on the Connections tab. With a plain vanilla ISP, you may need to have the "Use a proxy server" checked on the LAN settings page shown in **fig. 79**. Most likely, you will need to have it checked if you dial into your corporate local area network. Check with your ISP or network administrator to find out what you need to do with the LAN settings.

You also need to make sure that the network settings are correct in the Network control panel in Windows. The Internet and Network settings work hand-in-hand. Please see the instructions outlined in **Appendix C**, *How to Set Up the Network Control Panel.* I wouldn't advise changing any of these settings unless you have America Online or CompuServe 2000 and are NOT on a network. For any other situation, check with your specific ISP to see what they recommend for the settings here.

Fig. 79 Local Area Network settings.

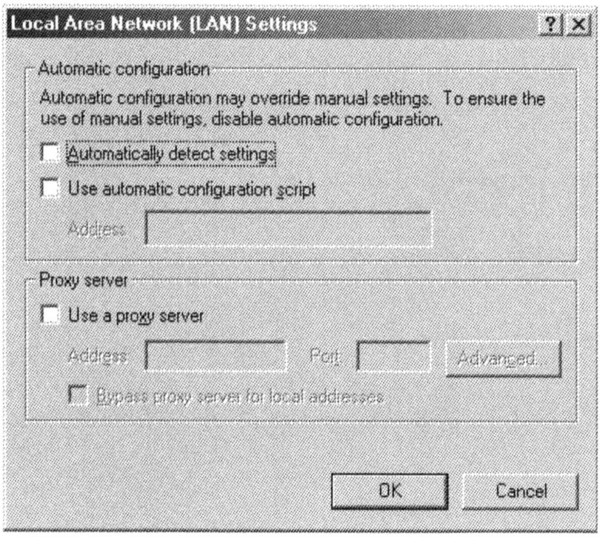

How to purge the browser cache

An important thing that you need to check from time to time in the Internet control panel is the cache file. The cache consists of the History and the Temporary Internet Files. Periodically, you need to delete these files because if they get too full, you may not be able to get to the Web. The instructions to delete these files using several different methods follow:

Please follow the steps that follow to purge your cache folder. The steps vary depending on which version of Microsoft Internet Explorer (MSIE) you are using. If you have a version of Internet Explorer that is less than 4.0, you really need to upgrade the browser. Upgrade to the latest version that is out at the time if your system can handle it. If you can't get to the Web anymore, the only reason why may be because you have an outdated browser even if it has been working for a long time. Sometimes, Web sites, especially secure sites, update their security so that it requires the latest version of the browser to get there. That is one possible reason why an old version of a browser would fail out of the blue.

To purge the cache with MSIE 4.0:

Click the START button then SETTINGS and CONTROL PANEL

Open up the Internet icon

Click on DELETE FILES where it talks about the Temporary Internet Files.

Put a check in the box where it states "Delete all subscription content." And click OK.

When that is done, click Clear History at the bottom and click OK.

You are done at that point, and just click OK at the bottom to close the Internet Properties window.

To purge the cache with MSIE 5.0:

a. Click the START button then SETTINGS and CONTROL PANEL

Open up the Internet Options icon

Click on DELETE FILES where it talks about the Temporary Internet Files.

d. Put a check in the box where it states "Delete all offline content." And click OK.

e. When that is done, click Clear History at the bottom and click OK.

f. Your are done at that point, and just click OK at the bottom to close the Internet Properties window.

Notice that in this respect, IE 4.0 and 5.0 are identical except what the check box is labeled in **step d.** when you click on Delete Files and what the icon is named in step **b.** It is either Internet or Internet Options

3. **Manually delete the cache:**

a. Click the START button on the Windows Taskbar.

b. Select FIND, then FILES of FOLDERS. (Windows Me is START>SEARCH>FOR FILES OR FOLDERS)

c. In the NAMED field, type the name of the file. In this case, Temporary

Internet Files. You will need to enter the search criteria like this:

temporary?internet?files or else it will find too many files.

d. Be sure the LOOK IN field is showing the C drive.

e. Click FIND NOW. (Windows Me will be SEARCH NOW)

f. When the Temporary Internet Files folder is found in the results window,

double-click to open the folder. See illustrations **fig. 81** & **fig. 82**.

g. Select EDIT from the Menu bar.

h. Choose, SELECT ALL to select all the files in the folder.

Press the DELETE key on the keyboard to delete the files or click FILE
on the toolbar then DELETE.

Fig. 81 Search for and delete the Temporary Internet Files.

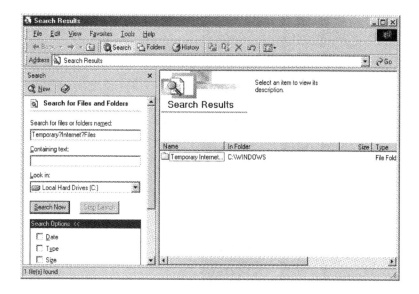

**Fig. 82 Shows what happens when you double-click
on the Temporary Internet folder and click on Edit>Select All.
Then all you have to do is hit the Delete key on the keyboard.**

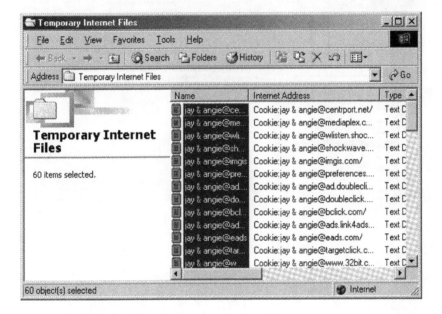

Advanced way to purge cache

Here is yet another way to purge the cache that is really more thorough than
the way you can do it in Windows. Using this procedure, you delete any
contents in the History folder and the History folder itself. There are some
occasions where the actual folder itself becomes corrupt and you want to
remove everything. This is the way to do it in Win 95 and Win 98.

Click on **Start>Shut down>Restart Computer in MS-DOS mode** and click **Ok**. When you are at the C:\Windows prompt type **Deltree history cookies** and hit **Enter** key. Type **Y** for Yes and hit **Enter** for both files. Type **Deltree Tempor*** and hit the **Enter** key. Type **Y** for Yes and **Enter**. When it returns to a C prompt, type WIN and hit the **Enter** key to restart the computer.

If you have another version of Windows besides Windows 95 or Windows 98, such as Windows Me, you will not have the restart in DOS mode option. To get a DOS prompt, click **Start>Programs>MS-DOS prompt**. If you don't see that option, click **Start>Run**. On the run line type **command** and click **Ok**. You will be at the DOS prompt in a DOS window. You need to be at a C:\Windows prompt, so if it says C:\Windows\Desktop, type **cd..** and hit the **Enter** key to jump up one directory level. Then just follow the same instructions as outlined before with the deltree commands. Deltree is a DOS command that tells the computer to delete the file specified and all of the subdirectories within that file. Incidentally, you can use the method for Win Me also in Windows 95 or Windows 98, but you generally want to reboot the computer after deleting the cache. Restarting in DOS mode serves as a reboot while the DOS window does not.

Sometimes a browser may become damaged and it is necessary to remove it. If you have checked all of the settings and used the deltree method to get rid of the cache and you still can't get to the Web, you may want to try the following instructions. They will tell you how to uninstall and reinstall the Web browser in Windows 95. Sometimes, things don't go so smoothly and it is necessary to manually remove the browser. Manual removal of the Web browser can be found in Appendix M, *Advanced Web Browser Removal.*

How to remove browser if things go smoothly in Windows 95

First of all **only attempt this if you have Windows 95!**

Go to the control panel by clicking on **Start>Settings>Control Panel.**
Double-click on **Add/Remove Programs** and Click once once on
Microsoft Internet Explorer 5 and Internet Tools shown in **fig. 83.**
Click on the **Add/Remove** button. Choose the option that says, "Restore
the previous Windows configuration" and click **Ok** (see **fig. 84**). Follow
the onscreen prompts from there. You may or may not have the Microsoft
Internet Explorer listing in there. If it is not listed, look for Microsoft
Internet Explorer 4.01 or it may say some other version number or it
could even say Internet Explorer 3.xx or some other version number. If
you have anything that resembles those listings, click once to select it and
click on the **Add/Remove** button. Again follow the onscreen instructions
to remove IE. At the end it will probably tell you that it is closing all windows and will attempt to restart the computer. Then it will say that it
couldn't close all programs, and that you need to manually close them.
Just do whatever it tells you to do on the computer screen and manually
close everything and restart Windows.

Fig. 83 Add/Remove programs applet in the control panel.

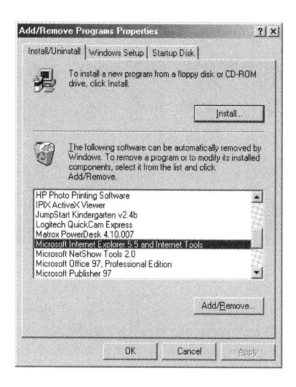

**Fig. 84 Screen shown after selecting Microsoft Internet Explorer and
Internet Tools and clicking on Add/Remove.**

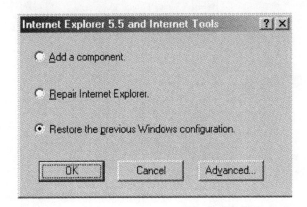

If you did have a Microsoft Internet Explorer 5 and Internet Tools listing,
follow the instructions previously stated and go back to control panel and
Add/Remove Programs and look for either another Microsoft Internet
Explorer listing or an Internet Explorer listing. If one of these is present,
click on it and click Add/Remove and follow the onscreen prompts to
uninstall it. Sometimes, an Internet Explorer listing will not show itself
until you restore the previous Windows configuration from the Internet
Explorer 5 and Internet Tools listing. At any rate, you want to make sure
that all versions of the browser are removed, and that's the purpose of
going back in and removing an Internet Explorer listing if there is one.
Three important things here to point out:

Microsoft Internet Explorer 5 and Internet Tools represents IE version
5.x.x. An Internet Explorer listing represents IE 4.x.x or less. Typically, an

Internet Explorer listed in there will represent IE 3.0.2, which came with the original Windows 95.

The listing will remain in Add/Remove even after the program is uninstalled. Don't let that worry you. It is just listed in there and it does not mean that the program is still on the computer.

3) If the browser doesn't remove this way, you typically need to either reinstall Windows or manually do a complete blowout of the Internet Explorer Web browser. See **Appendix M**, *Advanced Web browser removal*, for instructions on how to manually uninstall the Web browser. For further help, or to reinstall Windows, check with your computer manufacturer or Microsoft.

Next, run a thorough ScanDisk and Defrag by clicking on **Start>Programs>Accessories>System Tools>ScanDisk**. Put a dot in the circle next to **Thorough** and put a check in the box that says, "Automatically fix errors" as shown in **fig. 85**. Click on the **Advanced** button and check the boxes as shown in **fig. 86**. Click on **Ok** and click on **Start**.

Fig. 85 Scandisk

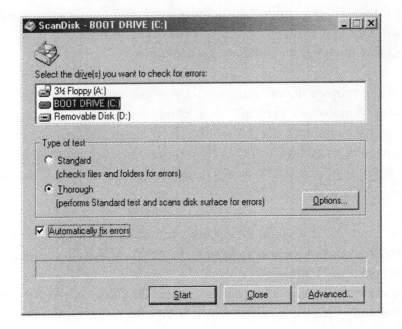

Fig. 86 Scandisk Advanced settings.

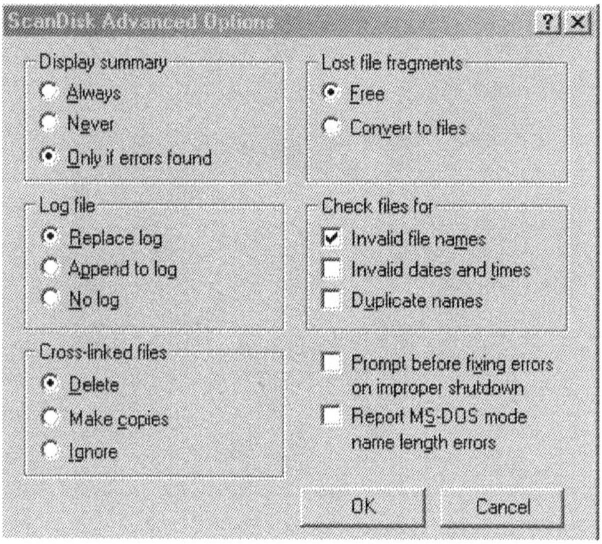

After that, run the Disk Defragmenter. **Start>Programs> Accessories>System**

Tools>Disk Defragmenter as shown in **fig. 87**. All you have to do on that one is click on **ok** and Run it even if Windows tells you that you don't have to.

Fig. 87 Disk Defragmenter

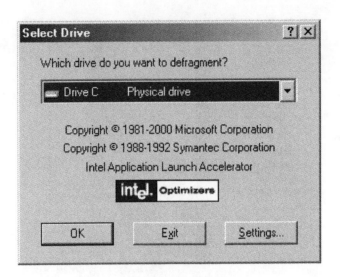

After that completes, shut the computer all the way down safely and turn it back on after about 20 seconds. You are now ready to reinstall the Web browser. If you have America Online or CompuServe 2000, the Internet Explorer Web browser can be extracted from the CD. In any other situation, check with your ISP support to find out your best solution for reinstalling the Web browser. Incidentally, THIS SHOULD NOT BE TRIED ON WIN98. To remove the Internet Explorer Web browser in Win 98, you will need to follow some unsupported-by-Microsoft-instructions. This information can be found on the Microsoft Web site.

There are keyboard shortcuts that you can use for Internet Explorer just like you can use in Windows. To see these, look at **Appendix P,** *Internet Explorer Keyboard Shortcuts.*

Appendix C

How to set up the Network Control Panel

Make sure the Internet properties are configured correctly

You need to check the Internet Properties since these work hand in hand with the Network control panel. If one of them is out of whack, you may not be able to get to the Web even if one or the other is configured perfectly. These are both located in the control panel. Enter the control panel by clicking on **Start>Settings>Control Panel** or Double-click on **My Computer** and Double-click on **Control Panel**. Once in the Control Panel, you will see a bunch of icons that should be in alphabetical order. You should have one called either Internet or Internet Options. If it says Internet, you have Internet Explorer version 4.x.x or less. If the icon is called Internet Options, you have Internet Explorer version 5.0 or above. You can make almost any tweaks or adjustments to Internet Explorer through this icon. Double-click on the **Internet** or **Internet Options** icon then click on the **Connections** tab at the top. If your icon is named Internet (IE ver. 4.xx or less) and you are using an ISP with a proprietary dialer like AOL or CompuServe 2000, you want to select "Connect to the Internet using a LAN." If you use Dial-up networking (nearly any ISP but AOL or CompuServe 2000), select "Connect to the Internet using a modem."

If your icon is named Internet Options (IE ver. 5.0 or above), on the Connections tab select "Never dial a connection" If you have AOL or CompuServe 2000. Choose "Always dial my default connection" If your ISP uses Dial-up Networking, and if you have AOL and a generic ISP, or you use DUN to connect to your office network, choose "Only dial if a

189

network connection is not present." Also, click on the **LAN settings** button at the bottom of this screen. This section here should have nothing checked unless your ISP tells you specifically to check something. Anything checked here, like Automatically detect or use a proxy server, has the ability to override any other settings on the Connections tab. Sometimes you will need the proxy server checked if you are on a network or dial into your office LAN. Illustrations of these screens can be seen in **Appendix B,** *How to Set Internet Properties in the Control Panel.*

Network beware

Many ISPs may not work if your computer is networked. If you are networked, and you do encounter problems, it will usually be accessing the Web. You will probably be able to establish a connection to your ISP, but you may find that the Web browser doesn't work. Usually there is some way to figure out how to get around problems here, but it may be very difficult or take a lot of jury-rigging. This is why few ISPs will support their software on a network. They won't say that it won't work, but they sure won't guarantee that it will. And unless they "officially" support their software on a network, you can jump up and down all you want but they will not help you if it is clear that the network configuration is screwing things up. This holds true even if it worked before. Many times something will work on a computer when it really shouldn't have in the first place, and when it fails, it is just because you were lucky for however long it worked in the beginning. After all, you really can't expect tech support to help you with something that they don't support. On that note, let's look at what this Appendix is really about, the Network control panel.

Network control panel

The Network control panel is usually located just below the Internet icon in the Control panel. Remember these icons are in alphabetical order. I can't speak for every ISP, but I will mention what the settings need to be in this area for a few ISPs. Basically, if the settings and adapters aren't in here and set as follows, you won't be able to get to the Internet. You may be able to sign on, and you might even be able to use your e-mail because these things usually aren't accessing the Internet and they don't require a Web browser. However, if you try to get to the Web, you will encounter problems if your network control panel is not configured properly. You may see an error message of some sort like "Internet Explorer cannot open the Internet site, a connection to the server cannot be established" or you may just see a blank white or gray screen when it is supposed to load a Web page. There are several other possible reasons why you can't get to the Web like a bad Web browser, but chances are the problem lies in the Network control panel. For this reason, you may likely have trouble reaching the Web through your ISP if you are on a network. A network requires that you have certain network adapters with certain settings in the Network control panel as shown in **fig. 88**. Your ISP requires the same thing, and there is a decent chance that some of these adapters or settings may contradict each other or they just can't co-exist.

Fig. 88 Network Control Panel.

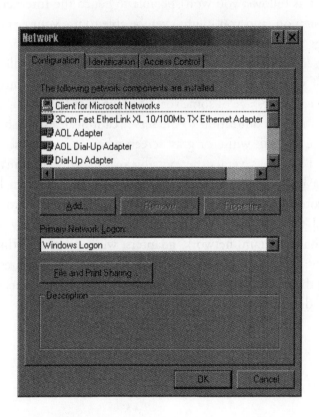

You may see all kinds of adapters in the network applet, but most people really only need 2 of them. These 2 are TCP/IP and AOL Adapter for AOL or CompuServe 2000. Or, TCP/IP and Dial-up Adapter for a standard ISP. Sometimes you may need Client for Microsoft Networks for an ISP. If you see an Ethernet adapter of some sort, it usually indicates you are on a network, but a lot of manufacturers are including a network card with a new computer purchase so you might see an Ethernet adapter in there even if you are not on a network.

You may see a number of other various adapters in the Network control panel. Some of these include ISP/SPX, NETBEUI, TCP/IP, Dial-up adapter, Microsoft Virtual Private Networking adapter, NDISWANà Microsoft Virtual Private Networking adapter, or Dial-up adapter #2

(VPN Support). If you have AOL or CompuServe 2000, all you really need to connect and access the Internet are AOL adapter and TCP/IP. CompuServe 2000 uses the adapter called AOL adapter in the Network Control panel. This is just the name of the adapter, and because of programming issues it was just easier to keep it that way than to make a separate adapter called CompuServe adapter. Below are the proper network settings outlined for CompuServe 2000 or AOL.

Network settings for CompuServe 2000 or AOL

You need to make sure that the network settings are correct in the Network control panel in Windows. To check this, please follow the instructions outlined below.

On the Windows Desktop, click on the **Start** button then click on **Settings** then click on **Control Panel**. In the control panel, double-click on the **Network** icon. At the bottom, change the Primary Network Logon to Windows Logon if it isn't already. Click once to highlight the item at the top that says **TCP/IPàAOL Adapter** (it might just say TCP/IP) then click on **Properties**. Make sure there is a dot in the circle next to "Obtain an IP address automatically." (**fig. 89**) Click on the **DNS configuration** tab at the top and make sure there is a dot next to "Disable DNS." (**fig. 90**) Click on the **WINS Configuration** tab at the top and make sure that the dot is next to "Disable Wins Resolution." (**fig. 91**) If any of these are not set like I stated, please put the dot where it says that it should be. After that just click **Ok** and **Ok** again. It will pause for a moment to build a driver and tell you to restart the computer. Go ahead and restart and sign back online when the computer comes back up and all should work OK. If it still does not work, and you are not on a network and you do not have any other Internet providers besides AOL or CompuServe 2000, go back into the **Control Panel** then open up the **Network icon**. Click on the first item to highlight it and click on **Remove**. Click on the second item and click **Remove** and follow suit until every single network component is gone. Make sure the Primary Network Logon at the bottom is set to Windows Logon and click **Ok**. Restart the computer when prompted.

Fig. 89 Obtain IP automatically.

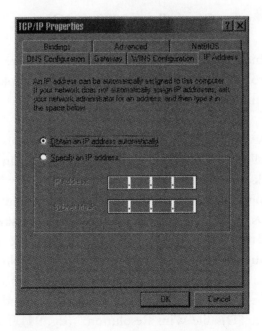

Fig. 90 Disable DNS.

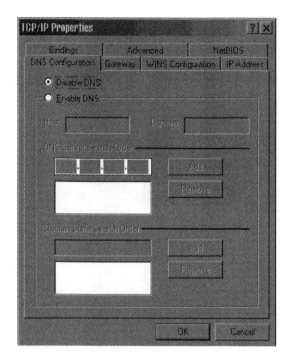

Fig. 91 Disable Wins Resolution.

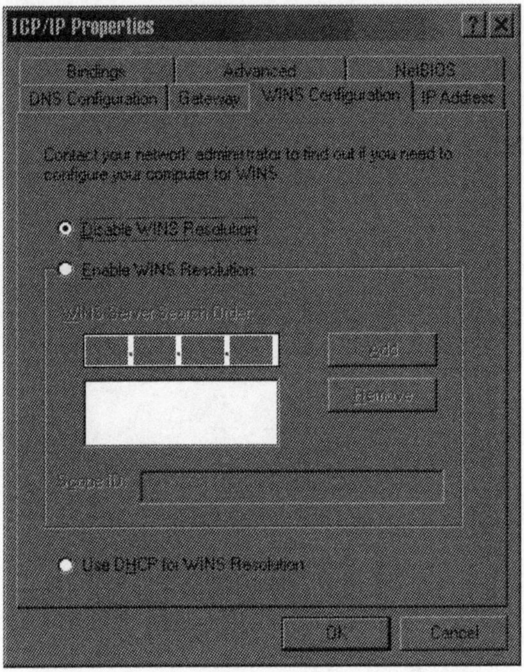

If it asks for the Windows disk, put it in. If you don't have the disk, you may be out of luck until you can get one, but try to type the path C:\Windows\System and finally C:\Windows, if the first doesn't work, where it says "Copy files from" and click **Ok**. If it still doesn't find the file, click Skip File or Cancel. After the computer boots back up, the Control Panel should still be open. Open up the Network again and click on **Add>Adapter>Add** and choose **America Online** on the Manufacturers list on the left and click **Ok**. Click **Add>Protocol>Add** and choose

Microsoft on the left and **TCP/IP** on the right and click **Ok**. Adding the TCP/IP adapter is illustrated in **fig. 92** and **fig. 93**.

Fig. 92 Add TCP/IP adapter.

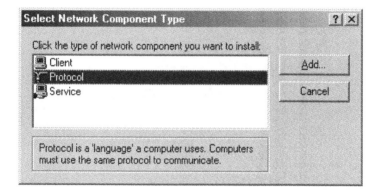

Fig. 93 2nd Add TCP/IP window.

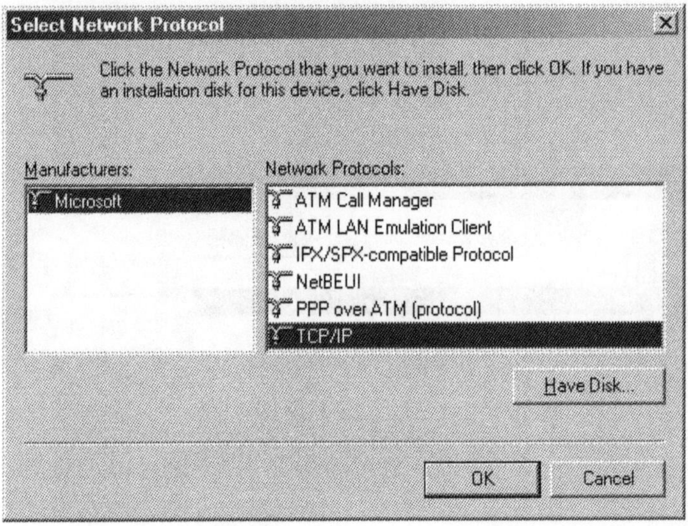

TIP If you don't have a Windows CD and the computer asks you for one, try and borrow one from a friend. If you type the path C:\Windows\System, and it still doesn't find your file, you can try to search for the file that it's looking for by using Start>Find>Files or Folders. Just bring that window up while leaving the window up that is asking you to put in the Windows CD. When you click on Find Files or Folders, or Start>Search>For Files or Folders if you have Windows Me, type in the file that it's looking for, and set the Look In box underneath the Named or Search for files or folders named line to My Computer. If it finds the file, all you have to do is type the path on your other window where it says Copy Files From.

You should now have only AOL adapter and TCP/IPàAOL adapter listed. If there is anything else, remove them one by one. If they all remove, repeat the above procedure but add TCP/IP first and then AOL adapter and remove any excess adapters. If they still don't add properly, your problem is most likely a damaged Network control panel and it may be necessary to call Microsoft technical support or reinstall Windows to correct the problem. However, as long as you have at least AOL adapter and TCP/IP, just go ahead and ignore any other adapters that may be in there at this point and see if you can access the Web.

Fig. 94 Bindings of AOL Adapter.

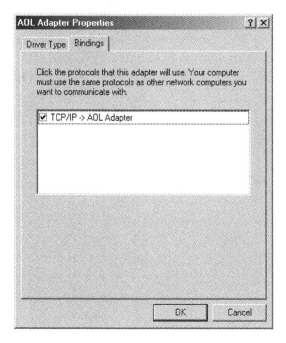

Next check the properties of the adapters. Click once on **AOL adapter** and click **Properties** then **Bindings** at the top. The only thing that should be listed here with a check next to it is TCP/IP as shown in **fig. 94**. It may say TCP/IPàAOL Adapter and that is the same thing. Once you have made sure that the TCP/IP is the only one there with a check mark click **Ok**.

Check the TCP/IP adapter properties again. Click once to highlight the item at the top that says **TCP/IPàAOL Adapter** then click on **Properties**. Make sure there is a dot in the circle next to "Obtain an IP address automatically." Click on the **DNS configuration** tab at the top and make sure there is a dot next to "Disable DNS." Click on the **WINS Configuration** tab at the top and make sure that the dot is next to "Disable Wins Resolution." If any of these are not set like I stated before, please put the dot where it says that it should be. Click **Ok** and make sure that the Primary Network Logon is Windows Logon and click **Ok** again. Say Yes to restart the computer when prompted. Try the Internet again and it should work or else you may have a serious problem like a completely damaged Web browser.

Narrowing down the problem

One way to check this is to download another browser like Netscape and see if it works. Now that your network settings are correct, the only other thing it could be is a damaged browser for the most part. If Netscape works, it tells you that Microsoft Internet Explorer is damaged. If Netscape doesn't even work, it will tell you that Windows is damaged or at least one crucial file is damaged such as the wsock32.dll. Of course, it will be difficult to download Netscape if you can't get to *www.netscape.com*. However, some ISPs have a 16-bit version of their software such as America Online version 4.0. The 16-bit version of AOL 4.0 uses an internal browser, and it is not dependent on the browser that is built into Windows. Therefore, an option may be to install the 16-bit version just to get to the Internet in the first place so that you can download another browser.

The following are other settings that you may need to check if you still cannot get to the Web on CompuServe 2000 or AOL:

In addition to checking the Connections tab in Internet Options as outlined before, you need to clear the browser cache and check a couple of more things in the Internet area.

No matter what version of the Internet Explorer you have, the procedure is pretty much the same to delete the cache files. When you first come to the General button, which is the first page that will come up when you open the Internet or Internet Options icon (see **fig. 95**), you will see something that refers to the Temporary Internet Files. Click on where it says **Delete Files** and put a check in the box that says either "Delete all offline content" Or "Delete all subscription content" as shown in **fig. 96** and click **Ok**. When that seems like it is done (Your mouse will turn back into a pointer when finished), click on **Clear history** toward the bottom part of the page and click **Ok**. You will have just cleared the browser's cache, which are folders that contain a history trail of everywhere you have been on the Internet. The cache is nothing that you will notice is missing and has nothing to do with your favorite places or bookmarks. As a matter of fact, if these folders get too full it can prevent you from getting to the Internet.

Fig. 95 Internet Options General tab.

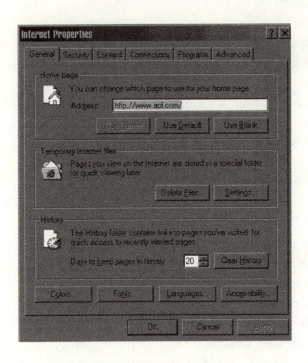

Fig. 96 Delete offline content that stores if you tell IE to save a Web page for offline viewing.

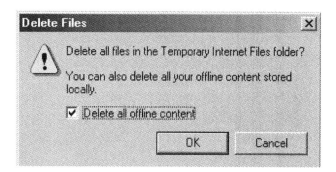

Click on **Programs** at the top. Click on **Reset Web Settings**. Say Yes to follow through with this. It will have a check box that asks about the home page, just leave the check in the home page box and click Yes. Also, make sure that there is a check in the lower left corner where it says, "Internet Explorer should check to see whether it is the default browser." Click **Apply** at the bottom then **Ok**. If Apply is grayed out, just click **Ok** to close the window.

Back to the Network control panel

If you have what we'll call a standard ISP or a provider that uses Dial-up Networking, most of the time you only need the TCP/IP adapter and Dial-up Adapter as far as the adapters in the Network control panel. The Dial-up Adapter is necessary for Dial-up networking. Sometimes you need a client with a DUN Connection such as Client for Microsoft Networks or Microsoft Family Logon. Family Logon doesn't seem to be as stable of an adapter as Client for Microsoft Networks, however.

So let's say you have a standard ISP and your connection quits working. This could of course be due to any one of dozens of things or it could be several adjustments that need to be made up to and including uninstalling & reinstalling DUN or even Windows. Most of these operations are beyond the scope of this book, and instructions for removal & reinstallation of DUN and the like can be found at the Microsoft Knowledge Base at *www.microsoft.com*.

Sometimes you just want to clear all of the components out of the Network Control Panel and rebuild the adapters before trying some of the more extreme steps like uninstalling DUN, uninstalling the Web browser, or reinstalling Windows. Here's how to do it:

Uninstalling all components in the Network control panel

Remove all items out of the network control panel by clicking on the 1st item and clicking remove. Follow suit on all the rest of the listings no matter what they are. You will probably find that after removing the 3rd or 4th item, all the rest will go with it. Look at **fig. 97** to see how an empty Network control panel should look. If you had a listing in there that was labeled something like Client for NetWare Networks, and you are not on a network, that was probably the problem. If you have an adapter that is labeled something like 3Com Fast Ethernet 10/100Mb TX Ethernet Adapter or NIC Ethernet Adapter, and you remove it, the computer will detect new hardware when you restart it. That's because this is a NIC card (Network Interface Card), and it's actually a physical piece of hardware that's inside of your computer. If you've tried a lot of stuff and you still can't connect to the Web, you may want to disable the NIC card. You would want to leave the NIC card listing in the Network control panel and follow the instructions to disable the NIC card outlined in **Appendix Q**, *Instructions for Disabling Hardware*.

Fig. 97 Empty Network Control Panel.

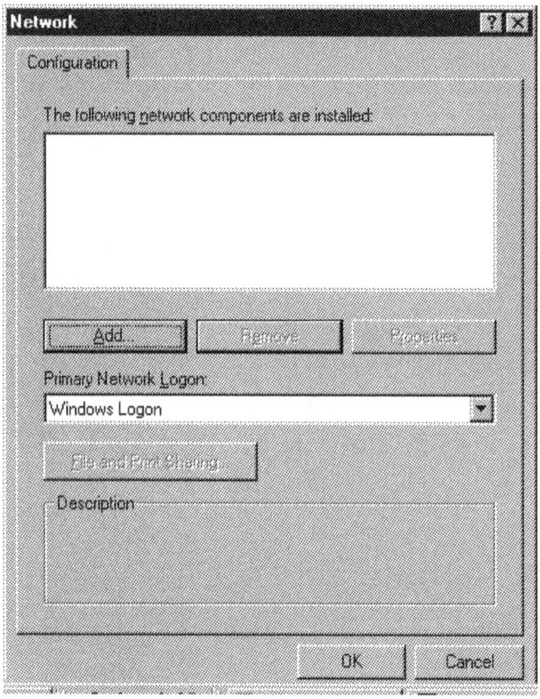

Once everything is gone out of the Network control panel, make sure the Primary network logon is Windows logon at the bottom of the Window you will be looking at. Click **Ok** at the bottom. Windows will copy some files or build a driver database, and it will prompt you to restart the computer. You say Yes to this. If it asks for the Windows disk, put it in. If you don't have the disk, you may need to get it in order for everything to work again. However, until you can get one, you can try to type the path C:\Windows\System and finally C:\Windows, if the first doesn't work, where it says Copy files from and click **Ok**. Hopefully it will find the file it is looking for.

If it doesn't find the file by then, and you don't have the Windows disk, you can click SKIP FILE but it probably isn't going to work again until Windows can extract these files from the disk.

As a last ditch effort, you can try to search for the file that it is looking for by clicking on **Start>Find>Files or Folders** as previously mentioned in this chapter. Where it says NAMED, type in the file name that Windows needs as shown in **fig. 98**. Underneath the Named line, where it says, "Look In," select My Computer and click **Find Now** to the right. If it finds the file, it will give you the path where it is on your system to the right of where it lists the file at the bottom, and that path is what you will need to type on the Copy files from line shown in **fig. 99**.

Fig. 98 Search for a file that Windows is looking for

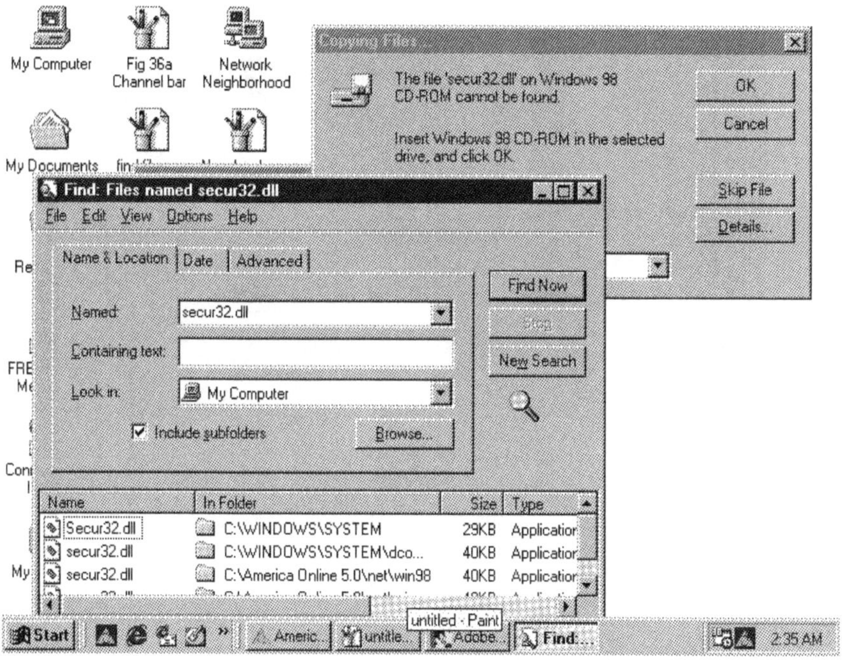

**Fig. 99 Type the path of the file on the line labeled Copy files from:
so that Windows can find it.**

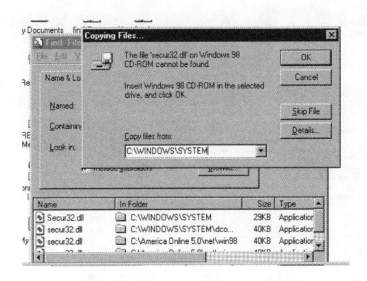

You may wonder why it worked all this time and now it needs the Windows disk for a file. It's the same reason why things will work for a long time and one day they may just fail when there have been no changes made. This is true of computers, automobiles, or just about anything else.

A full cache may be your only problem

Your problems accessing the Internet may just be a full cache that needs to be emptied, or most of the time the Primary Logon in the Network control panel just needs to be switched to Windows Logon which it should have been all along (For AOL or CompuServe 2000 anyway). The reason why it works this way is a difficult concept for new computer users to grasp. Basically the logon switch forces Windows to copy files and therefore refresh the files in the Network control panel, and this will restore a problem that may have presented itself because of a corrupt file. Sometimes, it needs to get a file from the Windows CD because the one on the system corrupted. It's not really unusual to have a corrupt file on a computer; that's just the nature of the beast. If it can't get that file, it just won't work again even if it had been working for months and months before. Sometimes during a file copy process a message will come up that says, "A file being copied is older than the one currently on the computer. It is recommended that you keep the existing file. Do you wish to keep the existing file?" Y/N as shown in **fig. 100**. Normally, we would want to go with Windows recommendation and say "Yes" here. Although, if you go through this whole procedure (And you've tried everything else), you might try repeating the whole procedure and say "No" to the keep the existing file question. I have seen it work both ways before to fix a problem of not being able to reach the Internet. I will say "Yes" to keep the existing file first, however. Why sometimes yes works and sometimes no, I really don't know, but I stopped questioning quirky things like that on a computer a long time ago. The bottom line is that you have to know what ultimately works and what doesn't. I know that if I say "Yes" to that question and I still can't get to the Web, I am going to do it again and say "No." I don't waste my mental energy worrying about why that may be.

The reason for copying a file is that sometimes the file on the computer is damaged. It goes to copy a file from the CD, which will be a fresh unadulterated file of this type. Windows says to you that you are about to replace a file that already exists since it sees that a file on the Windows CD has the same name as one already on your computer. There is no definitive right or wrong answer here on whether to say yes or no. As a rule say yes, however, and if whatever the problem is still exists try it again and say no. The reason why we would normally say yes is to go with Windows advice for one thing. Furthermore, a program you installed or a Windows update of some sort may have updated the file that already is on your computer. The reason why we might say no to keep the existing file is that for one thing the file on the computer might be corrupt. Furthermore, sometimes Windows is wrong. The way files are labeled might lead Windows to think that what appears as the newer file is really the older of the two files. Just as an example: a certain file on your computer might have a version number 5.34.274 and the one on the CD is version 3.26.126, and the one on the CD is newer even though it doesn't appear that way from the number.

Fig. 100 A file being copied...

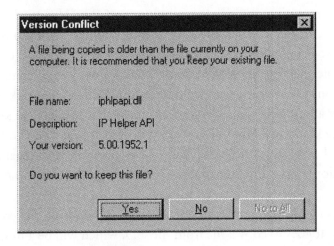

Back again to the Network control panel

Kind of got off on a tangent, but let's get back to the Network CP when you have a standard ISP (Not AOL or CompuServe 2000). You click **Ok**, and it copies some files. It might or might not ask for the CD, and then it will ask you to restart the computer and you say Yes. When the computer comes back up, the Control Panel should still be open. Double-click on **Network** again. Click on **Add** and choose **Adapter** then **Add** again and choose **Microsoft** on the left and **Dial-up Adapter** on the right and click **Ok**. Click **Add** then **Protocol** then **Add** again. Choose **Microsoft** on the left then **TCP/IP** on the right and click **Ok**. Like I said you may want to go ahead and select a Client if you are using DUN. Click **Add** then **Client** then **Add** again and choose **Microsoft** on the manufacturer's list on the left and **Client for Microsoft Networks** on the right and click **Ok**.

You should now have 3 adapters in the Network Control panel. Dial-up Adapter, TCP/IP, and Client for Microsoft Networks. If you have any extras that showed up, remove them one at a time by clicking on one and clicking on **Remove**. If everything disappears, add all the adapters back in a different order like say Client for Microsoft Networks, TCP/IP and Dial-up Adapter. Again if you end up with extras remove them one at a time. This time they should remove properly, if they didn't in the first place, and just leave those 3 adapters. If extra things keep adding and you just can't narrow it down to the needed 3 after several time of trying, your whole problem might be a hosed Network Control Panel.

Network control panel properties for a standard ISP

Once you have the adapters added properly, you need to check the properties: Click on **Dial-up Adapter** then click **Properties** and click on the **Bindings** tab at the top. The only thing that should be listed here with a check next to it is **TCP/IP** (It may say TCP/IPàDial-up Adapter). If anything else is checked here, just uncheck it and click **Ok**. Click once on the **TCP/IPà Dial-up Adapter** then click **Properties**. Normally this should be selected on "Obtain an IP address automatically." However, some ISPs may have you specify an IP address, which you would need to get from the ISP. If you need to specify an IP address, your ISP uses what is called a static IP address. This means that the IP doesn't change, and there will be a Primary & Secondary IP in the format something like 134.78.414.13 and 134.178.412.15 for the Primary & Secondary, respectively.

After you check the **IP address** tab click on **DNS configuration** at the top and make sure it's set on Disable DNS then click the **WINS config-uration** tab. Put a dot in the circle next to where it says Disable Wins Resolution if it's not already there. Then click **Ok** and set the Primary Network Logon to Client for Microsoft Networks (for a standard ISP not AOL or CompuServe 2000) if it isn't already. Click **Ok** at the bottom and say Yes to restart computer. If it asks for the Win CD, put it in. Remember these settings were described for a standard ISP and not CompuServe 2000 or AOL, which is covered at the beginning of this appendix. These settings described for an ISP should work for any ISP that uses Dial-up networking. But be sure to check with your ISP or system administrator to make sure or if you have any doubts whatsoever.

More on IP addressing

Most ISPs use what is called a Dynamic IP address, which means that it changes every time that you sign on. America Online and CompuServe 2000 use a Dynamic IP address, and that's why you don't need to fill out any of that information with Internet Explorer and the Internet Connection Wizard or any other program that requires an Internet Connection; that's why you select Obtain an IP Address Automatically for the TCP/IP properties in the Network control panel. The Internet Connection Wizard might ask you for a primary and secondary IP address. AOL or other ISPs that have a dynamic IP address will fill that in for you. When using programs that require an Internet connection, it is necessary to connect to certain ISPs, such as AOL or CompuServe 2000 first. You connect first and minimize the program. That way AOL is running in the background when you launch the Web browser or any program you have that needs an Internet connection. Since AOL is running, it will fill in the IP addresses each time since they will change from session to session. In other words, since this information will change every time that you connect, there is no way to actually fill this information in. Also, the program itself that requires an Internet connection would need to be configured correctly as well as the Internet connections tab. When configuring programs that require an Internet connection, such as a Web browser or Quicken or Real Player, you want to select something like "Connect using a modem" if you are using Dial-up Networking. Select something like "I have a direct connection to the Internet" or "I have a LAN connection" or something to that effect if your ISP doesn't use DUN like AOL or CompuServe 2000. A dynamic IP address has a greater security measure generally because it is a lot more difficult for someone to hack into your computer if the IP number changes every time that you sign on to your ISP.

Appendix D

128-bit encryption

The SSL (Secure Sockets Layer) of your Web browser is what allows the browser to gain access to secure sites on the Web. These secure sites are typically found when banking or shopping online. Currently, the highest level of security is 128-bit encryption. Upgrading your browser to a more current version will allow you access to secure sites with higher encryption ratings.

When upgrading your Web browser, you are given the option to download the higher encryption level (128-bit SSL) when you accept the conditions found on the Export Restrictions screen. Only legal residents of U.S. and Canada who agree to the Export Restrictions outlined in the upgrade process will receive a version of the highest security. Visit *www.microsoft.com* to obtain the latest version of the Microsoft Internet Explorer with 128-bit encryption.

If you see https://www.fidelity.com, your browser has not gone berserk on you, but this is a secure web site. The extra "s" at the end of http stands for secure. Now to reach this secure site, you'll need 128-bit encryption. In plain English, a 128-bit browser is much more secure than a 40-bit browser. As mentioned before, 128-bit encryption is only legal in the US and Canada. Outside of the United States, the most that can legally be used is 40-bit. Interestingly, Microsoft Internet Explorer comes in the 40-bit and 128-bit varieties and Netscape comes in the 56-bit and 128-bit flavors. Many times with a brand new computer you will get the 40-bit browser because the hard drive, if not the entire system, was made outside the U.S. The Windows software may have been installed overseas as well.

All you need to do in this case is point your browser to www.microsoft.com and download the 128-bit upgrade or IE 5.05 w/128-bit encryption—the latest version out at the present time. Just look for the word download or browser or something like that on their site and click on it and follow the path from there. Microsoft usually puts a fairly noticeable link on their Web site for the latest version of their browser. You can also run the Windows Update by clicking on **Start** then **Windows Update** usually located at the top of the Start Menu. Make sure that you have an active connection to the Internet, and this will take you to the Microsoft Web site where all of the latest Windows updates will be offered including the latest version of Internet Explorer.

When opting to download the browser, you will have a choice of how to download it. There will be 2 choices: **1)** *save program to disk*, and **2)** *open program from current location* (not necessarily in that order). It is best to choose open program from current location because that way you don't have to find the file on your hard disk, but it will start to run automatically when it is done downloading. And don't psyche yourself out and think that you have to be some computer expert or a network administrator to install this thing from here. Most programs these days are pretty intuitive actually. If it runs from current location, all you have to do is click on **Next, Ok, Finish, Yes,** or whatever the choice is to proceed with the operation. Do what the computer tells you to do; if it suggests restarting then restart.

Appendix E

File extensions

.$$$ temporary file

.@@@   Backup ID file

.000   Geoworks file

.2GR   286 Grabber Support File

.386   Intel 80386   processor specific file (Windows 3)

.3GR   386 Grabber Support   File

.ABK   automatic backup file (CorelDRAW)

.AD   screen saver data   (After Dark)

.ADF   Adapter Description File (IBM)

.ADN   Add-In   Utility (Lotus 1-2-3)

.AFM   outline font description (Adobe Type 1   PostScript font)

.AI   Metafile (Adobe Illistrator)

.ALL   WordPerfect master printer file

.ANM   animation file (Deluxe Paint   Animator)

.ANN   Help Annotations (MS Windows)

.APP   Application   (R-Base)

.ARC   compressed file archive created by ARC   (arc602.exe/pk361.exe)

.ARC   compressed file archive created by SQUASH   (squash.arc)

.ARJ   compressed file archive created by ARJ   (arj241.exe)

.ARS   Audio Resource File (WordPerfect)

.ASC   ASCII   text file

.ASM   ASSEMBLY source code file

.ASP   Association of   Shareware Professionals OMBUDSMN.ASP notice

.AVI   Audio Video Interleaved   animation file (Video for Windows)

.AWK   AWK script/program

.BAK   backup file

.BAS   BASIC source code file

.BAT   batch file   (DOS)

.BBS   Bulletin Board System announce or text info file

.BGI   Borland Graphic Interface

.BIB   Bibliography

.BIN   binary file

.BIO   OS2 BIOS

.BIT   bitmap X11

.BK!   document backup   (WordPerfect for Win)

.BK1   timed backup file for document window 1 (WordPerfect for Win)

.BK9   timed backup file for document window 9 (WordPerfect for Win)

.BLD   BASIC Bload Graphics

.BKP   backup file   (Write)

.BLK   temporary file (WordPerfect for Win)

.BMK   Help Bookmarks (MS Windows)

.BMP   BitMaP graphics file (Windows 3) (PC   Paintbrush)

.BSC   Boyon Script (Boyon Communications)

.C   C   language source code

.CAL   calendar file (MS Windows)

.CAT Catalog

.CBL COBOL Source Code

.CCH chart (CorelChart)

.CDF Comma Delimited File

.CDR vector graphics file (CorelDRAW native format)

.CDX Compact Index (Fox Pro)

.CEL graphics file (Autodesk Animator)

.CFG configuration file

.CGM Computer Graphics Metafile vector graphics (A&L—HG...)

.CH Header File (Clipper)

.CHK recovered data file by CHKDSK (DOS)

.CLP clipboard file (MS Windows)

.CMD batch file (OS/2)

.CMF Creative Music File sound file (Soundblaster command file)

.CNF Configuration

.COB COBOL language source code

.COD Code List or Object List

.COM command   (memory image of executable program) (DOS)

.CPF   Fax (The Complete   Fax)

.CPI   Code Page Information (MS-DOS)

.CPL   control panel file   (MS Windows 3.1)

.CPS   backup of startup files by QEMM (?)   autoexec.cps

.CPT   compressed Mac file archive created by COMPACT PRO   (ext-pc.zip)

.CRD   cardfile (MS Windows)

.CRF   Cross-Reference File   (MASM)

.CSV   Comma Seprated Value

.CUT   bitmap graphics file   (Halo)

.DAT   data file in special format or ASCII

.DBD   Definition   file (dBase)

.DBF   database file (dBASE III/IV—FoxPro—dBFast)

.DBG   Debug file

.DBK   database backup (dBASE   IV)

.DBT   Datebase memo text (dBase)

.DBV   Datebase memo text   (Clipper)

.DCT   Dictionary

.DEF   defaults—definitions

.DEM   demonstration

.DES   Description

.DHP   Dr. Halo Picture

.DIB   Device-Independent Bitmap graphics file (MS Windows)

.DIC   dictionary

.DIF   Data Interchange Format (databases)

.DIR   dialing   directory file (Procomm Plus)

.DLL   Dynamic Link Library (Windows—OS/2)

.DOC   document text file

.DOS   text file containing DOS   specific info

.DOT   Templet file (Word for Windows)

.DRS   Driver   Resource file (WordPerfect)

.DRV device driver eg. for   printer

.DRW Draw (Micrographics Designer)

.DTA Data

.DV   Script (DESQview)

.DVR Driver

.DXB Drawing Interchage Binary   (AutoCAD)

.DXF Drawing Interchange Format (AutoCAD)

.EML Electronic Mail

.ENC encoded file—UUENCODEd file (Lotus 1-2-3—uuexe515.exe)

.EPS   Encapsulated PostScript vector graphics (Adobe   Illustrator)

.ERR Error file

.EXE   directly executable program   (DOS)

.EXT   extension file (Norton Commander)

.FAQ Frequently Asked   Questions text file

.FAX fax graphics image (WinFax Pro)

.FLC   animation file (Autodesk Animator)

.FLI   animation file (Autodesk Animator)

.FNT   Font file

.FON font file (many—Windows3 font library)

.FON log of all calls (Procomm Plus)

.FOR FORTRAN language source code

.FOT TrueType font file (MS Windows 3.1)

.FPT   Database memo text (Fox Pro)

.FRM Report form file (x-Base)

.FRS   Font Resource file (WordPerfect)

.FXS   Winfax Transmit Format graphics file (WinFax)

.GBK Back-up (Grammatik)

.GEM Graphical Environment (Digital Resource)

.GEO GEOS specific file (application) (GeoWorks)

.GIF   Graphics Interchange Format bitmap graphics file (CompuShow)

.GIM Graphics link (Powerpoint)

.GIX   Graphics link (Powerpoint)

.GL   animation file (GRASP GRAphical System for Presentation)

.GLX   Glossary (MS-Word)

.GMF   Fax (GammaFax)

.GNA   Graphics link (Powerpoint)

.GNX   Graphics link (Powerpoint)

.GRB   MS-DOS Shell Monitor file (MS-DOS 5)

.GRF   Graph

.GRP   group file (MS Windows—Papyrus)

.H   Header: Include file (C)

.HDR header for messages (mail) left by remote users (Procomm Plus)

.HEX Intel Hexadecimal format file

.HLP   help information

.HPL   HP LaserJet

.HST   history file (Procomm Plus)

.HYP   Hyphenation

.ICO   icon (Windows3)

.ID   disk   identification file

.IDX   index (many)

.IFF   Amiga Image File   (Commadore)

.IFS   system file (OS/2) hpfs.ifs

.IMG   bitmap graphics   file (Ventura Publisher—GEM Paint)

.INC   Include file

.INF   information text file (ASCII)

.INF   setup installation support file (MS   Windows SDK)

.INI   initialization file

.INT   Object file

.JAS   graphics file

.JBD   datafile (SigmaScan)

.JPG   graphics file JPEG   Joint Photography Experts Group format

.JTF   Fax (JT Fax)

.LBM   bitmapped graphics file (Deluxe Paint/Amiga)

.LBR   Library

.LET   Letter

.LEX   Data files for spell checker (Word for Windows)

.LGO   startup logo code (MS Windows)

.LHA   compressed file archive created by ? (lha213.exe)

.LHW compressed Amiga file archive created by   LHWARP

.LHZ   Compressed file (LHA)

.LIB   library file (several   programming languages)

.LOG   log file

.LRS   Language Resource file   (WordPerfect)

.LST   list file (archive index—compiler   listfile)

.MA   Program file (hDC Microapps)

.MAC bitmap graphics   file (Macintosh MacPaint)

.MAP   Address map file

.MAX   Visioneer Paperport HP scanner file

.MCX   Fax   (Intel)

.MDX Index file (dBase IV)

.ME   Opening Information (i.e.: READ.ME)

.MEN Menu

.MH   Fax (TeliFax)

.MID   MIDI file (MS Windows)

.MKI   japanese graphics MAKIchan format (MagView 0.5)

.MNU Menu

.MOD Module file

.MOD Sound file

.MPC Microsoft   Project

.MPG MPEG animation file

.MPP   Microsoft   Project

.MPV   Microsoft Project

.MPW Microsoft Project

.MPX   Microsoft Project

.MRB Multiple Resolution Bitmap graphics file (MS   C/C++)

.MSG message text file (ASCII)

.MSP bitmap graphics file   (MS Windows 2.x Paint)

.NDX Index (dBase III+)

.NEW new   info

.OBJ object (machine-language) code

.OLD backup   file

.OPT Options

.ORI Original

.OUT Outlines

.OVL overlay file (part of program to be loaded when needed)

.OVR Compiler   overlay

.PAK compressed file archive created by PAK   (pak251.exe)

.PAL color palette file

.PAS PASCAL source code   file

.PC   text file containing IBM PC specific info

.PCC cutout   picture vector graphics (PC Paintbrush)

.PCD Photo-CD Image graphics file   (hpcdtoppm)

.PCL   HP Printer Control

.PCL   Freelance   Graphics

.PCT   bitmap graphics file (Macintosh b&w PICT1—color   PICT2)

.PCW   text file (PC Write)

.PCX   bitmapped graphics (PC   Paintbrush)

.PDF   Printer description (Lotus, Borland)

.PDF   Adobe Acrobat file

.PFA   outline   font description (Readable PostScript)

.PFB   outline font description   (Adobe Type 1 PostScript font)

.PFC   text file (First Choice)

.PFM   Printer Font Metrics

.PGL   HP Plotter or Freelance Graphics

.PGM   PBM Portable Gray Map graphics file

.PGP   support file (Pretty Good   Privacy RSA System)

.PGP   Program Parameter (AutoCAD)

.PHO   Phone   list

.PIC bitmap graphics file (Macintosh b&w PICT1—color PICT2)

.PIC bitmap graphics file (many eg. Lotus 1-2-3—PC Paint)

.PIF Program Information File (Windows 3)

.PIF vector graphics GDF format file (IBM mainframe computers)

.PIT compressed Mac file archive created by PACKIT (unpackit.zoo)

.PIX Alias image file (SDSC Image Tool)

.PKA compressed file archive created by PKARC

.PLL Prelinked library (Clipper)

.PLN spreadsheet (WordPerfect for Win)

.PLT HPGL Plot File (Hewlett-Packard)

.PM PM graphics file

.PNT Macintosh painting

.PPT Presentation table file (Powerpoint)

.PRD Printer driver (MS-Word)

.PRF Preferences (Grammatik)

.PRM parameters (many)

.PRN   text file (Lotus 1-2-3—Symphony)

.PRO   Profile

.PRS   Printer resource file   (WordPerfect)

.PS   PostScript file (text/graphics) (ASCII)

.PUB   public key ring file (Pretty Good Privacy RSA System)

.PUB   publication   (Ventura Publisher)

.PUB   Microsoft Publisher file

.PW   text file (Professional Write)

.PX   Primary index (Paradox)

.QDI   Dictionary (Quicken)

.QDK   backup of   startup files created by Optimize (QEMM)

.QDT   Data (Quicken)

.QIF   Quicken Interchange Format

.QLB   Library file (Microsoft   Quick)

.QMT   Memorized list (Quicken)

.QNX   Index   (Quicken)

.RAW   raw RGB 24-bit graphics file

.RC   Resource Script File

.REC   recorded macro file (MS Windows)

.REF   cross-reference

.REG   registration file (Corel programs)

.REM remarks

.RES   Compiled Resource file

.RIC   Bitmap (Rhcoh)

.RLE   Utah Run Length Encoded rasterfile graphic file (SDSC Image Tool)

.ROL   Adlib Songfile

.RTF   Rich Text Format text file (Windows Word)

.RTF   Windows Help file script

.SAM text file (Samna—Lotus Ami/Ami Pro)

.SAV   backup file

.SBB   Label definition file (Superbase)

.SBD   Definition file (Superbase)

.SBF   Data file   (Superbase)

.SBK   Function key file (Superbase)

.SBM   Macro file   (Superbase)

.SBP   Program file (Superbase)

.SBQ   Query file   (Superbase)

.SBT   text editor file (Superbase)

.SBU   Update file   (Superbase)

.SBV   Form file (Superbase)

.SCR   script   (Kermit)

.SDF   Standard Data File

.SEA   Self-Extracting compressed   Macintosh file Archive

.SET   Driver settings (Lotus) Image Settings   (Paradox)

.SH   unix ASCII file archive created by SHAR   (unshar.zip)

.SHK   compressed Apple II file archive created by   SHRINKIT

.SHP   Bitmap (NewsMaster)

.SIT   compressed Macintosh archive created by STUFFIT (unsit30.zip)

.SLK   Symbolic Link   format

.SMM macro (Ami Pro)

.SND   digitized sound file   (Macintosh/ATARI/PC)

.SNG   song (midi sound) file (Atari   Cubase)

.SPL   print spooling file (MS Windows)

.SQ2   Compressed   file

.STF   Structured File (Lotus Agenda)

.STY   Style

.SUM   Summary file (Grammatik)

.SU   Supplemental Dictionary   (WordPerfect)

.SWP swap file (DOS)

.SYD   backup of startup files   created by QEMM (?) autoexec.syd

.SYM Synonym

.SYS   System   file

.TBK   Toolbook

.TDF   Trace Definition File (OS/2)

.TFM Tagged Font Metric

.TGA Truevision Targa graphics file

.THD Thread

.THS Thesaurus

.TIF Tagged Image File Format bitmap graphics (PageMaker—CorelDRAW)

.TLX Telex

.TMP Temporary file

.TRM terminal settings (MS Windows)

.TST Test

.TTF TrueType Font file

.TUT Tutorial

.TXT text file

.UU compressed ASCII file archive created by UUDE/ENCODE

.UUE compressed ASCII file archive created by UUENCODE (uuexe515.exe)

.VAL Validity Checks (Paradox)

.VBX Visual Basic eXtension (Visual Basic)

.VGA VGA display driver (many)

.VGA VGA display font (many)

.VOC audio file (Soundblaster)

.VRS Graphics driver (WordPerfect)

.VST Truevision Vista graphics file

.WAV Microsoft Waveform audio file

.WDB database (MS Works)

.WEM Express Data File (hDC Windows)

.WFM graphics file (Corel Symbol & Typeface)

.WK1 Lotus worksheet R.2

.WK2 Lotus worksheet R.2x

.WK3 Lotus worksheet R.3

.WKB document (WordPerfect for Win)

.WKE Lotus worksheet R.1A or MS-Works worksheet

.WKQ spreadsheet (Quattro Pro)

.WKS spreadsheet (Lotus 1-2-3 version 1A—Symphony 1.0—MS Works)

.WKZ Compressed worksheet (Borland)

.WMF Windows MetaFile vector graphics   (Windows 3)

.WPB Button Bar (WordPerfect)

.WPD Window Postscript   Description

.WPD Document (WordPerfect versions 6 and up)

.WPG WordPerfect Graphics Format bitmapped file (DrawPerfect)

.WPK Keyboard   (WordPerfect)

.WPM Macro (WordPerfect)

.WPP Color Printing   Pallette (WordPerfect)

.WPS text document (MS Works)

.WPX Fax   (WorldPort, Fax Manager, JetFAX, OAZ Communications)

.WQ! Compressed   Spreadsheet (Borland)

.WQ1 Spreadsheet (Borland)

.WQ2 Spreadsheet   (Quatro Pro 5)

.WR1 Symphony

.WRI   text file (Windows   Write)

.XLA   add-in macro sheet (MS Excel)

.XLC   chart (MX   Excel)

.XLM   macro (MS Excel)

.XLS   worksheet (MS Excel)

.XLT   template (MS Excel)

.XLW   workspace (MS Excel)

.ZLW   workbook (MS   Excel)

.ZIP   compressed file archive created by PKZIP or Winzip   (PKZ204G.EXE)

.ZOO   compressed file (Dhesi10/7/99 6:48 AM

*if your file isn't listed on this page, check out
http://www0.delphi.com/navnet/faq/extguide.html **or**
http://kresch.com/exts/ext.htm. **Both are excellent references for file**
extensions, and the latter lets you search for the file extension.

Appendix F

How to use Search Engines:

Allow me to mention briefly what a ***search engine*** is before I tell you how they work and some tricks for using them. A loose definition of an engine is something that allows you to do a lot of work with less effort than you would exert by yourself. As far as searching the 'Net, all of the major search engines do a good job of bringing a lot of information to your fingertips with a minimal amount of effort.

A search engine is a computer program, like a Web browser, that searches a ***database***. A database is information that is contained in one place in some semblance of order. Obviously, the more information a search engine has in it's database, the more effective it's going to be. It's like the more information that you have in your brain, the more likely you are to get the big bucks on "Who Wants to be a Millionaire."

How do these search engines build their databases?

Search engines use ***robots***, sometimes called bots, to comb through ***Web servers***. The major search engines may cover hundreds of Web servers on a daily basis; each Web server may contain thousands and thousands of Web sites each site containing anywhere between a few pages to hundreds of pages. Remember that a ***server*** is a computer that is dedicated to a specific purpose. You can use a computer for word processing and that sort of thing and serve Web pages, but most machines that serve Web pages are dedicated servers that do nothing else. This is definitely the case with the large search engines and portals such as Yahoo. Instead of someone using these Web servers to do word processing or for personal use, they are dedicated computers that store Web pages and serve them up to people that visit the Web sites that reside on a particular server. These programs that traverse the Internet and gather information to store in a search engines database are often referred to as **Web crawlers** or **Spiders**. They usually roam late at night when Web traffic is low; that way they don't congest the Internet.

Search engines employ different methods of obtaining information. Their Web crawlers may index the title of Web pages only, and still others index every word on Web pages that they visit. An engine may take into consideration how often a word occurs in a Web page or even the placement of that word or words. Some of the smarter engines even take the proximity of words into account.

Many search engines record a Web site's **Meta tag**. A Meta tag is something that Web masters usually insert into their Web pages for the main purpose of facilitating a Web crawlers job of finding and referencing their site on search engines. The Meta tag is located in the header of a page; there is normally one Meta tag that lists all of the keywords that are relevant to a Web site. They are supposed to be words that actually appear in the site somewhere. Another Meta tag describes a site in a short 1-2-sentence summary. It is the latter that is usually shown in the results of a search. For example, a Web master of a computer tutorial site would enter a tag like the following into the html code of their Web site: *<meta name="description" content="One of the best resources for novice computer users on the Web. This site is for beginner computer users, and offers free tips that can be printed from the Web.">* In the search results on search engines, there would be a hyperlink that said *"One of the best resources for novice computer users on the Web. This site is for beginner…"* if it brought up this example Web site on a search for Beginner computer tips or something similar.

Furthermore, search engines vary in the ways that they physically search for information. Engines have different classifications based on how they conduct their searches. A true search engine combs through its entire database based on keywords or key phrases that you type in. It will then display relevant Web sites, called hits, which match your search criteria. A quintessential *search engine* is Alta Vista.

A *multiengine* is a strong tool—especially if you learn how to use it properly. MetaCrawler is classified as a multiengine. MetaCrawler doesn't actually maintain it's own database rather it has the ability to search several engines at once, sift through the irrelevant hits, and deliver a comprehensive list of results to you.

A *search directory* is similar to a search engine, but instead of blindly shuffling through databases, a search directory searches databases that are more specifically designed by subject, and it searches from general subject matter to specific.

Another genre of search engine is a combination *search engine* and *search directory*. These sites offer the option to search the entire database or to search for a specific subject matter by category. Infoseek and Lycos employ this kind of search technology.

In addition, there is a new breed of search engine on the forefront that employs a highly sophisticated proprietary search technology. Google (*www.google.com*) is one such engine. Google specifically uses software called **PageRank(TM)** that boasts the ability to methodically search out your subject matter in a way that no other engine currently employs. Because of the efficiency of Google's search algorithms, and because they have thousands of computers networked together, you can expect a speedy and accurate response to your search query.

We now know that search engines use different techniques to gather their data in the first place and they technically work on one of four principles.

Along the same lines, each engine offers several different ways to search and to refine your search. Although engines all work on basically the same principle as far as actually searching with them, there are special techniques you can use to expedite your search; these will vary from engine to engine. You should refer to the Help files or FAQ on the search engines that you use to find out just what types of searches are permissible. The Help files will tell you what type of operators can be used on a specific site. After you familiarize yourself with several engines, you will not only know how to use the search tools that are indigenous to that site, but you will learn what engines are better for different types of searches. If you can become proficient using search engines, you will find them extremely useful; you will be able to find virtually any kind of information in a matter of minutes.

Keyword Search

The most common method that can be used across the board with all engines is the *keyword search*. You simply type in a keyword or words or even a phrase, and the engine combs through its database and returns the relevant hits. Of course, what the engine determines as relevant depends on how the Web crawler indexed the information in the database in the 1st place. As I mentioned, some engines develop an index based on the title of Web pages and some look at the Web page Meta tag. Some search through every single word in a Web page and use a mathematical algorithm to build its database based on factors such as how frequently a word is used, where it is placed in the document, and it may even cross-reference that information with another factor such as the Meta tag.

A lot of Web masters have employed every trick in the book to try and get their Web page to pop up on various search engines. These include using an incredibly long Meta tag that may contain every word that could remotely relate to the Web site's subject matter. I have heard some people discuss importing the entire Oxford English Dictionary into their site since a search of nearly any word would possibly cause that site to appear in search results. Others may use such techniques as using words like porn, sex, etc. in the Meta tag since words like that are the more popular terms that people search for on the Internet. Other techniques have been to scatter keywords throughout the Web document and make the text of those words the same color as the background so they cannot be seen by the naked eye. A Web crawler would pick up on these "invisible" words, however.

I could go on and on about ploys to make a Web site appear on a search engine, but that's not what this article is about. I wanted to mention it though because if you plan on making a Web site, be careful of these tactics. Most search engine Web masters have caught on to these more obvious techniques by now, so they will likely not do you that much good at this stage in the game.

The ***conceptual search*** employs artificial intelligence to methodically search the database instead of just blindly going after the search based solely on the keywords that you type in. Excite is the best-known search engine that uses this sort of technology.

In the best case scenario, a conceptual search returns relevant hits even if they differ from the search terms that you typed in. They are able to do this using mathematical algorithms that determine the frequency and placement of words in a document. They can normally go one step further and determine the location of words in a document in relation to other words thus taking some of the ambiguity out of the search for you. For example, the artificial intelligence understands that "fan" can mean a football fan or a fan that ventilates a room; it can tell the difference between a basketball court and a court of law.

The problem with a conceptual search

Conceptual searching is a great idea, but like computers it is far from perfect yet. This kind of search depends on many factors such as linguistic analysis, algorithms, and cross-referencing documents. Because of the complexity of these factors, there are bound to be some mistakes made by some of the search engines that use this kind of method. However, using a conceptual search will often be able to determine what you actually mean and not just what keywords you type in and thus give you more accurate hits.

Although search engines use different techniques, all conceptual searches use a method known as ***clustering*** to find what you are looking for. Clustering can decipher different denotations by examining how words are positioned in relation to other words. For example, a conceptual search engine can reason that if the word star is used in a space exploration context, it would stand to reason that words such as planet, solar system, and nebulae would appear in the document as well. If the word star is used in another context, some related words might include Hollywood, actor, or actress. Because of the way this works, you are better off using a lot of words, almost a sentence, to describe your search. You may type "red giant stars in the universe" without quotes, and the engine will reason that if a document contains words such as universe, comet, or black hole, it will be relevant to your search and it won't give you Web pages about a baseball star from the New York Giants.

The faux pas of keyword searching

The reason why conceptual searching is superior to only searching by keywords is that the keyword search is unable to distinguish between different contextual meanings; it can't tell the difference in the word black between black ice, black plague, or black lung disease. Furthermore, it can't tell the difference between synonyms; if you type in sense of smell for your search query, you will not get hits back on pages that used the word olfactory instead of smell. In other words, your search will be limited to the actual words that you typed in for your search. Whereas a contextual search can use quantitative analysis to serve relevant pages to you that are outside of the realm of the actual criteria that you provided.

Search Operators

Operators are ways to refine your search because often, whether with key-word or conceptual searches, many irrelevant hits are returned or many relevant ones may be excluded. All search engines can use some operators and some are specific to certain engines. Be sure to check the Help files on the search engine that you are on to see what kind of operators you can employ.

Boolean search

You can use the words AND, OR, and NOT to refine your search with Boolean operators. There are what is called ***proximal locators*** that can also be used; these include the words NEAR and FOLLOWED BY. When using Boolean search words, they need to be capitalized and do not leave a space between your search words and the Boolean operator.

The word AND narrows your search by requiring that both or all words be present in a document for it to come up on a search engine. For example, if you are a coin collector, but you are looking for coins outside of the Unites States you may want to type the search words coinsANDforeignANDrare. This will require that the documents that are returned are relevant to all 3 of your search words and thus eliminate a lot of the irrelevancies.

The word OR might be used if you don't want to cut too much out of your search. If you search for a subject and it comes up with little or nothing, try the OR operator to extend your search. Let's say that you search for real estate and it comes up with hundreds of hits, but what you really want is real estate in Florida. You would type real-estateANDFlorida. If that returned too few hits, you would try FloridaANDreal-estateORpropertyORland.

The word NOT is used to eliminate extraneous results. You would use this most often if you anticipated irrelevant hits. You may search for modemsANDcableNOTtelevision reasoning that a search engine may very well give you hits about television because you used the word cable even despite the fact that modems were in your search also.

NEAR specifies that your search words be within a certain proximity to one another. FOLLOWED BY means that one word must directly follow the other one. ADJ (adjacent) is synonymous with FOLLOWED BY.

Phrase searching

It can be quite an advantage to be able to search with a phrase. Search engines that allow phrase searching usually require that you enclose the phrase in quotation marks. For example, I searched for "chocolate starfish and hotdog flavored water" on google.com, and it came up with several sites pertaining to Limp Bizkit despite the fact that the search words are not related at all to the words limp or bizkit.

Symbolic searching

These types of searches allow you to use + and − signs to refine your query. These are really used as a replacement for the AND and NOT Boolean operators. There are many different combinations of operators that may be executed on any given search engine. Just take a minute to read the Help files and find out what they offer. Some engines offer proprietary search techniques that would be beyond the scope of this article to even go into. There is not a standard for search engines across the Internet and that's why it is so important to learn exactly what you can and cannot do with particular search engines. On many engines you can combine techniques to customize your search even more. If the engine allows it, you can type in +software+computer+linuxNOT"Microsoft Windows" if you are looking for Linux software. For the most part, search engines all work on the same principles: You type in a search word or phrase and with the click of your mouse, you watch as a list of hyperlinks appears in front of you. The hyperlinks will be descriptions of each hit, and all you have to do is click on the hyperlink to go to the one that sounds like it has the description that applies to your search the most. Try many search engines and just experiment with them. You may find one or two that you like the best, and you may reference half a dozen of them that you will use for different circumstances. Don't be scared to try them though. As of this writing, they are all free so you have nothing to lose.

Appendix G

Computer problems

Why am I having so many computer problems?

This question may not be as easily answered as you might think; there is probably not a clear-cut answer. There are a lot of things that can go wrong with a computer because there are so many possible configurations. There is so much hardware and software available nowadays that it is nearly unfathomable.

Why could you be having so much trouble with your computer? Well, if you call a technical support help desk, they may not know for sure no matter how knowledgeable the person is that you're talking to. The reason why one may hem and haw before giving an answer to such a broad question is that there may not be a definitive answer. That would be like asking why there is so much red tape and bureaucracy in the government or the military.

Keep this in mind before asking why you have so many computer problems. If you call technical support once or twice and they are able to fix your issue, then you had a more clear-cut problem that was straightforward and had a textbook answer. If you have called a support line half a dozen times, and you still have the same problem(s), then you have one of those annoying issues that falls outside of the lines of a normal problem. Believe me that it won't be due to lack of trying that your problem won't be fixed. Most likely it won't be due to lack of knowledge either. I mean you may get 1 or 2 techs out of 6 calls to a support line that might not be that knowledgeable: No company can afford to send all of it's representatives to train-

251

ing for 6 months to a year to learn everything that they might actually need to know in real-world situations before actually starting the job. Therefore, a lot of the training that companies provide will only give answers to solve textbook problems.

A lot of times it will be up to the representatives to think for themselves, which some people are better at than others. Also, a lot of answers to your more complicated problems are learned on the job (OJT or On the Job Training). So you might get a couple of reps that unknowingly lead you astray; to get 6 or more reps in a row that don't know their stuff would be highly unlikely at almost any company. Maybe it would be about as unlikely as the computer problem that you are experiencing.

Furthermore, if a certain problem still exists after dozens of fixes have been tried, there is some problem that exists on your end. Yes that's right: It's your computer, your phone line, your something. Consider this: Most software (and this is especially true with big name brands like Microsoft, AOL, IBM, CompuServe, Intuit, etc.) has been Alpha tested, Beta tested, tested some more, retested, tested some more, and then tested some more before it is released to the general public. It has been determined that the software can run on most computers that meet the system requirements set forth by the software manufacturer. So if you always have problems with software, or with certain software, make sure that your computer meets all of the system requirements. If you still have problems, make sure your computer exceeds (at least a little bit and in most areas) the system requirements. Some of the system requirements set forth by software manufacturers are pretty liberal, and software will only work with the minimum if everything else is perfectly configured on your system, which is usually not the case.

For example, As of this writing, America Online has some 25 million members plus or minus a few hundred thousand. The software runs fine on probably at least 24.5 million of them. Therefore, if you are one of the few unfortunate soles that has trouble with this program, it is something on your end, period. If it were the AOL software in this example, then 25 million computers wouldn't be running the program successfully.

If you have problems with certain software, It might be due to something that you are unaware of or something that isn't spelled out one way or the other in the system requirements such as that you are on a network. A lot of software, including AOL, is not supported on a network. This is not to say that it will not work. Manufacturers that don't support their software on a network just don't guarantee that it is going to work, and they are not obligated to help you fix it or reinstall your network if something goes wrong. In other words, it is up to you if you want to try to run software on a system or within a configuration that falls outside the companies guidelines of support; you have to accept the inherent risks that may come along with this and if you can't make it work, they can't either.

So okay you're telling me it's my computer so what can I do about it?

Again, this may not be so simple or clear-cut especially if you've called tech support numerous times and your problem still exists. The good news is that many very annoying problems are actually easily fixed. You should not get too frustrated because this will just impede your progress in figuring out what the problem is—which probably isn't too difficult with the right guidance. If you end up throwing your computer out the window, you will be even madder when you cool down and come to the realization that you've thrown $1000, or maybe more, out that window. Remember that Computer Science is not perfect.

Additionally, don't assume that just because you have a new computer that you don't need an update of some sort. Remember again that computers aren't perfected yet, and it is not like getting a toaster or a microwave oven where it is a pretty safe bet that you will have years of trouble-free usage of the appliance right out of the box. In a perfect world, you would be correct in the assumption that a new computer would work perfectly and you shouldn't need to upgrade or update anything for a long time.

The computer industry changes very rapidly (in case you didn't notice), and if you think about it, even a modern car is subject to a recall or it might need a newer part for the air-conditioner to comply with a regulation that has just been enacted by the EPA soon after the car is driven off the lot. The good news is that in most cases, the manufacturer will absorb the cost of the update or upgrade; it will cost you a little time to find out how to get an updated driver for that video card or to drive the car to the dealership to get that new part installed, however. Another positive thing is that despite the possible imperfections of a computer, you normally will not need to upgrade any of the hardware right off the bat with a brand new computer. Of course if you choose to add a peripheral or a completely different piece of hardware that expands the capabilities of the base system, such as a scanner or a joystick, that will be up to you and it would not be necessary for the basic operation of the system. You will probably need to get some updated drivers, however. Drivers are software programs that tell a piece of hardware how to communicate with the computer. Hardware manufacturers are always striving to improve the functionality of their product. As a result, they may produce an updated driver at any time—even the very day that you bought your computer!

This is what happens sometimes: A hardware manufacturer makes a video card let's say. Then a newer operating system, such as Windows 2000, emerges after the video card is produced. The video card manufacturer realizes that the video card needs different instructions to perform to peak capacity on this new operating system, so they write an updated driver. Scenario number 2 might be that the video card performed well in all of the benchmark tests that were conducted before the video card was released to the public. It is then realized that the card behaves irregularly with just certain programs that may or may not have even existed when the first driver was written. A manufacturer cannot possibly test their product with every single program out there or else nothing would ever be released and all of the hardware companies would go broke and be out of business. A third scenario might be that a modem manufacturer sells a modem, and after it has gone to market they realize that they can make a certain improvement to the driver to make the modem perform even better or to ignore phone line noise more or something like that. They will then write a patch or driver to improve the functionality of the modem.

Keep in mind that when computers are put together, they may sit in a warehouse for months before they are even shipped to a retail store. At the store, they will likely sit around for a while before someone buys the system. By the time that you get your computer home, it is likely that the manufacturer has written updated drivers for some of the hardware inside of your computer. Don't be surprised if you don't need an updated driver the very day that you bring your computer home.

You may not realize that you need a new driver unless you have an incompatibility problem with a certain program. For example, you may have problems connecting to your ISP, and an updated modem driver will fix it. Or, you may install a piece of software, and while running that program, your colors on the screen look splotchy. Normally, that problem would indicate that you need an updated video driver for your video card. A video card controls how graphics are rendered on your computer screen. Of course, in both examples, the problem could be myriad of things; the driver may not be the problem. Sometimes a device just needs to be uninstalled and reinstalled, for instance.

A computer is not a toaster

A computer is really just an electronic device like a toaster or a stereo, so you really shouldn't let it scare you. However, you don't install software on your stereo or TV, and you aren't likely to take your toaster apart and put a new component in it like you could with your computer. Needless to say, there are lots more variables you are dealing with on a PC than most other electrical devices. To complicate matters even more, computers are not perfected yet. They have come a long way in a short time, but they really have a long way to go in the developmental stage.

Maybe about the year 2050 they will be pretty much perfected. Well, I don't know if I'd use the word perfected, but they will probably be as reliable as the automobile is today by then. I hate to say it, but I believe that we are living in the biggest time-crunch of all time. I think that our time-poor society exemplifies how imperfect Computer Science really is. It also reiterates the fact we are in the midst of the Information Age. Think about how much time we had before computers. Weren't computers supposed to save us time? It wasn't totally clear to me at first why I had a lot less time than I used to. When I scrutinized my situation, here's the conclusion that I came to:

1) Since computers are a hobby of mine, and are needed for my profession, they naturally occupy a lot of my time.

2) I really don't spend more time doing things on a computer that I could have done more quickly with older technology as a rule. I am pretty computer literate though. I could imagine someone that wasn't so computer savvy spending a lot of time just spinning their wheels getting the thing to work.

3) Although I don't usually spend more time doing things on a computer that I could have done on a typewriter, there is simply a lot more to do. In this Information Age, there seems to be infinite knowledge that I want to grasp. It is to the point sometimes where it overwhelms me so much that I end up just trying to figure out what to read first or what to do first. I click on a link in e-mail and next thing I know I'm off on a tangent for an hour or two. Then I end up not getting anything done, but I spend all of my time just trying to figure out what to do or doing something that I had no plans to do in the first place. I have 3 or 4 e-mail boxes that are very active and just as many that aren't that active; I spend hours on some days just wading through that e-mail.

Computers will save us time one of these days

So there you have it in a nutshell. My synopsis is that computers will eventually give us more leisure time, but the bad new is that it probably won't be in our lifetime if you are old enough to be reading this article now in the year 2000. The world will probably enjoy a lot of leisure time in some rather distant future that might resemble the Jetson's cartoon show or the Star Wars movie. You see we've been caught in a unique era where we are too technologically advanced to be primitive, but we are not advanced enough to be considered Space Age. Our designation could be compared to a teenager when you are too old to be a child but too young to be considered an adult. Or, it's like turning 30: You are too old to be young and too young to be old. To put this in perspective, as advanced as our civilization really is, we would probably be laughed at by aliens out there that might have the know-how to travel to earth from whatever distant galaxy that they might come from. If there are Aliens out there, as portrayed in a lot of our movies and television shows, they would probably look at our computers and it would be like us looking at the Cotton Gin or something.

Some people enjoyed a lot of leisure time in the 19th century before industrialization. Then again, a lot of people had to work on farms from dusk till dawn. This may not have been a whole lot worse than slaving over a computer at the office for 14 hours a day but just different work. While physical work may be a lot more grueling, it still takes up just as much of your free time working at the office if you are there 10-12 hours a day or more. It is a good thing that there is greater longevity nowadays. Basically it's the same thing as it's always been in the Computer Age as far as leisure time is concerned. It is true that we don't have kids working 14-hour days in sweat shops because of regulatory agencies like OSHA. But we have adults working 14-hour days in offices sometimes 6 or 7 days a week. Furthermore, because of longevity we are seeing older people working later in life, and some of them even work long hours as well. I think that we will see more elderly people in the work force as the Social Security system falters and as the mortality rate gets even lower. People can also work later in life because not as many jobs nowadays require very physical work. It just isn't possible for most 60 or 70 year olds to perform the backbreaking labor that is necessary in most factories, but they can sit in front of a computer.

Never enough thyme

Our civilization probably had the most leisure time in the mid 1900s, perhaps from 1945-1960, before computers were really thought of. In the early 1900s technology still wasn't very developed and we were right in the midst of the Industrial Age where people had to slave away in hot factories day in and day out. Then came World War I, and the Great Depression era was not too far behind. A decade after that was World War II that had our country and others hustling and bustling. That's why I figure that in that time frame (1945-1960), it might have been one of the best times to live in modern history. I mean we had some technology such as the automobile. The television was on the forefront during this period also. Things didn't seem as competitive then, and life was certainly more predictable and less complicated. That period, and maybe even as far as the '70s, was when we could usually go to school, get a job, work 30 years and retire with a decent pension plan and a Social Security check. You would live out the remaining 10-20 years of your life doing what you wanted to do with little or no financial worries. In other words, the Information Age has made things more complex which is probably the understatement of the century. This complexity has put time-restraints on our lives that we have never seen before. Because Computer Science is not perfect, and we have not figured out a way to harness all of the information available, it has taken quite a time-toll on our lives.

Appendix H

Attaching files to e-mail using AOL or CompuServe 2000

Attaching files using America Online

1. On the Mail screen, click the Attachments button. The Attachments window appears.

2. Click the Attach button.

3. Browse your hard disk or floppy disk directory for the file you want to

attach.

4. Click to highlight the file's name, and click Open. The file name appears on the Attachments window. If you change your mind and decide not to send the file, click the Detach button. Repeats steps 2 and 3 until you have attached all the files you wish.

5. When you are satisfied with your attachments, click OK.

6. Fill in the address, subject, and body of your e-mail normally. Even if your attachment contains your primary information, it's customary to include some kind of a "cover letter" in the e-mail message box.

7. Click the Send Now button in the upper-right corner of your mail form. You'll see a blue status bar indicating that your file is being sent with the e-mail.

If you attached multiple files, the AOL software will automatically zip them for you before it sends the mail.

Note: The recipient must have software that is compatible with your file. For example, if you send someone a WordPerfect file, your recipient must have either WordPerfect or a word processing program capable of opening WordPerfect files.

Also make sure the file is compatible with your recipient's computer; a Macintosh machine may not be able to read some Windows files, and vice versa.

Attaching files using CompuServe 2000

1. On the Create Mail screen, click the Attachments button. The Attachments window appears.

2. Click the Attach button and then click the Add button.

3. Browse your hard disk or floppy disk directory for the file you want to

attach.

4. Click to highlight the file's name, and click Open. The file name appears on the Attachments window. If you change your mind and decide not to send the file, click the Detach button. Repeats steps 2 and 3 until you have attached all the files you wish.

5. When you are satisfied with your attachments, click Attach.

6. Fill in the address, subject, and body of your e-mail normally. Even if your attachment contains your primary information, it's customary to include some kind of a "cover letter" in the e-mail message box.

7. Click the Send button. You'll see a blue status bar indicating that your file is being sent with the e-mail. If you attached multiple files, the CompuServe software will automatically zip them for you before it sends the mail.

Note: The recipient must have software that is compatible with your file. For example, if you send someone a WordPerfect file, your recipient must have either WordPerfect or a word processing program capable of opening WordPerfect files.

Also make sure the file is compatible with your recipient's computer; a Macintosh machine may not be able to read some Windows files, and vice versa.

Appendix I

Internet Acronyms

Many people use **shorthand** to speed up their typing. Shorthand is simply an online form of acronyms or abbreviations. Here is a list of the most common acronyms you are likely to run into in email, IMs, chats and message boards.

Depending on where you are online, you may encounter different sets of **shorthand**. While no one set of acronyms is necessarily complete, this list should cover most any abbreviation you are likely to come across:

2U2 = To You, Too
AAMOF = As A Matter Of Fact
AFAIK = As Far As I Know
AFAIC = As Far As I'm Concerned
AFAICT = As Far As I Can Tell
AFK = Away From Keyboard
ASAP = As Soon As Possible
BAK = Back At Keyboard
BBL = Be Back Later

BBFN = Bye-bye for now
BITMT = But In The Meantime
BOT = Back On Topic
BRB = Be Right Back
BTW = By the way

BYKT= But you knew that
C4N = See ya For Now

CMIIW = Correct me if I'm wrong
CRS = Can't Remember "Stuff"
CU = See You
CUL(8R) = See You Later
CWOT = Complete Waste Of Time
CYA = See Ya

DIIK = Damned if I know
DITYID = Did I Tell You I'm Distressed?
DIY = Do It Yourself
EOD = End Of Discussion

EOL = End of lecture
EOT = End of thread
EZ = Easy
F2F = Face To Face
FAQ = Frequently Asked Questions
FBOW = For Better Or Worse

FITB = Fill in the blank
FOAF = Friend Of A Friend
FOCL = Falling Off Chair Laughing

FOTCL = Falling off the chair laughing
FWIW = For What It's Worth
FYA = For Your Amusement
FYI = For Your Information
/ga = Go Ahead
GAL = Get A Life

GBTW = Get Back To Work
GFC = Going For Coffee
GFETE = Grinning From Ear To Ear

GLG = Goofy little grin
GMTA = Great Minds Think Alike

GOK = God only knows
GR&D = Grinning, Running & Ducking

GTG = Got To Go
GTGTTBR = Got To Go To The Bathroom
GTRM = Going To Read Mail
HAND = Have A Nice Day

HHOJ = Ha, ha, only joking
HHOK = Ha Ha Only Kidding

HHOS = Ha, ha, only serious
HTH = Hope This Helps
IAC = In Any Case
IAE = In Any Event

IANAL = I am not a lawyer
IC = I See
IDGI = I Don't Get It
IMCO = In My Considered Opinion
IMHO = In My Humble Opinion
IMNSHO = in My Not So Humble Opinion
IMO = In My Opinion
IMPE = In My Previous/Personal Experience
IMVHO = In My Very Humble Opinion

IOTTMCO = Intuitively Obvious To The Most Casual Observer
IOW = In Other Words
IRL = In Real Life
ISP = Internet Service Provider

IWBNI = It would be nice if
IYKWIM = If You Know What I Mean

JADP = Just another data point

JASE = Just another system error
JIC = Just In Case
J/K = Just kidding
KISS = Keep It Simple Stupid
L8TR = Later
LD = Later Dude

LOL = Laughing Out Loud

LOT = Lovely and talented
LTNS = Long Time No See
MorF = Male or Female, or person who asks that question
MTCW = My Two Cents Worth
NRN = No Reply Necessary
ONNA = Oh No, Not Again!
OTOH = On The Other Hand
OTTOMH = Off The Top Of My Head
OIC = Oh I See

OOC = Out of character
OTF = On The Floor
OLL = Online Love

PCMCIA = People Can't Memorize Computer Industry Acronyms
PLS = Please

PMJI = Pardon my jumping in
PU = That Stinks!
REHI = Hello Again (re-Hi!)

RL = Real life
ROFL = Rolling On Floor Laughing
ROTF = Rolling On The Floor
ROTFL = Rolling On The Floor Laughing

ROTM = Right on the money
RSN = Real Soon Now
RTDox = Read The Documentation/Directions
RTFM = Read The Frickin' Manual

RUMOF = Are you male or female?
RUOK = Are You OK?

SITD = Still in the dark
S!MT!!OE!!! = Sets! my teeth!! on edge!!!
SNAFU = Situation Normal; All Fouled Up
SO = Significant Other
SOL = Smiling Out Loud (or You're Out of Luck)
TANSTAAFL = There Ain't No Such Thing As A Free Lunch
TAFN = That's All For Now
TEOTWAWKI—The End Of The World As We Know It
THX = Thanks
TIA = Thanks In Advance

TIC = Tongue in cheek
TLK2UL8R = Talk to you later
TMK = To My Knowledge

TMOT = Trust me on this
TOS = Terms Of Service
TPTB = The Powers That Be
TSWC = Tell Someone Who Cares
TTBOMK = To The Best Of My Knowledge
TTFN = Ta-Ta For Now
TTYL(8R) = Talk To You Later

TTYTT = To tell you the truth
TWIMC = To Whom It May Concern
Txs = Thanks

TYVM = Thank you very much
URL = Web Page Address

WADR = With all due respect
w/b = Welcome Back
w/o = Without
WRT = With Regard To
WTG = Way To Go
WU? = What's Up?
WWW = World Wide Web
WYSIWYG = What You See Is What You Get
Y2K = Year 2000
YGIAGAM = Your Guess Is As Good As Mine
YGWYPF = You Get What You Pay For

YOYOW = You own your own words
YMMV = Your Mileage May Vary
ZZZ = Sleeping

You'll notice that different chat communities can develop different 'dialects' or accents. If you see an acronym or smiley used, you can figure it's pretty safe to use it yourself. If you use acronyms and the majority of people in the room don't seem to understand, it's probably not something commonly used in that community.

Some chats on AOL use protocol. That means that rather than having an open chat where everyone talks at once, a host leads the chat. If you have a question, you type

?

If you have a comment, you use

!

Then you wait for the host to acknowledge you. It's also common to send a

/ga

For "go ahead" into the room indicating that you've finished with your question or comment.

Appendix J

Downloading files from the Internet

One thing that you need to realize is that downloading files from the Internet is different from downloading files from e-mail. The outcome is essentially the same: You transfer a file to your computer and execute it if it is an executable file (which we'll talk about more at the end of this article) or open it if your computer has a program installed on it that is capable of reading your file.

However, you need to realize that downloading from e-mail and downloading from the Internet are really 2 different procedures.

With E-mail, you usually receive some sort of message, and the mail may or may not have a file attachment. Sometimes an e-mail may contain no other message but to tell you that a file is attached. To download the file you click the **Download** button or **Download Now** or whatever it is called in your e-mail program. It comes up with a dialogue box that asks you where you would like to download the file.

When you download from the Internet, you will normally get a message that asks if you want to *download the file to disk* or *open the file from it's current location*. If you download the file to disk, it is saved somewhere on your hard drive. You have to find it and click on it to start the installation or to open the file if it is not an executable program. If you opt to open the file from its current location, it will run automatically, and it saves you from having to find the file on your computer and execute it. If this makes no sense to you or you still don't have a full understanding of all of this, read on.

Perhaps you need a little background information to really grasp this concept. When you opt to download a file from either e-mail or the Internet, a dialogue box will pop up and you can choose where you want to download it to. When downloading from the Internet, you will only get that dialogue box when you choose the save to disk option. If you open the program from current location, it will open itself as I have mentioned and the file usually will automatically go into a folder on the C drive called My Download Files. The file will have a name on the line labeled File Name in the download dialogue box. You can erase this and name the file anything you want. Just type in there what you want to call it. At the top of this window there will be a drop-down list. This is where it says Save In: A drop-down list is where you can click the little down arrow looking symbol {?} and it drops down several choices from which you can click on and select.

Whether you download from e-mail or the Internet, you will end up with the same window with the dropdown list—provided that you selected the save to disk option when downloading from the Internet. The dropdown list shows every drive on your computer, Desktop, and My Computer. The drives usually consist of 3 ½ floppy (A:), (C:) drive, and your CD-ROM drive that may be labeled D, G, M, Q or maybe even another letter. There will be any other drive that you may have on the computer, but these might be all of the choices except for Desktop and My Computer. Desktop will put the file on your main computer screen (The one that

comes up when you first turn the computer on with all the icons, the START button, etc) and My Computer is just another way to access all of the drives on the computer, but you can't actually download anything directly to My Computer.

If you want to save your file to a 3 ½" floppy disk, put a blank floppy in the floppy drive. Choose 3 ½" inch floppy (A:) from the dropdown list in the download window. Type whatever you want to call the file where it says File Name (or leave it the way it is if the file name is acceptable to you) and then click the **Save** button, which will usually appear in the lower-right hand corner of the window. If you want to save the file to your main drive or C drive, choose (C:) from the dropdown list. This may be named something else like Harddrive (C:), HP Pavilion (C:), or 80917(C:), but the C will be in there somewhere.

The thing about the C drive is that it has a lot of subdirectories. You can drill down through these files and choose to save a file in one of the subdirectories on the C drive. You could even make a new directory just for this purpose. You can always save your downloaded files to this same directory so you always know where all of the files that you download are.

Instructions to make a directory:

Open up **My Computer** and double-click on the **C drive** or Hard Drive.

Click **File** in the upper-left corner and choose **New>Folder**. This will produce a new folder named New Folder. It may be necessary to scroll down to the bottom of the entire window to see the one that says New Folder. You can promptly hit the **Delete** key to get rid of the name that Windows gave this folder and type in whatever you want to call it—maybe Downloads—then hit the **Enter** key to confirm your choice of names.

If you already hit the **Enter** key before renaming it and it won't let you back in where the name is, just rename the file yourself. Right-click on it and left-click on **Rename**. Hit the **Delete** key to get rid of the present name or just start typing and it will get rid of the name automatically. Type in what you want for a name and hit the **Enter** key to confirm.

You could choose **Desktop** from the download dropdown list. That way the file will download to the Desktop, which is your main computer screen. The Desktop is the screen that comes up when you first turn your computer on. You know, the one with all of the icons and the START button. Choosing Desktop makes it easy to locate your downloaded file because it will be right there where all of the other icons are. If you forget where you downloaded the file, you can choose the **Find Files** feature in Windows to find it. It is a good idea to make a note of the file name just in case you have to search for it using the Find Files feature.

Another way to make a directory is to right-click on the **Desktop** and left-click on **New>Folder**.

The folder will have the name New Folder, but you can name this whatever you want. Right-click on the folder and choose **Rename**. Hit the **Delete** key on your keyboard to get rid of the name. Type in whatever you want to replace it with and hit the **Enter** key to confirm your choice.

How to use Find Files or Folders:

Click on Start>Find>Files or Folders. Where it says Named, type in whatever the name is of the file that you downloaded. This is why it is important to pay attention to the name of any file you download. You might even want to write this information down. Underneath the Named line, there will be a dropdown list labeled Look In. Select (C:) drive or My Computer if you can't find C drive or if you think that you might have possibly downloaded the file to another drive besides C. By choosing My Computer, you will tell it to look in ALL of the drives on the computer. Make sure the box is checked that says include subfolders. Now just click on Find Now on the right-hand side of this window, and a little magnifying glass with move around in a circle while it is looking. You may get a message right away that says, "There are no items to show in this view."

As long as the magnifying glass is still moving around, just ignore this message. It should come up with your file at the bottom. After it is all said and done, if you get the message "There are no items to show in this view," the file does not exist on the computer if My Computer is selected where it says Look In. Or you misspelled the file name, or you down-loaded the file to a floppy disk that is not in the floppy drive now. You might need to redownload the file and pay more attention to where it is downloaded. If your file is found, just click on the little icon to the left of the file name that will be located at the bottom portion of the window; the program should open or do whatever it is supposed to do. It will say something like 1 file found in the lower-left corner—of course provided that the computer only found 1 file on the whole system with the name that you specified.

How to search for files or folders with Win Me

If you have Windows Me, you need to click **Start>Search>For Files or Folders...**

Type your search word where it says **Search for Files or Folders named**. All of the other principles, such as the Look In box are really the same as in older versions of Windows. Just click on Search Now at the bottom when you are ready to search for your file.

If you don't make a conscience effort to choose a download location, the file will download to a default location if you are downloading from e-mail. This will be wherever your mail program wants to put the file, which will usually be a designated download folder. Interestingly, if you choose "open the file from it's current location" when downloading from the Internet, by default it will download a copy of the file into the folder called My Download Files, located on the C drive. While it will start the installation automatically if you choose this option, it still saves a copy so you don't have to redownload the file if you need to reinstall the program.

What is an executable file?

An executable file is actually a self-contained program that has a specific purpose. It might be a game, a word-processor or office suite, a tax program, or a number of other things. There are many categories of programs these days. What I mean by self-contained is that it doesn't take another program to open these types of files. What defines an executable is that you can just double-click on the file or icon itself and the program will start running. Windows itself is the program that is actually needed to open an executable. Well, that's provided that the program is designed to run in a Windows environment, which most of them are these days.

Every file on a computer has a 3-letter extension. The extension on an executable is .exe. When you get a program on a CD, like say your ISPs program, it is an executable. That is why it installs if you double-click on the icon that represents the program; in most cases the CD-ROM drive is set up to auto run, so all you have to do is put the CD in and it will start automatically. Once that program is installed, you don't need the CD anymore (but you always want to keep it because you might need to reinstall your program some time in the future). The program is installed on your computers big drive (or C drive) at that point, so you don't have to put the CD in every time that you want to run that particular program.

If you download an executable file from the Internet, you just need to double-click on the program to kick it off, or if you choose "open from current location" it will start itself when the file is finished downloading. Open from current location would kind of be equivalent to putting a CD in the CD-ROM drive when auto run is enabled. In both cases, it will start to run the program automatically. So whether you install a program from a CD or download it from the Internet, you are just transferring an executable file to your hard drive. Once it is on your hard drive, it should not be necessary to redownload or reinstall the file unless the program becomes damaged or you reinstall Windows and lose all of your personal information on the computer. Furthermore, in most cases, you could copy the executable file from a CD to your hard disk. This is just a matter of copying a file from one disk to another. Your hard disk is kind of like several CDs stacked one on top of another. That way if your program became damaged, and you lost your CD, you would be able to reinstall without putting the CD in. Of course if you reinstalled Windows, it would erase the copy that you made of that file unless you copied it to a different drive other than C or you backed up your files.

There are many programs that offer you the option to do a partial installation. What this means is that it copies enough of a CD-ROM to your hard drive to run the program, but a lot of extra information is on the CD that is not copied to your hard drive. As you access that information, you will be prompted to insert the CD. Microsoft Publisher installed most of the program to my computer, but when I try to insert certain graphics, it prompts me to put the CD in so it can access that information. Programs such as Publisher would take up quite a chunk of hard drive space if you opted for the custom install and copied the entire thing to your hard drive.

If the file has another extension besides .exe, you will usually have to have a certain program that is capable of opening that particular type of file. Some programs you will probably have on your computer and some you won't. See Appendix E, *File Extensions* for a list of file extensions and what applications are needed to open them.

Appendix K

Description of ASCII and Binary Files

ASCII (TEXT)-stands for American Standard Code For Information Interchange. In simpler terms this is a computer standard for representing upper and lower-case Roman letters, as well as numbers and control characters on a US Standard 101/102 key keyboard.

ASCII files are commonly referred to as TEXT files or messages; they will appear in plain English such as the words you are currently reading. These types of messages do not require any special type of program for reading, rather they can be viewed by a simple text editor.

BINARY- Binary files are basically defined as all non-ASCII files that consist of eight-bit strings of data (versus seven bit for ASCII). These types of files include programs, graphics, documents, spreadsheets, and all other such files that require a compatible type of program for viewing as the file was created with.

Appendix L

Alt Commands

Alt 15 ¤ Alt 20 ¶ Alt 21 § Alt 33 ! Alt 34 "
Alt 35 # Alt 36 $ Alt 37 % Alt 38 & Alt 39 '
Alt 40 (Alt 41) Alt 42 * Alt 43 + Alt 44 ,
Alt 45—Alt 46 . Alt 47 / Alt 48 0 Alt 49 1
Alt 50 2 Alt 51 3 Alt 52 4 Alt 53 5 Alt 54 6
Alt 55 7 Alt 56 8 Alt 57 9 Alt 58 : Alt 59 ;
Alt 60 Alt 63 ? Alt 64 @
Alt 65 A Alt 66 B Alt 67 C Alt 68 D Alt 69 E
Alt 70 F Alt 71 G Alt 72 H Alt 73 I Alt 74 J
Alt 75 K Alt 76 L Alt 77 M Alt 78 N Alt 80 O
Alt 81 Q Alt 82 R Alt 83 S Alt 84 T Alt 85 U
Alt 86 V Alt 87 W Alt 88 X Alt 89 Y Alt 90 Z
Alt 91 [Alt 92 \ Alt 93] Alt 94 ^ Alt 95 _
Alt 96 ` Alt 97 a Alt 98 b Alt 90 Z Alt 91 [
Alt 92 \ Alt 93] Alt 94 ^ Alt 95 _ Alt 96 `
Alt 97 a Alt 98 b Alt 99 c Alt 100 d Alt 101 e
Alt 102 f Alt 103 g Alt 104 h Alt 105 i Alt 106 j
Alt 107 k Alt 108 l Alt 109 m Alt 110 n Alt 111 o
Alt 112 p Alt 113 q Alt 114 r Alt 115 s Alt 116 t
Alt 117 u Alt 118 v Alt 119 w Alt 120 x Alt 121 y
Alt 122 z Alt 123 { Alt 124 | Alt 125 } Alt 126 ~
Alt 128 Ç Alt 129 ü Alt 130 é Alt 131 â Alt 132 ä
Alt 133 à Alt 134 å Alt 135 ç Alt 136 ê Alt 137 ë
Alt 138 è Alt 139 ï Alt 140 î Alt 141 ì Alt 142 Ä
Alt 143 Å Alt 144 É Alt 145 æ Alt 146 Æ Alt 147 ô
Alt 148 ö Alt 149 ò Alt 150 û Alt 151 ù Alt 152 ÿ

Alt 153 Ö Alt 154 Ü Alt 155 ¢ Alt 156 £ Alt 157 ¥
Alt 158 P Alt 159 ƒ Alt 160 á Alt 161 í Alt 162 ó
Alt 163 ú Alt 164 ñ Alt 165 Ñ Alt 166 ª Alt 167 º
Alt 168 ¿ Alt 169 _ Alt 170 ¬ Alt 171 ½ Alt 172 ¼
Alt 173 ¡ Alt 174 « Alt 175 » Alt 179 ¦ Alt 225 ß
Alt 227 ¶ Alt 230 µ Alt 241 ± Alt 246 ÷ Alt 248 °
Alt 249 • Alt 250 · Alt 252 n Alt 253 ² Alt 800
Alt 02222 ® Alt 05555 ³ Alt 08888 ¸ Alt 01234567 ‡ Alt 098745

Without glasses....
§(©¿©)§ = alt 21, alt 808, alt 0169, alt 424, alt 0169, alt 809, alt 21
With glasses.....
§(@¿@)§ = alt 21, alt 808, shift 2, alt 424, shift 2, alt 809, alt 21

Some pictures appear different in different chat areas....also note ..the "shift 2" must be on your keyboard....NOT on the keypad....

Pic Examples..
ô¿ô = Face——————- Alt 147, Alt 168, Alt 147
â¿â = Face——————- Alt 131, Alt 168, Alt 131
-¿ô = Wink——————- Alt 638, Alt 168, Alt 147
-¿- = Sleeping— Alt 638, Alt 168, Alt 638
:Þ = Sticking Tongue out——————- : , Alt 0222
† = Cross—————— Alt 0134
+†+ = Crosses—— + , Alt 0134 , +
§§(^o^)§§ = Bozo The Clown—————- Alt 789 twice, (^ o ^), Alt 789 twice
¦:) = Face w/eybrows——————- Alt 1478, : ,)
©aaaaaa© = handcuffs Alt 0169, Alt 0170 x6, Alt 0169
Smiley Emoticons..
:) = Smile

:o = Surprised
:O = REALLY Surprised
:D = Laughing/smiling
:+ = Kiss
:* = Whistle
;) = Wink
:x = My lips are sealed
}:(= Mad
=) = Smily face
:(= Frown
:'(= crying
0:) = Angel (Halo is a zero)
(\O/) = Angel
\o/ \o/ \o/ = Praising God
Cute Ass Emoticons..
(_!_) a regular ass
(__!__) a fat ass
(!) a tight ass
(_._) a flat ass
(_^_) a bubble ass
(_*_) a sore ass
(_!__) a lop-sided ass
{_!_} a swishy ass
(_o_) an ass that's been around
(_O_) an ass that's been around even more
(_x_) kiss my ass
(_X_) leave my ass alone
(_zzz_) a tired ass
(_o^o_) a wise ass
(_13_) an unlucky ass
(_$_) Money coming out of his ass
Cute Boobie Emoticons..

(.)(.) Boobies
(.)(.) Bigger Boobies
(O)(O) Pamela Anderson-Lee boobies
(,)(,) Boobies with pierced nipples
. . Very Little Boobies
(*)(*) Implanted Boobies (very pert)
( ) ( ) Nursing Mom boobies
(.) (.)
(^)(^) Madonna Boobies
-<.><.>- Teeny Bikini Boobies
—(.)(.)— Regular Bikini Boobies
—-(.)-(.)—- Mondo Bikini Boobies
x x No boobies
(/)(/) Feminist Boobies
()() Wonderbra Boobies

Keyboard and Alt Pics
Shift+ 6 (small I) Shift+ 6 = ^i^ Angel
Alt+15 Alt+168 Alt+15 = ¤¿¤
Alt+147 Alt+168 Alt+147 = ô¿ô
Alt+0169 Alt+168 Alt+0169 = ©¿©
Alt+40 Alt+126 Alt+168 Alt+148 Alt+41 = (~¿ö)
Alt+40 Alt+126 Alt+168 Alt+126 Alt+41 = (~¿~)
Alt+174 Alt+147 Alt+168 Alt=147 Alt=175 = «ô¿ô»
Alt+132 Alt+168 Alt+132 = ä¿ä
Alt+0139 Alt+808 Alt+249 Alt+168 Alt+249 Alt+809 Alt+0155 =
‹(•¿•)›

ALT+ 0139 Alt+350 Alt+0155 Space Alt+0139 Alt+808 Alt+249
Alt+168 Alt+249 Alt+809 Alt+0155 Space Alt+0139 Alt+350
Alt+0155 = ‹^› ‹(•¿•)› ‹^›

ALT+ 0139 Alt+350 Alt+350 Alt+0155 Space Alt+0139 Alt+808
Alt+249 Alt+168 Alt+249 Alt+809 Alt+0155 Space Alt+0139
Alt+350 Alt+350 Alt+0155 = ‹^^› ‹(•¿•)› ‹^^›

Alt+249 = •
Alt+0139 Alt+350 Alt+350 Alt+0155 = ‹^^›
Alt+168 = ¿
Alt+0134 = †
Alt+136 Alt+168 Alt+136 = ê¿ê
(~¿~) = tired....
‹(•¿•)› = all ears....
<3 <3 <3 = Hearts
()))__*crayola*__))) = Crayola Crayon
(::waving::) = Waving
(:D) = Big Grin
{{{a screen name here}}} = Personal Cyber hugs
{{{}}} = Cyber Hugs
@————— Rose
@—-}—-}————
{^@^} = Pig
<*{{}}>

Foreign character

Alt Commands

To get foreign characters, hold *ALT* and type the number using the
numeric keypad.

French Characters

à 133

ç 135 Ç 128
é 130 É 144
è 138
ù 151

German Characters

ä 132 Ä 142
ö 148 Ö 153
ü 129 Ü 154
ß 225

Spanish Characters

é 130
á 160
í 161
ó 162
ú 163
ñ 164
Ñ 165
¿ 168
¡ 173
ü 129

Other Useful Characters

w 119
x 120
y 121
z 122
{ 123

| 124
} 125
~ 126
Ç 128
ü 129
é 130
â 131
ä 132
à 133
å 134
ç 135
ê 136
ë 137
è 138
ï 139
î 140
ì 141
Ä 142
Å 143
É 144
æ 145
Æ 146
ô 147
ö 148
ò 149
û 150
ù 151
ÿ 152
Ö 153
Ü 154
¢ 155
£ 156

¥ 157

P 158

ƒ 159

á 160

í 161

ó 162

ú 163

ñ 164

Ñ 165

ª 166

º 167

¿ 168

_ 169

¬ 170

½ 171

¼ 172

¡ 173

« 174

» 175

ß 225

Appendix M

Advanced Web Browser Removal

Complete Web browser removal tips. If all else has failed try this:

If you have tried "everything" to get to the Internet and it just doesn't work, you will need to try to blow out Internet Explorer and the associated .dlls in order to try and fix the problem. Dynamic Link Library (dll) files can be shared by multiple programs. Some .dlls come with a Windows installation, and some may be installed with certain programs. But most of the time they already exist in Windows and many programs use these same dlls so that every time you install a program it doesn't have to keep installing the same dll files. That is why they are dynamic; they can be used by many programs, including Windows, at the same time. **Only follow the instructions in this article if you have Windows 95 and all other possible solutions have been exhausted**. This isn't for the technically weak, and you won't be able to do this with Windows 98 because the Internet Explorer Web browser is integrated into the operating system so tightly, that for all practical purposes it can't be removed without completely destroying the operating system. You can actually remove the Windows 98 browser, but that is far beyond the scope of this book, and instructions can be found in the Microsoft Knowledge Base. However, Microsoft doesn't even support the removal of the Web browser on Windows 98. If all kinds of things have been tried on your Windows 95 machine, and the Web browser won't work, an alternative might be to use another browser like Netscape. You can download it for free at *http://www.netscape.com.*

By the time you even think about trying these instructions, you need to be at the end of your rope.

You need to have tried all of the conventional fixes short of reinstalling Windows. Reformatting your hard drive and reinstalling Windows might be your best bet if that is feasible for you. If you still can't get to the Web after seemingly everything has been tried, chances are you either deleted a file improperly, you have some sort of Windows file manager or Anti-virus program that inadvertently wiped out some crucial files, or the Web browser or operating system has just become damaged for some other reason. At any rate, this is a last ditch effort to restore your computer before the final step of reinstalling Windows.

I have to put the disclaimer in here too: Anything that you try as a result of anything in this article, or anywhere in this book, is **AT YOUR OWN RISK!** Neither I, the publisher, nor anyone associated with this book accepts any responsibility for any problems caused to your computer as a result of using any information in this book. The information in this book is for educational purposes only. Anything you might decide to try is your own responsibility.

Don't be too upset if a technician recommends reinstalling the Windows operating system. Microsoft actually recommends formatting your hard drive (this means erasing everything on the entire computer) and reinstalling Windows about once a year in order to keep the Windows registry free from errors. It might just be time to reformat your hard drive and start over. Sometimes Windows is basically beyond repair, and it will be faster and work a lot better if you format and reinstall Windows. **Make sure you back up any important files before you might try this!!**

The first step is to open the **Control Panel** and then **Add/Remove** pro-grams. Click once on the **Microsoft Internet Explorer 5.0 and Internet Tools** listing and click the **Add/Remove** button.

Choose the option that says, "Restore to previous Windows configura-tion" and follow the onscreen prompts to do so. (You won't have that list-ing if you don't have Internet Explorer 5.x.x; if that's the case, just go on with the rest of the instructions as if you had already restored to the pre-vious configuration). After that, reboot the computer if it doesn't prompt you to anyway. Go back to Add/Remove programs and click on the Microsoft Internet Explorer 4.x.x listing and click Add/Remove. Again, follow the onscreen prompts to remove the program. Go back into the Add/Remove programs in the control panel one more time for good meas-ure and see if there is any listing for Microsoft Internet Explorer or Internet Explorer 3.x.x or Internet Explorer anything. An old Internet Explorer listing may not surface until you have selected Microsoft Internet Explorer and restored to previous configuration.

If there are no other listings of Internet Explorer, continue on with the rest of the instructions. There may be no listing for Microsoft Internet Explorer, but just one for Internet Explorer. And there may not be any listings at all. Windows 95 usually came with Internet Explorer 3.02 or Internet Explorer 3.x.x. Typically what happens is that a newer browser ends up being installed or overlaid over this old browser. This can cause problems; if the browser fails, all versions need to be removed, and a clean install should be run so that it does not overlay over an old version of the browser.

If one of these listings says that it can't be removed, just continue on with the instructions that follow. No listings of Internet Explorer might indi-cate a damaged Windows registry, and following the instructions may fix it and it may not, but you are looking at reinstalling Windows anyway at this point, so you really have nothing to lose. No listing of IE could also indicate that it isn't installed. However, if you have been getting to the Web and all of a sudden it stopped working, you can bet that you have IE on the system unless someone else removed it behind your back or something like that. You can try to install Internet Explorer and see what happens. I haven't gone into great detail with these instructions because if they make no sense to you, you really should not attempt this operation anyway.

If you are installing Internet Explorer, and you come across an error message such as "The Internet is likely busy," follow the instructions in the following tip to resolve the problem. I have seen instances where even after following the instructions in the tip, the error will still occur. In those instances, I believe that Windows is pretty much completely damaged and you will probably need to format the drive and start over. You could try the complete browser removal instructions and see what happens, but that will rarely work if you still get the Internet is busy message after renaming the 4 files.

*Tip

PROBLEM CAN OCCUR WHEN INSTALLING INTERNET EXPLORER

ERROR MESSAGE: *Setup was unable to download all the required components For this installation. TheInternet is likely busy. Please try setup again later and select Smart Recovery to continue downloading.*

CAUSE: URLMON.DLL, URL.DLL, WININET.DLL, and WINTRUST.DLL FILES ARE INCOMPATABLE WITH NEW INSTALLATION OF INTERNET EXPLORER RESOLUTION:

To resolve this problem, rename the Urlmon.dll file, Url.dll, Wintrust.dll, and the Wininet.dll file, and then reinstall Internet Explorer. The files are located in the Windows\System folder in Windows 95

HOW:

REBOOT IN MSDOS MODE AT C:\WINDOWS (TYPE) CD SYSTEM THEN TYPE ren url-mon.dll urlmon.old (ENTER) THEN TYPE ren wininet.dll wininet.old (ENTER)

THEN TYPE ren url.dll url.old (ENTER)

THEN TYPE ren wintrust.dll wintrust.old (ENTER)
THEN TYPE WIN (ENTER)
REINSTALL Internet Explorer

Complete Browser Removal:

RESTART IN MS-DOS MODE

Start>Shutdown>Restart in MS-DOS mode

You should be at the C:\Windows prompt. Type in the following commands and hit ENTER after each one. Then it will confirm that you want to delete the files.

Type a Y for Yes and hit the ENTER key again.

DELTREE COOKIES

DELTREE JAVA

DELTREE HISTORY

DELTREE TEMPOR~1 (the ~ is called a tilde and it's in the upper-left corner of most keyboards)

DELTREE OCCACHE

Change directories to the C:\Windows\System by typing the command below:

cd windows\system

WE NEED TO RENAME THE FILES BELOW BEFORE INSTALLING INTERNET EXPLORER AGAIN. AFTER TYPING EACH OF THE COMMANDS BELOW AND HITTING ENTER, IT WILL NOT SAY THAT THE FILE HAS BEEN RENAMED, BUT IT WILL JUST GO BACK TO THE WINDOWS\SYSTEM PROMPT AND WAIT ON THE NEXT COMMAND.

*If any of the files below give a response like "File not found", just skip that one and go to the next one.

ren inetcpl.cpl inetcpl.old

ren ole2.dll ole2.old

ren ole32.dll ole32.old

ren oleaut32.dll oleaut32.old

ren olepro32.dll olepro32.old

ren olethk32.dll olethk32.old

ren setupwbv.dll setupwbv.old

ren softpub.dll softpub.old

ren stdole2.tlb stdole2.old

ren urlmon.dll urlmon.old

ren wininet.dll wininet.old

ren wintrust.dll wintrust.old

RESTART (either type WIN and hit enter or press CTRL+ALT+DELETE twice to warm boot computer)

Click on Start>Find>Files or Folders and search for and delete the following

files: If a message comes up that says the file(s) cannot be deleted, just click OK and go on to the next step.

IEXPLORE.EXE

MSHTML.DLL

SHCVW.DLL

Run Scandisk and Disk Defragmenter afterwards

To run these utilities, click **Start** then **Run**. Make sure that nothing is typed on the line labeled Open. If there is something there, erase it. Type on the Run line **scandisk** and click **Ok**. Put a dot in the circle next to the Thorough box (not Standard) and make sure there is a check in the box labeled Automatically Fix Errors. Next just click on **Start** and wait for it to run.

After the Scandisk, click **Start** then **Run** again. Erase Scandisk from the Run line and type **defrag** and click **Ok**. On the defrag window all you have to do is make sure that it is going to defrag drive C (it will normally be set on this already) and just click on **Ok**. Windows 95 will almost always say that you don't have to run a defragmenter unless the drive is literally about to fall apart, but choose to run it anyway no matter what Windows says. After the defrag, click **Start>Shut Down>Shut Down Computer**. Shut the system off for at least 15 seconds and turn it back on. At this point you are ready to try reinstalling the browser.

Reinstall Internet Explorer from CD or download it and make sure that no anti-virus programs are running while you are downloading or installing the browser.

*If you still can't get to the Web, you might try one last thing: Go in the control panel again and open up Add/Remove programs. Remove the Microsoft Internet Explorer that you just installed, then reinstall it again. The purpose of this is to put the files back in and uninstall it again, which is sometimes necessary to straighten out a jumbled registry. The Windows registry is a hierarchical type of system that controls the most rudimentary functions of Windows. The registry is the main factor that made Windows 95 so much of a technological advance over Windows 3.1. Windows 3.1 had system files called Autoexec.bat, Config.sys, Windows.ini, and System.ini, respectively. Although these pesky files carried over into Windows 95 and beyond, they really don't make that much of an impact on the system like they did with Windows 3.1. The system registry basically took the place of the system files. The registry is much more 3-dimensional than the 4 system files in Windows 3.1. Actually, Windows 3.1 did have some sort of registry, but it was hidden and did not exist for all practical purposes. It is not advisable to try and edit the registry unless you are a computer expert, but you can make changes to the Windows operating system that even the control panel will not allow using the **regedit** utility. One small mistake in the registry and you can render Windows useless, however.

*If the computer does not boot after renaming the files, just rename everything back to .dll and you will be back to where you started from. In other words, just do the manual browser removal instructions in reverse order.

*If you still can't get to the Web after this procedure, before throwing in the towel, try the instructions that follow. Don't attempt this if you are on a network, and you may need to find out the settings for the network adapters for your particular ISP. Also, the following instructions do not apply to Windows NT or Windows 2000 although they can sometimes straighten out a problem getting to the Web on Windows 98 or Windows Me as well as Windows 95.

Open up the **Control Panel** and then the **Network** applet. Click on the first item listed there, no matter what it is, and click **Remove**. Click on the second item and click **Remove**. Follow suit on the rest of them until the whole window is blank. Make sure that the Primary Network Logon at the bottom is set to Windows Logon. Click **Ok**. Windows will build a driver information database and prompt you to restart. It may ask for the Windows disk. If it does, put it in. If you don't have it, you will need to get one because that is probably why you haven't been able to get to the Web: One of the network adapters corrupted on you, and it will need to extract a fresh file from the Windows disk in order to work again. If you get a message "A file being copied is older than the one currently on the computer. It is recommended to keep your existing file." Click YES to keep your existing file. If you still can't get to the Web, you may consider repeating this whole procedure and saying NO to the message. After that is done, reboot the computer when it prompts you too. When the computer boots back up, launch your ISP. It may ask for the Windows CD here also or you may get a message that a file is being copied like when you closed the Network control panel. These things may occur here instead of when closing the Network control panel. Reboot if it asks you too and sign on and see if you can get on the Internet now.

If you are using America Online or CompuServe 2000, after the computer boots back up, when you have removed all of the Network control panel items, open up the Network applet before launching the program and click on **Add>Adapter>Add** and choose **America Online** from the manufacturer's list and click **Ok**. Click **Add>Protocol>Add** and choose **Microsoft** from the manufacturer's list on the left and **TCP/IP** on the right. Click **Ok**. You should now have AOL Adapter and TCP/IPàAOL Adapter only in the network window. If there is anything else, remove them one by one. If it removes everything after just removing one or two of the components, add them again in reverse order (TCP/IP first and then AOLàAdapter) then remove any extra adapters. If you can never get it down to only those 2 adapters, then your problem most likely is a corrupt Network control panel and Windows may need to be reinstalled to correct it.

At the bottom, change the Primary Network Logon to Windows Logon if it doesn't say that already. Then click once to highlight the item at the top that says **TCP/IPàAOL Adapter** then click on **Properties**. Make sure there is a dot in the circle next to "Obtain an IP address automatically." Click on the **DNS configuration** tab at the top and make sure there is a dot next to "Disable DNS." Click on the **WINS Configuration** tab at the top and make sure that the dot is next to "Disable Wins Resolution." If any of these are not set as stated, please put the dot where it says to. Click **Ok** and click on the item that says **AOL Adapter**. Click **Properties** and then click **Bindings** at the top of that window. The only thing that should be listed here with a check in the box to the left of it is **TCP/IP**. It may say **TCP/IPàAOL Adapter** and that would be the same thing. If anything else has a check in it, remove it. After that just click **Ok** and **Ok** again, it will pause for a moment to build a driver and tell you to restart the computer. Go ahead and restart. Sign back on to your ISP when the computer comes back up and everything will normally work.

Appendix N

Why don't I get 56k?

I'll try to put this in English. There are 2 ways that a modem will report speed. One is DTE and the other is DCE. DTE is ***Data Terminal Equipment*** and DCE is ***Data Communication Equipment***. DTE is how fast the data moves from the Central Processing Unit (the brain) of the computer to the modem or more simply put, how fast the information travels inside of the computer. DCE is how fast the information travels across the telephone line. Get it?

Data Communications

Modems operate from commands in the modem configuration in an online service or in Windows that are called the command set and they tell the modem how to perform. These modem commands are usually rooted in Windows, but when there is an Internet provider involved, usually that software will have a modem command string (commonly called a modem string) that will take precedent over or override the commands in Windows. Whatever the case, the Internet provider's or Window's commands are telling the modem how to connect to the Internet. Within these commands, there is a command to make the modem report either DTE or DCE.

Incidentally, some modems will report DCE (the actual speed) and it is virtually impossible to make them report the other speed or DTE. Remember that DCE is how fast the information is traveling through the phone lines and DTE is how fast the data travels through the computer.

Therefore, if your modem had a command in the modem string that was making it report DTE, It probably would say *Connecting@57,600* when connecting to your ISP. DTE will report what we call a standardized protocol. There is a group called the ITU (International

Telecommunications Union) formerly the CCITT (Consultative Committee of International Telephony and Telegraphy) that makes up these protocols. They went in the order 2400, 9600, 14,400, 28,800, 33,600, and 57,600. If you've ever been in most ISP's setup, you'll notice that there are these choices for PORT or MODEM Speed. The exception may be that the speeds 2400 and 9600 will not be there because they are very slow and old protocols in today's standards.

If the modem is reporting DCE, which is the actual true speed in which the modem is transmitting data over the phone lines, it will say 44,000 Kbps or 39,200 or 34,100 or some non-standard speed. The best that I can get on my computer that has a 56k modem is 43,333 Kbps. This is reporting the true speed, and I get this on a regular basis. One sure sign of line noise is an inconsistency in the connect speed. i.e. 38,000 kbps one time and 26,400 kbps the next. I am totally content with this speed because with line noise and many other factors it is the best I could hope for with an analog modem.

You will not get an actual 56k connection although sometimes it might say that on the screen when the modem reports DTE. The FCC (Federal Communications Commission) limits the data transfer rates on analog modems to 53.3 bps to inhibit cross-talk over the phone lines. Cross-talk is when you hear another party's conversation on your phone line or someone might hear yours that is not supposed to. In addition, you would only actually get a speed of 56 Kbps in an impossible-to-achieve laboratory condition. If you notice, modem manufacturer's claim that 56k modems will connect at up to 56k. The key words there are "up to." Incidentally, the phone company is only obligated to provide you with a phone line clean enough for a 9600 kbps data transfer. You can jump up and down all you want, but the only solution these days to get close to a 56k connection may be either to move or pay the price for a cable modem, ADSL line, or T1 line.

Take a look at the following modem string: **AT&F&C1&D2X1W0^M**.

The W0 in the modem string will report DTE. If the string had a W1, you could just change the 1 to a 0 (zero) and this would report the Data Terminal Equipment (DTE) speed. Remember this is going to say on your computer screen that the modem is connecting@28,800, 57,600, or another standard protocol. If the speed on the computer is set to 115,200, it will say *connecting@115,200* even if it's a 56k modem.

If the modem string has a W1, such as **AT&F&C1&D2X1W1^M**, it will report the Data Communications Equipment (DCE). This is going to be the true speed (more or less), but it can always be plus or minus a couple of thousand bps. Another way to adjust what the modem reports is to add **S95=0** which will report Data Terminal Equipment (DTE) speed, and **S95=1** will report Data Communications Equipment (DCE). Some modems will only report the DCE or the true speed and they will not lie. US Robotics modems will only report DCE.

DCE   **DTE**

A T & F & C 1 & D 2 X 1 S 9 5 = 1 ^ M
AT&F&C1&D2X1S95=0^M

Some phone lines just are not capable of 56k speeds. You can run a line test to see if this is the case in your area. Go to the following Web page to run a **Line Test: www.3com.com/56k/need4_56k/linetest.html** and print out the instructions on that page if you have a printer and then sign off from your ISP. If you don't have a printer, jot down the main points of the directions like the phone number that you need to dial and then disconnect from your ISP. You need to perform this line test in a program called HyperTerminal. This is a communications program that should already be installed on your computer. Click on **Start** then choose **Run** and type **Hypertrm** and click **Ok**. This will come up to a screen that asks for a Name and an Icon. Ignore the Icon part of it, and type in Test for the name and click **Ok**. On the next screen, don't do anything for the area code (leave it alone whether it is typed in there or not) and type in the entire phone number that it gives you on the Line Test Web page on the line labeled Phone Number. Click **Ok** and on the next page click on **Dial**. From there just follow the instructions on the Line Test page.

If HyperTerminal is not installed on your computer, you can easily add the program if you have the Windows CD. You will know if the program is not installed on your computer if you type **hypertrm** on the Run line, click **Ok**, and you get a message "Cannot find 'hypertrm' (or one of it's components). Make sure that path and file name are correct and that all required libraries are available." To install HyperTerminal, Just click on **Start>Settings>Control Panel**. Double-click on **Add/Remove** programs then click the **Windows Setup** tab at the top. Click on the **Communications** listing then click on **Details**. You will see maybe half a dozen or so things that you can choose from. Click on the checkbox to put a checkmark next to HyperTerminal. Click **Ok** and on the next window, click **Apply** then **Ok** again. The computer will prompt you to put in your Windows CD. Do so and click **Ok**. It will extract what files it needs to install HyperTerminal, and probably prompt you to restart the computer. If it tells you to restart, do so. If it does not tell you to restart, close all windows and restart the computer yourself. While the computer is restarting, eject the Windows CD and put it in a safe place. Follow the instructions above to enter HyperTerminal and conduct the Line Test.

A modem string looks something like this:

AT&F&C1&D2X1S95=1^M. Each command tells the modem to do a certain thing, and you can usually see a complete list of these commands and what they do in your modem manual or on your modem manufacturer's Web site. These often vary from modem to modem, so I won't go into it in much detail. The subject can get very technical. Basically, if you take a look at the modem string you will see an X1. This command causes the modem to blind dial, meaning that it will pick up the phone line and attempt to dial whether it gets a dial tone or not. You might want to add an X1 to your modem string if you are getting a "no dial tone" message a lot because of voice mail or fax tones. You see, modems hate line noise and they are very sensitive to noise. Like a dog, a modem can hear noise that a human ear cannot pick up. Thus, a modem can detect a noisy phone line even when it appears totally clear to the human ear. If you have the voice mail feature on your telephone, there will be a stutter tone when you pick up the receiver if you have messages waiting. The stutter tone will keep the modem from recognizing a dial tone sometimes, so you can play your voice messages out to solve this problem. As a workaround, however, you can add an X1 to the modem string, which will usually make the modem able to dial out even with messages.

Another thing that may work is to add several commas before the phone number that the modem dials. Each comma represents ¼ of a second pause. Therefore, 3 commas would make the modem pause ¾ of a second which might be long enough to let the stutter tone go by and get to a normal dial tone. The format of the phone number in your ISP's setup would need to look like this: **,,,682-9987**.

You need to make sure that your modem has the latest driver. A driver is a little software program that tells a piece of hardware (such as your modem) how to communicate with the computer. You can have an outdated driver even if you just bought your computer today. The reason why is that modem manufacturers figure out better programs to write to enhance the capabilities of their modems sometimes. As they may do so, they will usually post these on their Web site with instructions for downloading and installation. If it is not on their Web site, they will send you the software (driver) on a disk sometimes; you may just have to pay a nominal fee for shipping in a case like this. So maybe the modem manufacturer will make an updated driver the day after you purchase your computer. That's just the way it is with computers, and you will want to install the new driver to make your modem all it can be. Below I have outlined some good Web pages for modem drivers and even other drivers in some cases. You should always check your modem manufacturer's site first, but these Web sites below will give you some pointers if you can't find an updated driver any other way. Some of the ones included are not huge Web sites, but they are all good ones. As of the date of this writing, all of the Web sites listed were up and running. Due to the nature of the Web, things are subject to change on a daily basis, so I apologize in advance if some of the sites are no longer there by the time that you read this. Also, some of the sites listed below will give you much more in-depth information about modems—probably a lot more than you care to know.

Name of Web site	URL
Modem manufacturer's drivers page	http://www.modemhelp.org/drivers.html
56k=v.unreliable	http://808hi.com/56k/rockhcf.htm
Modem initialization	http://www.unf.edu/~drolfe/dmod/dr-main.htm string reference

Modem speed test page	http://homepage.eircom.net/~leslie/test-page.htm
V.90 standard	http://www.v90.com
LT WINMODEM drivers	http://www.digitan.com/download.htm
Windows device drivers	http://fixwindows.com/drivers.htm
Driver guide (Printer, modem, Sound card, video card, etc.)	http://www.driverguide.com
Drivers page	http://www.multiwave.com/support/download.htm

Appendix O

Emoticons

:) Generic smiley
8) Four-eyed smiley
:-) Smiley, with nose
B-) Cool smiley wearing sunglasses
:-() Wide mouthed smiley
;-) Winking smiley
:-(Frowney
:-> Devilish smiley
:-{) Smiley with a moustache
{:-) Smiley with a brushcut
>:-(Very angry smiley
:-o Talking smiley
:-O Shouting smiley
:-D Laughing smiley
:O Shocked smiley
:*) Intoxicated smiley
O:-) Angelic smiley
:-)~~ Drooling smiley
|-O Yawning smiley
x-(Dead smiley
#8^0-|-< Full-bodied smiley

More Emoticons

0:) or 0:-) = Angel
:II or :-II = Angry
:@ or :-@ = Angry or screaming
>:-(= Angry, annoyed
|-I = Asleep
;)=) or ;-)=)= Big grin
:1 or :-1 = Bland face
:o or :-o = Bored
:c or :-c = Bummed out
:'(or :'-)= Crying/sad
:> or :-> = Devilish grin
:6 or :-6 = Eating something sour
}) or }-) = Evil
:] or :-] = Friendly
:(or :-(= Frowning
:/ or :-/ = Frustrated
8) or 8-) = Glasses
:D or :-D = Grinning
{ } = Hug
:*) or :-*) = Kiss
:x or :-x = Kissing
:))) or :-))) = Laughing or double chin
:.) or :.-) = Laughing tears
:$ or :-$ = Mouth wired shut
:X or :-X = Mute
:l or :-I = Not talking
:Y or :-Y = Quiet aside
:[or :-[= Real downer
:< or :-< = Sad
:> or:-> = Sarcastic
B) or B-) = Shades
=:) or =:-) = Shocked

:Z or :-Z = Sleeping
:) or :-) = Smiling
:O or :-O = Surprised
:() or :-() = Talking
:P or :-P = Tongue out
:& or :-& = Tongue-tied
I) or I-) = Trekkie
:^(= Unhappy, looking away
;) or ;-)= Winking
:} or :-} = Wry smile

Strange Emoticons

Not all *smileys* are used to express emotions. Sometimes, people have too
much free time on their hands and create emoticons that are simply
bizarre. You may never find a use for the following smileys, but they are
worth mentioning:

_O-) = Aquanaut
:=8) = Baboon
@:-] = Baby
=:-) = Bad hair day
(:-) = Bald
:o) = Boxer's nose
*:o) = Bozo the Clown
:-{#} = Braces
:-E = Bucktoothed Vampire
:-F = Bucktoothed Vampire with one tooth missing
cl:-= = Charlie Chaplin
C=:-) = Chef
%-) = Cross-eyed
O-) = Cyclops

#-) = Dead
<:-) = Dunce's hat
}:-> = The Devil
:-[= Dracula
:-3 = Has eaten a lemon
<<<<(:-) = Hat salesman
(-: = Left-handed smiley
8:-) = Little girl
:-{} = Lipstick
:-.) = Madonna or Marilyn Monroe
(8-o = Mr. Bill
:<) or :-{ = Moustache
.-) = One-eyed
:@) = Pig
:-? = Pipe smoker
P-) = Pirate
K:P = Propeller beenie
=:-I = Punk Rocker
[:] = Robot
*<-:-{{{ = Santa
*<;{o> = Santa
(:)-) = Scuba-diving
.^) = Side view
:-Q = Smoking
?-(= Sorry, I don't know what went wrong
%-) = Stared too long at monitor
B:-) = Sunglasses on head
8-) = Swimmer
=|:-)= = Uncle Sam or Abe Lincoln
X-) = Unconscious
[:-) = Wearing a Walkman
{:-) = Wig

Appendix P

Internet Explorer keyboard shortcuts

You can use shortcut keys to view and explore Web pages, use the Address bar, work with favorites, and edit.

Viewing and exploring Web pages

Press this	To do this
F1	Display the Internet Explorer Help, or when in a dialog box, display context help on an item
F11	Toggle between Full Screen and regular view of the browser window
TAB	Move forward through the items on a Web page, the Address bar, and the Links Bar
SHIFT+TAB	Move back through the items on a Web page, the Address bar, and The Links bar
ALT+HOME	Go to your Home page
ALT+RIGHT ARROW	Go to the next page

ALT+LEFT ARROW or **BACKSPACE**	Go to the previous page
SHIFT+F10	Display a shortcut menu for a link
CTRL+TAB or **F6**	Move forward between frames
SHIFT+CTRL+TAB	Move back between frames
UP ARROW	Scroll toward the beginning of a document
DOWN ARROW	Scroll toward the end of a document
PAGE UP	Scroll toward the beginning of a document in larger increments
PAGE DOWN	Scroll toward the end of a document in larger increments
HOME	Move to the beginning of a document
END	Move to the end of a document
CTRL+F	Find on this page
F5 or **CTRL+R**	Refresh the current Web page only if the time stamp for the Web version and your locally stored version are different

CTRL+F5	Refresh the current Web page, even if the time stamp for the Web version and your locally stored version are the same
ESC	Stop downloading a page
CTRL+O or **CTRL+L**	Go to a new location
CTRL+N	Open a new window
CTRL+W	Close the current window
CTRL+S	Save the current page
CTRL+P	Print the current page or active frame
ENTER	Activate a selected link
CTRL+E	Open Search in Explorer bar
CTRL+I	Open Favorites in Explorer bar
CTRL+H	Open History in Explorer bar
CTRL+click In History or Favorites bars	Open multiple folders

Using the Address bar

Press this	To do this
ALT+D	Select the text in the Address bar
F4	Display the Address bar history
CTRL+LEFT ARROW	When in the Address bar, move the cursor left to the next logical break (. or /)
CTRL+RIGHT ARROW	When in the Address bar, move the cursor right to the next logical break (. or /)
CTRL+ENTER	Add "www." to the beginning and ".com" to the end of the text typed in the Address bar
UP ARROW	Move forward through the list of AutoComplete matches
DOWN ARROW	Move back through the list of AutoComplete matches

Working with favorites

Press this	To do this
CTRL+D	Add the current page to your favorites

CTRL+B	Open the Organize Favorites dialog box
ALT+UP ARROW	Move selected item up in the Favorites list in the Organize Favorites dialog box
ALT+DOWN ARROW	Move selected item down in the Favorites list in the Organize Favorites dialog box

Editing

Press this	**To do this**
CTRL+X	Remove the selected items and copy them to the Clipboard
CTRL+C	Copy the selected items to the Clipboard
CTRL+V	Insert the contents of the Clipboard at the selected location
CTRL+A	Select all items on the current Web page

Appendix Q

Instructions for Disabling Hardware

Open up the **Control Panel** and then the **System** applet. Click on **Device Manager** at the top. Look for the hardware that you want to disable. If it is a network card, it will be in the Network Adapters section. In that case, you would click on the **+** sign next to Network Adapters. Click on the network card listing once (or whatever hardware you are disabling) to highlight it and click on **Properties** at the bottom left of the page. Put a check in the box that says *Disable in this hardware profile* at the bottom left of the page you will be on now. Uncheck the box labeled **Exists in all hardware profiles** it if is checked. Click **Ok** twice and restart the computer if it prompts you to.

Appendix R

Internet Terms Glossary

17Real Life and On the 'Net

Backbone

In real life-That which separates your head from your butt, or which your brother-in-law needs more of.

On the Net-The main high-speed physical network that connects other networks to form the Net.

Bandwidth

In real life-The unit of measure used to describe the cross-sectional size of Meatloaf's back-up group

On the Net-A measure of the amount of data that can be transmitted in a given period of time. Usually defined in bits per second (bps).

Client

In real life-The one who ensures that lawyers can afford the best accommodations when on holiday.

On the Net-Software ·that requests data from a server (such as a newsreader, Web browser or FTP program)

Point-to-Point Protocol (PPP)

In real life-The rules governing which of the UN member countries gets the blame when the world goes pear-shaped.

On the Net-The rules that enable a dial-up connection (you) to connect to a host computer (your ISP).

Dial-up Service

In real life-A number you call when you haven't had a date in over a year.

On the Net-A temporary connection to your ISP, usually through a modem.

ISDN

In real life-Short for Innovations Society Doesn't Need.

On the Net-Integrated Services Digital Network. A totally digital high-speed connection. Line charges are higher and you'll have to invest a few hundred bucks in specialized equipment.

Post Office Protocol (POP)

In real life-Defines who gets to drop-kick packages marked FRAGILE.

On the Net-A protocol that manages your Internet mail until you pick it up from your ISP.

Point of Presence (POP)

In real life-Indicating that someone has entered the room by sticking your finger in the air and yelling, "Who the hell let HIM in here?"

On the Net-Areas where you can dial in to your account without placing a long-distance call, reducing your phone bill to something potentially payable.

POTS

Plain Old Telephone Service-Means the same thing no matter how you're connected.

Server

In real life-"Do you want fries or roast potatoes with that?"

On the Net-Software that provides data requested by a client.

System Administrator (SysAdmin)

In real life-The ISP guy you're not allowed to talk to.

On the Net-The ISP guy who won't talk to you because he's too busy doing all the work at your ISP.

Internet Glossary

Anonymous FTP-Some Internet sites have publicly accessible files that can be downloaded. You can log into these public sites using Anonymous FTP. The user id is usually ANONYMOUS and the password is usually your Internet screenname, user id, or e-mail address.

Applet-A small application or utility, such as a mortgage calculator program, that performs only one task and is designed for use within larger programs.

Because of their small size, many applets are available online as free software.

They also may be easily incorporated into Web pages.

Archie-A tool used to access FTP sites via Anonymous FTP.

ASCII-Standard for the codes that computers use to represent all of the upper and lower case letters, numbers, and all of the other symbols on a standard keyboard. There are 128 standard ASCII codes that are represented by a 7 digit binary number-0000000 through 1111111.

Backbone-1 A cable that is capable of high-speed connections that forms the primary thoroughfare of a network. **2** The backbone is a communications cable that runs across the United States that has 11 interconnect points. All ISPs and networks eventually route back to one of those points.

Bandwidth-Loosely referred to as the amount of data that can be transferred over a network connection.

BITNET-Stands for **Because It's There Network**-Educational sites that are separate from the Internet. Listservs originated on BITNET, and e-mail can be sent back and forth from the Internet to BITNET even though they are separate entities.

Boolean-A standard system of logic that uses operators such as AND, OR, NOR, and NOT and is used to find information with search engines. To search for a document that includes the words "January" and

"March," but not "February," the Boolean expression would be "January AND March NOT February."

CCITT-French organization that is called the Comité Consultatif International de Telegraphique et Telephonique. In English they are the Consultative Committee for International Telephony and Telegraphy. It's an organization that plays a major role in the United National International Telecommunications Union (ITU). The CCITT is responsible for making technical recommendations about communications systems worldwide. Every four years, CCITT updates the standards, most recently in 1996.

Client-Software that requests data from a remote server; a Web browser is a client and your ISP software is a client.

Cookie-A method used by Web site operators to track visitors. Cookies are designed to recognize users' IDs or passwords when they revisit a Web site.

After a particular Web server places the cookie on the computer user's hard drive, each subsequent request to the same server will contain that cookie.

Cyberspace-A term used to describe the far reaches of the Internet and its nearly infinite boundaries much like space in our universe. The term was coined by William Gibson in his novel *Neuromancer*.

Domain Name-The unique name of a collection of computers connected to a network.

On the Internet, domain names typically end with a suffix denoting the type of location of a site. For example, ".com" usually denotes a for-profit company; ".edu" an educational institution and ".gov" a government agency. Country domains include ".jp" (Japan) and ".cs" (China).

Domain Name Service-Program that runs on an Internet-connected computer system (called a DNS server). Provides automatic translation between domain names (such as watt.seas.virginia.edu) and IP addresses (128.143.7.186). Enables Internet users to continue using a familiar name (such as www.yahoo.com) even though the service's IP address may change.

Ethernet-Common method used to network computers. Ethernet can transfer data at about 10MB per second. A newer protocol called fast Ethernet can handle data transfers at up to 100MB per second.

File Transfer Protocol-Allows for the exchange of information between computers-part of TCP/IP protocol. You can have secure access that requires a user id and password or public access called Anonymous FTP. With Anonymous FTP

The user id is usually ANONYMOUS and the password is usually your Internet screenname or user id.

Finger-Internet software tool used for locating people on other Internet sites.

Firewall-A software and hardware implementation that protects an internal network from penetration and damage originating from an outside network. Also, a security model that allows a company to connect its internal network to the Internet—Allows for PUBLIC ("Sacrificial") and PRIVATE servers.

Flame-A derogatory comment that may be generated due to an inappropriate comment made on a newsgroup or message board. In other words, if someone makes a racial slur or threatening post to a message board, they will likely get flamed by other readers of that message board.

Gateway-Software that translates data from the standards of one system to the standards of another. A Mail Gateway is a machine that connects similar or dissimilar electronic mail systems and translates and transfers messages between them.

Graphics Interface Format-GIF (Pronounced "jiff"). A method used to compress and transfer graphics images into digital information; it is commonly used to transfer graphics files on the Internet because of its excellent display of solid colors on all Web browsers.

Gopher-Grouping of information servers throughout the Internet. Displays Internet documents and services as lists of menu options. If you select a menu choice, Gopher either displays a document (usually text only) or transfers you to a different Gopher system.

Hit-Loosely defined as a visit to a Web site. A Webmaster might say that his site got 100,000 hits this month meaning that 100,000 people requested his page via their Web browser in one month. More technically, a hit means a single request from a Web browser for a single item from a Web server. Since each Web page consists of many constituents, one Web page would literally be many hits: The HTML page would be one hit and each graphic on the page would be one hit. Hits are used to roughly measure the amount of load on a Web server, but it is almost impossible to figure since the definition of a hit is so vague.

Host-A computer on a network that makes services available to other computers on a network. Like a server, a host is likely to be a powerhouse machine but it doesn't necessarily need to be.

Hyperlink-An icon, graphic, or word in a file that, when clicked with the mouse, automatically opens another file for viewing. World Wide Web pages often include hyperlinks that display other Web pages when selected. Usually these hyperlinked pages are related in some way to the first page. Hyperlinks include the address or names of the files to which they point, but typically this code is hidden from the user.

Hypertext Markup Language-(HTML)-A language used to create electronic documents, especially pages on the World Wide Web, that contain connections called hyperlinks. Hyperlinks allow users to jump from one document to a related document by clicking an icon or a hypertext phrase. For instance, you might jump from a company logo or name on a Web page to the company's home page on the Internet.

Hypertext Transfer Protocol-(HTTP)-Protocol used to exchange information on the Web. When you see a URL that begins with "http://," you know that address points to a Web page.

Internet-The global Transmission Control Protocol/Internet Protocol (TCP/IP) network linking millions of computers for communications purposes. The Internet originally was developed in 1969 for the U.S. military and gradually grew to include educational and research institutions. Today, commercial industries, corporations, and home users all communicate over the Internet, sharing software, messages, and information. The most famous aspect of the Internet is the World Wide Web, a system of files saved in Hypertext Markup Language (HTML) format. An internet (lower case i) is formed anytime that you connect 2 or more networks together.

Internet Protocol-(IP)-The address of a computer on a Transmission Control Protocol/Internet Protocol (TCP/IP) network. IP addresses addresses are written as four groups of numbers (each group may consist of as many as three numbers) separated by periods. An example of an IP address is 119.173.115.11

Intranet-A network usually found in a corporate environment that may use a lot of the same protocols as found on the public Internet, but the Intranet will only be able to be accessed internally by employees. An Intranet may or may not have a connection to the Internet, but most of the time they do. Internet users would not be able to access the Intranet in that case because the company will have firewalls in place to prevent such penetration.

IRC-Stands for Internet Relay Chat. Very large chat facility on the Internet. There are channels on IRC like on a TV, and anything typed by a user on a channel is seen by everyone else on that channel; a private channel can be created so that only the user that created it and the people he invites will be able to see what is said or communicate within that channel.

Java-Object oriented programming language invented by Sun Microsystems. Many Web pages use small Java programs, called "Applets," to perform all kinds of functions such as calculators or even rather sophisticated games. Java in very versatile because you can use it to write nearly any computer application and it can be easily integrated into a Web page.

JavaScript-Invented by Netscape and not related to Java. JavaScript is also a programming language primarily used in Web pages to add neat features such as a scrolling banner. JavaScript is used in many cases to make a Web site more interactive.

Joint Photographic Experts Group-JPEG (Pronounced "jay-peg"). A color image graphics compression format in which a lossy compression method is used and some data is sacrificed to achieve greater compression.

List Server-Program that automates mailing list administrivia such as subscription and unsubscription requests. Two of the most common list servers are ListServ and Majordomo. ListServ is a common synonym for a mailing list, Listserv is actually the name of one particular mailing list maintenance program.

Mailing Lists-A discussion forum that takes place in electronic mail. A system that sends out regular e-mail messages related to a specific topic. To get the messages, subscribe to the list by sending an e-mail message to the list's subscription address list server. Usually the subscription address is Majordomo@whateverlistserv and for the subject of the e-mail you would put subscribe.

Modem-Acronym for modulator/de-modulator. The device that lets a computer transmit and receive information over telephone lines by converting digital data from computers into analog data that can be transmitted over phone lines. The opposite process takes place on the receiving end. Modems are the primary way computer users connect to outside networks, such as the Internet.

MOO-Mud, Object Oriented-A multi-user role-playing game. It is sort of line Dungeons & Dragons on the 'Net.

Mosiac-Web browser invented by the NCSA (National Center for Supercomputing Applications) that set the stage for the modern browsers we know today. Mosaic ruled the Web until Netscape Communications Corporation invented Netscape Navigator. Many other companies tried and failed to produce a viable Web browser until Microsoft's Internet Explorer surpassed the popularity of the Netscape Navigator.

MUD-Multi-User Dungeon or Dimension-Multi-user environment where there are many subjects ranging from fun interaction to serious software development. Most MUDs are text-based, and an advantage of a MUD is that what someone creates will normally remain even if they leave the MUD. Therefore, Things can be developed incrementally and methodically much like each successive generation of human beings carries over the knowledge of the last generation.

Netiquette-Slang for the unwritten rules of Internet courtesy.

Netscape-A Web browser that was derived from the Mosaic browser developed by the National Center for Supercomputing Applications. Mark Andreessen was the primary creator of Netscape. Mr. Andreessen left the NCSA to form a company called Mosaic Communications that became Netscape Communications Corporation. Netscape is second in popularity only to the Microsoft Internet Explorer.

Network-Two or more computers that are connected, usually by physical wiring, so that they can share resources such as printers, scanners, files, etc.

Newsgroup-A group of messages about a single topic. On the Internet, newsgroups bring together people around the world for discussion of shared interests. A single discussion forum in Usenet, such as rec.pets.cats or alt.internet.services. A format of newsgroups is usually main_category.sub_category1....sub_category

NIC-1 Network Interface Card that is used to network computers. Generally the NIC plugs into a slot on the motherboard, like the modem or sound card, and a wire is run from a NIC in one machine to the NIC in another machine to physically connect them. **2** Also can stand for Network Information Center. In general, this is any organization that handles affairs for a network. The main one on the Internet is InterNIC, which is where new domain names are registered.

NNTP-(Network News Transfer Protocol)-A protocol such as TCP/IP that is used to transfer USENET (Newsgroup) postings back and forth across the Internet.

Plug-Ins-Software that expands the features of main programs and adds multimedia capabilities to Web browsers. A plug-in is a small program that "plugs into" a large application (such as a Web browser) and runs as a part of that application.

POP-1 Post Office Protocol-Part of a standard Internet protocol for e-mail. POP is an incoming mail server and SMTP is an outgoing mail server. Usually with a mail client, you configure the POP & SMTP mail servers so you can send and receive e-mail. This information can be obtained from your ISP. **2** Another definition is Point of Presence. This refers to a location where you can connect to the Internet usually with an analog (dial-up) modem. Therefore, if AOL said that they were getting a Point of Presence in a remote city in Alaska, that would mean that they would have local dial-up access in that city where no access number may have existed before.

Portal-A site on the Web that offers a wide variety of resources, such as news articles, and services, such as E-mail, Web site hosting, and online shopping. Online services such as America Online were the first portals. Traditional search engines and computer giants such as Netscape and Microsoft are currently positioning themselves to take advantage of the Interest in portals.

Point-To-Point Protocol-(PPP)-A communications language that lets users connect their PCs directly to the Internet through their telephone lines. Considered more advanced than the Serial Line Internet Protocol (SLIP) connection it is quickly replacing, PPP offers more error-checking capabilities as well as several forms of password protection.

PSTN-(Public Switched Telephone Network)-Synonymous with POTS-Plain Old Telephone System.

Search engine-Software that searches through a database (a large cache of information) located on your computer. At Web-based search engines, users type a keyword query (descriptor words), and the search engine responds with a list of all sites in its database fitting the query description.

Secure Socket Layer-A method of securing the transmission of confidential data through the Internet.

Serial Line Internet Protocol-(SLIP)-An Internet protocol that lets users gain 'Net access with a modem and a phone line. SLIP lets users link directly to the 'Net through an Internet service provider (ISP). It is slowly being replaced with it successor, Point-To-Point Protocol (PPP).

Server-A computer, or software package, that performs certain functions for client software on remote computers. For example, a Web server serves up Web pages for individuals that access the Web sites stored on that server. Some servers have more than one server software package installed on it and some servers are dedicated to just one function.

Shareware-Copyrighted software distributed on a time-restricted trial basis either via the Internet or by being passed along by satisfied customers. Usually Shareware has a nominal fee that you must pay if you decide to keep it past the trial period which in most cases is 30 days.

Sometimes, the trial period will limit the functionality of the software, and sometimes the software will be fully featured even during the free trial.

SLIP-(Serial Line Internet Protocol)-A standard for dialing up using a modem over standard telephone lines to connect to the Internet. Considered somewhat antiquated, SLIP is being phased out by PPP or Point-to Point Protocol.

SMTP-(Simple Mail Transfer Protocol)-Protocol used to send e-mail on the Internet. Also known as an outgoing mail server. A POP server is the protocol used to receive e-mail on the Internet, thus it is an incoming mail server.

Spam-Unsolicited e-mail that is rampant on the Internet. The verb tense is spamming as in Jack's ISP acct was cancelled because they caught him spamming thousands of their customers to advertise his business.

SSL-(Secure Sockets Layer)-A protocol that ensures privacy of transactions between a Web browser and a Web server. URLs that begin with "https" mean that SSL is being used. Usually you will see this on Web sites where some sort of financial transaction can take place or where you are viewing sensitive information that you would not want anyone else to see. These sites will normally use a secure connection.

Streaming audio-An audio format experienced in real-time—users hear the audio file as it is downloaded without waiting for it to be completely downloaded.

Streaming video-Technology that allows a user to see the contents of a video file as it is downloaded without waiting for the entire content of the file to be downloaded.

Sysop-This is a System Operator that performs tasks necessary to upkeep a network that a System Administrator prescribes. A Sysop may also be responsible for the day-to-day operations of a forum, which is kind of like a combination chat room and message board.

T1-A type of data connection able to transmit a digital signal at 1.544 megabits per second. T1 lines often are used to link large computer networks together, such as those that make up the Internet.

T3-A type of data connection that is faster than T1. T3 is capable of data transfer at speeds of 44,736,000 bits-per-second.

Telnet-A command and application used to login from one computer to another or one computer to a server. Telnet is a command that is built into Windows and can be enacted at a DOS prompt.

Transmission Control Protocol/Internet Protocol-(TCP/IP)-A protocol governing communication among all computers on the Internet. It dictates how packets of information are sent over networks and ensures the reliability of data transmissions across Internet-connected networks.

Universal Resource Locator-(URL)-Address pointing to a certain site on the Internet. Examples are http://www.aol.com and ftp://mac.archive.umich.edu. It is a standardized naming or addressing system for documents and media accessible over the Internet. For example, http://www.disney.com includes the type of document (a Hypertext Transfer Protocol (HTTP) document), and the address of the computer on which it can be found (*www.disney.com*).

Unix-A computer operating system that has TCP/IP integrated into it. UNIX is the most common operating system for servers on the Internet; it is specifically designed to be used by many users at one time.

USENET-A large network of discussion groups called newsgroups.

UUNET-(UseNet)-"Bulletin board of the Internet". Contains a collection of more than 20,000 discussion forums called newsgroups.

Veronica-Searches Gopher sites for file names and directories and consists of index server and search tool.

VPN-(Virtual Private Networking)-A network where the main system is normally connected to the Internet, but the data sent from one location to another is encrypted (data is kind of sent through a tunnel from one location to another) so communication between machines using VPN are "virtually" private.

Web browser-Software that gives access to and navigation to the World Wide Web. Using a graphical interface that lets users click buttons, icons, and menu options to access commands, browsers show Web pages as graphical or text-based documents. Browsers allow users to download pages at different sites either by clicking hyperlinks (graphics or text presented in a different color than the rest of a document, which contains a programming code that connects to another page), or by entering a Web page's address, called a universal resource locator (URL).

Web server-A computer on which a Web page resides. A server may be dedicated, meaning its sole purpose is to be the server, or non-dedicated, meaning it can be used for basic computing in addition to acting as the server. Good performance from a Web server, especially for busy sites, is crucial.

Wide Area Information Server-(WAIS)-A Unix-based system linked to the Internet or a program that allows users to search worldwide archives for resources based on a series of key words. Also called a Search Engine and it often times generates a list of documents that contain many "false drops" (irrelevant documents that don't really pertain to the search subject).

World Wide Web-Newest Internet Resource-Graphical in nature. Also provides audio and video capabilities. Accessed via point-and-click actions in a Web Browser.

Web Browser-(Another definition)-A program that allows you to view Internet service resources. Examples: Netscape, Internet Explorer, Opera. A Browser may use other programs to enhance it called plug-ins or sometimes they are called helper applications but mostly helper apps were from the old days of the Browser.

Helper: program Web browser launches when it encounters a file it doesn't know how to handle on its own.

Plug-in: A concept devised by Netscape to allow application developers to tie their programs more intimately into Netscape. With a plug-in, the application launches within your Web browser main window.

Web Page-A document that is made for viewing on the World Wide Web. It is normally written in a programming language called HTML (Hypertext Markup Language) or some variation thereof. A Web browser can translate HTML into graphics and text so that a Web page appears how you see it on the Internet. Web pages have a unique URL (Universal Resource Locator) that is it's address and it allows people to find it easily on the Web.

Hyper Text Markup Language: (HTML) Language used to code text files for use in hypertext systems. Namely the language that Web pages are written in. When displayed using a World Wide Web browser, documents created with HTML may include text and graphics, formatting, and hypertext links to other information

Home Page: Document Intended to serve as an initial point of entry to a Web of related documents. It is also called a Welcome page. Contains general introductory information, as well as hyperlinks to related resources.

A well-designed home page contains internal navigation buttons, which help users find their way among the various documents that the home page makes available.

*If you don't find your Internet term on this page, you will probably find it in the Glossary at the end of this book.

*The real life and On the Net Internet Terms is from .net magazine issue 48, August 1998, page #78.

Appendix S

Resources

5 Anderson, Heidi V. *Windows Tips & Tricks Superguide To Troubleshoot, Customize & Tweak Windows 98, NT, 95, and 2000* "**Windows File Management**—Organizing Your Files & Folders Into A Logical Sequence," Volume 6 Issue 6 pgs 56-59.

(chapter 16)

Excerpts:

6 Jerome, Marty *PC Computing* Magazine

"The Internet is Crushing Whole Industries...Is Your Company Next?" Golden Opportunity—

February 2000 edition pgs. 102-104

(chapter 17)

7 Jerome, Marty *PC Computing* Magazine

"The Internet is Crushing Whole Industries...Is Your Company Next?"

February 2000 edition   pg 100

(chapter 17)

8 Jerome, Marty *PC Computing* Magazine

"The Internet is Crushing Whole Industries...Is Your Company Next?"

February 2000 edition pg 98

(chapter 17)

9 Jerome, Marty *PC Computing* Magazine

"The Internet is Crushing Whole Industries...Is Your Company Next?" Golden Opportunity—

February 2000 edition pg 103

(chapter 17)

10 Katz, Jon *Yahoo Internet Life: How America Uses the Net* (Special Anniversary Issue magazine) "How the Net changed America," pg 97

www.yuk.com * September 1999

(chapter 21)

11 Phelps, Alan *PC Novice Guide to Internet Basics* (Quick Answers to all your Internet Questions) *special reprint Guide to Series* "Understanding The Internet," Volume 6 Issue 10 p.6

* September 1998

(chapter 21)

12 Phelps, Alan *PC Novice Guide to Internet Basics* (Quick Answers to all your Internet Questions) *special reprint Guide to Series* "Understanding The Internet," Volume 6 Issue 10 p. 5

* September 1998

(chapter 21)

13 Burns, Joe Phd. "E-mail Netiquette" (newsletter sent via e-mail)

(chapter 22)

14 Phelps, Alan *PC Novice Guide to Internet Basics* (special reprint) "The Life of E-mail," Volume 6 Issue 10 p. 7

(chapter 22)

15 Meers, Trevor *PC Novice Guide to Internet Basics* (special reprint) "No Stamp Required," Volume 6 Issue 10 pg 64-65

(chapter 22)

16 *What if people bought cars like they buy computers?* unknown source. The piece was circulating via e-mail around the Internet.

(chapter 25)

17 Collins, Steve *.net magazine* "**Place Your Bets**—How to win at Net roulette" *Words For The Wise* (The real life and on the Net), issue 48, August 1998, page 78.

(**Appendix R**- Internet Terms Glossary)

18 Lichty, Tom *The Official America Online Tour Guide* version 3 pg 95-96

(Appendix T-MIME-Attaching Files to Internet Messages)

Appendix T

Mime

Attaching files to Internet messages

America Online and CompuServe 2000 use the same e-mail protocols. Below I have included information that I have extracted from AOL literature. The following article is in reference to the incompatibilities that may arise when sending mail across the Internet. It depends on such factors as the exact path that the e-mail takes and what kind of attachment was sent as to whether an attached file will come over as a .mim file. If you do get a mime file, the only way to read it is to get a program that is capable of decoding it such as Winzip available at *http://www.winzip.com.*

The Internet's e-mail system handles basic text files nicely, but doesn't reliably handle binary files—files like pictures or word processing documents. So, when you send an e-mail message with a file attachment to someone on the Internet, the AOL software automatically encodes or translates the attachment using a system called MIME. (MIME stands for Multipurpose Internet Mail Extensions.) MIME converts the binary attachment to a text format that can be handled by Internet e-mail. The message's recipient needs a program that can decode the MIME e-mail and turn it back into a binary file that the computer can work with.

When you receive MIME files...

When someone sends you a MIME-encoded file in e-mail, it needs to be translated back into a format that your computer can understand.

Depending on the mail system that the sender used, the AOL software may or may not be able to automatically decode the MIME file. If it was able to decode the file, the e-mail's file attachment will be in its original, binary format: such as .GIF, or .ZIP.

If AOL was unable to decode the MIME file, the attachment will be in MIME format, with a filename extension of .MME or .MIM. Download this file—it is simple to use a utility to convert the .MME file back to a binary file.

Windows users can use these applications to easily decode MIME files.

* WinZip: http://www.winzip.com

* MIME Decoders: Keyword MIME

After you've downloaded and installed these programs, please be sure to read the READ ME guide for information on how to use the decoder(s).

When you send an attachment to an Internet user...

When you attach a file to an e-mail message that you send to an Internet user, it will automatically be MIME-encoded.

In order to use the attachment, your message's recipient must have a MIME-compliant e-mail program or use software that can decode MIME files—to translate it back into a format that his or her computer can understand. If the recipient has a MIME-compliant e-mail program, the MIME attachment will probably be automatically decoded for him. If not, the recipient can easily translate the file using a utility program.

18*Attaching files to Internet messages*

"Because there's no universal standard for attaching files to e-mail on the Internet, you can't directly send files (or receive them) via Internet mail. Internet mail, like all e-mail, is pure ASCII text. Don't worry if you can't define the term *binary data*; just understand that it's not ASCII text and therefore not native to e-mail. With that said, it will seem contradictory when I tell you that you can attach a file to Internet mail, but it's true. A few comments follow:

If you attach a file to Internet mail, AOL will convert it to text before it's sent. This may seem anachronistic: how can you send a picture of a frog (or the sound of a frog), for example, as text? Simple: use a program that converts binary data into ASCII text. AOL does this for you, via a technique called *MIME* (Multipurpose Internet Mail Extensions) *base64 encoding*.

The recipient's e-mail program must understand MIME base64 encoding and be able to decode it. If that's not possible, the recipient will have to decode it manually. There are a number of programs that can do this, most notably a little shareware application called MIME64. It's available in AOL's libraries.

Downloading files from AOL's libraries is discussed in Chapter 5, "Transferring Files."

There are other binary-to-text-and-back techniques for transferring files on the Internet—one called—uuencoding comes to mind, and Macintosh users are fond of *BinHex*—and if someone sends an attached file to you, it might be encoded using one of these other techniques. If that happens, your AOL software will not be able to automatically decode the message and offer to download the file in your machine. You'll have to do this manually. A description of that process—a process that can take many forms depending on the encoding method used—is beyond the scope of this book; again, you can find answers (and ask questions) by visiting the keywords: **Mail Gateway**.

It should be apparent that file attachments to Internet mail are not universally supported, just barely standardized and fraught with the potential for error.

Both you and the intended recipient should be prepared for period of experimentation and adjustment. The system doesn't always work the first time it's tried."

For more information on this subject visit keyword **Mime** on AOL. To obtain a copy of the book that this passage came from visit keyword **Aolstore**.

Aladdin Systems, Inc.'s freeware Expander products allow you to decompress, decode, convert and access the most popular compression archive formats, including StuffIt® (.sit), Zip (zip), UUencode (.uu), MacBinary (bin), and BinHex (.hqx). Aladdin Expander for Windows™ also supports MIME/Base64 (.mime),

Arc (.arc), Arj (.arj), and gzip (.gzip), and more. With the addition of the StuffIt Engine™ (included with DropStuff™ and StuffIt Deluxe™), StuffIt Expander™ for Mac supports Mime/Base64, Arc, gzip, Lha, CompactPro, AppleLink, and more. These easy-to-use, universal file access programs are available for Windows, Macintosh and DOS. With comprehensive access to the most online file formats, Aladdin's Expanders are the only expansion utilities you need.

Aladdin Systems—StuffIt Expander file decompression freeware My favorite feature....after install it asks automatically if you wish it to be the default application for all these file types and it then automatically opens anything encoded that you double-click.

*Lichty, Tom The Official America Online Tour Guide version three, pgs. 95-96

Glossary

Accessibility Options—Applet in the control panel where you can make customizations to the keyboard, sound, display, and mouse to accommodate the hearing impaired and persons with other mobility and visual impairments.

Add New Hardware—**Applet in the control panel where you can install new hardware. You can let Windows search for the hardware or you can select the hardware driver from a list and configure it yourself.**

Add/Remove Programs—Applet in the control panel where you should go to safely uninstall programs. If you want to remove a program, it should be done through Add/Remove Programs if it is listed there. Add/Remove Programs also offers the option to make a boot disk by clicking on the Startup Disk tab; it can help you start your computer if it doesn't start normally. In Addition, the Windows Setup tab allows you to add components to Windows that weren't installed in the original installation such as Accessibility Options.

Adobe Acrobat—Application made by Adobe that is capable of reading PDF files. This program works cross-platform, on a Macintosh and an IBM compatible computer, and therefore, it is a widely used program. Another factor that adds to its popularity is because an Adobe file (PDF) will retain its formatting, look, and feel no matter what computer it is opened on as long as Adobe supports the operating system.

Active X—A program introduced by Microsoft that is used to instruct certain technologies how to involve COM (component object model) and OLE (object linking and embedding) functions. ActiveX can be incorporated within most programming languages. It lets Web site creators make interactive, multimedia Web pages and links to Microsoft Desktop products to the Web. For instance, through ActiveX controls, users could view Microsoft Word or Microsoft Excel documents through Microsoft Internet Explorer. Although the results of ActiveX controls may be similar to those of Java applets, Java is a programming language, while ActiveX is a set of controls written with Microsoft's Visual Basic.

ADSL—Asynchronous Digital Subscriber Line—High speed Internet connection that far exceeds the speed that an analogue connection can achieve. ADSL requires a special modem and a subscription from the telephone company. At the present time, ADSL is not supported in every calling area. Another advantage of ADSL is the ability to talk on the telephone and go online with only 1 phone line. **See DSL for another definition even though it is the same thing as ADSL.**

Advanced Technology Attachment Packet Interface (ATAPI)—An extension to the EIDE (Enhanced IDE) interface that supports CD-ROM and tape drives, which were left out of the original EIDE and IDE standards.

Advertising Banner—SEE BANNER

AOL—America Online—A popular online service that is known for its ease of use and convenience. AOL has a lot of proprietary online content that only AOL members can access. Because of the numbers of members that AOL has, they can often offer economic advantages on all types of goods and services.

Applet—A small application or utility, such as a mortgage calculator program, that performs only one task and is designed for use within larger programs. Because of their small size, many applets are available online as free software. They also may be easily incorporated into Web pages.

Application—A Program that can be installed on a computer to serve a certain function or functions. Most consumer software is applications that would include such things as games, word-processing programs, and spreadsheets.

Archie—Method of automatically gathering and indexing files on the Internet. This tool can sometimes be used to access FTP sites via Anonymous FTP (and download files) once it has zeroed in on the information that it searched for.

ARPANet—Advanced Research Projects Agency Network—A military project that started in the late 1960s that paved the way for the Internet as we know it today. ARPA consisted of many military computers networked together, and everything on the Internet was text-based at the time.

ASCII—American Standard Code for Information Interchange—The basic format that all text files are written in. It is a file comprised of 128 different code numbers that stand for the different characters in the alphabet. Any text file created with the DOS "edit" program is in ASCII format.

Asynchronous Digital Subscriber Line—See ADSL

ATAPI—See Advanced Technology Attachment Packet Interface

Attachments—Files that can be attached to e-mail and sent across the Internet. These files have a 3-letter extension that defines exactly what kind of file it is and what program is needed to interpret it.

Autoexec.bat—The abbreviated form of an automatically executed batch file. The Autoexec.bat file is a special batch file placed in the system's root directory that is automatically executed each time the computer boots.

Backbone—The main cable that has 11 interconnect points across the United States to which every network is connected to form the Internet.

Banner—Online advertising graphic. Usually located at the top of a Web page.

Basic Input Output System—(Pronounced bye-ose) See BIOS

Batch File—Text file that contains a list of instructions and is marked with the extension .BAT. When the file is run in DOS, each instruction is carried out in sequential order. A batch file can include any DOS command and can launch other programs.

Battery—A computer battery is round and it looks like a giant watch battery. It sits in a place on the motherboard and powers the system clock. It also maintains a steady trickle of energy that drives the system BIOS. On average, a computer battery will last 3-5 years and will need to be replaced.

Baud Rate—The rate at which your modem can send data. You will usually see this listed as BPS when you are buying a modem.

BBS—Bulletin Board System—A computer that allows you to call it and access a variety of functions. For example, many manufacturers have a BBS that contains recent software updates. If a customer needs them, they would call the BBS and download the files. The BBS is usually accessed via a Windows communications program called HyperTerminal. America Online has a BBS where you can download the latest version of their software; the number to call the AOL BBS is 1-800-827-5808.

Binary File—Any file that is not plain ASCII text. For example: executable files, graphic files and compressed (ZIP) files.

Binhex—Stands for BINary HEXadecimal, it is a method for converting non-text files (non-ASCII) into ASCII. This is needed because Internet e-mail can only handle ASCII.

See Also: **ASCII, MIME, and UUENCODE.**

BIOS—Basic Input Output System—Controls the input and output of the computer. Any information that is outputted from the computer or inputted to the computer is handled by this chip that is on the motherboard.

Bit—Single unit of information that has two values, 0 or 1 (contraction of binary digit).

Bitmap—Type of file format that is usually associated with the Paint program. A bitmap image is a rather detailed picture that normally has a large file size. Any bitmap can be used for an icon in Windows by simply renaming the bitmap with the icon extension (.ico).

Boolean—A standard system of logic that uses operators such as AND, OR, NOR, and NOT and is used to find information with search engines. To search for a document that includes the words "January" and "March," but not "February," the Boolean expression would be "January AND March NOT February."

Boot—The process of turning on the computer

BPS—**Bits Per Second**—Measurement of digital information transmission rates.

Browser—A software program that enables you to read Web pages; it is sometimes called a Web client.

Buffer—This is an area that is set up in memory to provide a faster way for the computer to process information; it holds recent changes to files and other information to be written later to the hard drive.

Bulletin Board System—See BBS

Bus—A physical pathway to connect internal peripherals such as video cards, modems and sound cards.

Byte—The primary unit of memory in a computer. A character is equal to one byte. In a byte there are 8 bits. Thus, each byte contains eight characters that are really different combinations of 1s and 0s.

Cable Modem—A device that uses a cable TV signal as a medium for connecting nodes on a wide-area-network. The main advantage of a cable modem is increased speed. Rates are a maximum of 56Mbps for data downloads, with a real-world rate of 3Mbps to 10Mbps. For uploads, the maximum is 10Mbps with a real-world speed of 200Kbps to 2Mbps.

Cache—(*Pronounced cash*) An area of memory that holds recently accessed information for faster retrieval the next time it is needed.

CD-ROM—A storage device that uses compact disks for read only storage. These devices use the same optical technology found in home stereo players.

Cell—The intersection of a row and a column in a spreadsheet, such as cell A1, the cell at the intersection of column A and row 1. Each cell is a box that can hold text, a numerical value, or a formula.

Central Processing Unit—See CPU

Channels—The path through which information flows from one device to another. This link can be either internal or external to the computer. Internally, a channel is more commonly called a bus. It is the physical link that facilitates the electronic transfer of digital information. A channel transfers information, for example, from the CPU to the keyboard. Externally, and typically in communications, it is a line or circuit that carries either analog or digital information, depending on the type of channel. Channel also can refer to an individual chat group using the Internet Relay Chat system.

Chassis—Part of the computer case. It is the backbone of the computer to which the motherboard, disk drives, and power supply are connected.

Client—Software that requests data from a server such as a newsreader, Web browser or FTP program.

Close Program Window—Accessed by pressing CTRL+ALT+DELETE on the keyboard. Close Program lists all of the programs currently running in the background and they can be closed one by one by clicking on a program listing to select it and click on End Task.

CMOS—Complimentary Metal Oxide Semiconductor—Storage area for your system BIOS. The BIOS writes the information that is entered into the CMOS setup in this special type of memory.

Cold Boot—The process of shutting the computer all the way down and turning it back on as opposed to a warm boot.

Complimentary Metal Oxide Semiconductor—See CMOS

Components—Components can be thought of as just a piece of a pie. When you say "a computer component," you are saying a piece of the computer that makes up the whole thing.

Config.sys—A text file that specifies the drivers and system parameters used in MS-DOS and OS/2. Config.sys controls some aspects of the operating system's behavior, and it contains commands about how to do things such as work with new hardware or adjust memory.

Conventional Memory—This is the first 640k of memory in your system (1024k=1MB). All programs must start in the first 640k of memory and then may use the rest of memory after starting.

Cookie—A method used by Web site operators to track visitors. Cookies are designed to recognize users' Ids or passwords when they revisit a Web site. After a particular Web server places the cookie on the computer user's hard drive, each subsequent request to the same server will contain that cookie.

Corrupt—To alter or partially erase information in memory or a file, rendering it unusable by the computer. Hardware or software failure can corrupt a file by rearranging the bits of data. Corrupted information is no longer readable.

CPU—Central Processing Unit—Also called the microprocessor. This chip acts as the "brains" of a computer. It controls the computer's actions and can find, decode, and carry out instructions plus assign tasks to other resources. Most IBM-compatible PCs use 386-, 486-, or Pentium class chips designed by Intel Corp.

Cursor—A visible indicator that tells you where you are positioned on the computer screen. The cursor is normally an arrow that moves around the screen as you move the mouse. You can have a custom cursor whereby you can make the symbol nearly anything that you want other than an arrow.

Daughter Card—A smaller card that plugs into a slot on the mother-board. Typically, a daughter card will serve as an expansion slot where other hardware cards can plug into. Some motherboards have what is called a riser card that is really the same as a daughter card; in either case, the card plugs into the motherboard so that it sits perpendicular to the motherboard. Other hardware, such as a sound card or ECP port may plug into the riser card.

DDE—See Dynamic Data Exchange

Dedicated Line—A communications line that is used solely for computer connections. A separate phone line that is used only so that your computer can connect to the Internet is a dedicated line. In other words, you may have 1 phone line that is used for normal phone calls and a 2nd phone line that is used for your computer.

Defragmenter—Disk Defragmenter is a Windows diagnostic program that should be run periodically; the more changes that you make to your file system (the more programs that you install and delete), the more often the defragmenter should be run. Disk Defragmenter closes the "holes" that are formed on the hard drive over time due to normal wear and tear. In addition, it rearranges the file structure and puts things into some semblance of order thereby allowing faster access to files by the hard drive.

Demodulate—The process whereby a modem translates an analog signal back into a digital signal that can be interpreted by a computer.

Desktop—The screen that comes up when a computer starts or is booted. The Desktop normally contains shortcut icons that point to the programs that are installed on the computer. Such things as the Start button, My Computer, and the Recycle Bin can usually be seen on the Desktop.

Device—Any component of your computer such as a printer, speaker, sound card, etc.

Device Driver—See Driver

Device Manager—Resides in the System applet of the control panel; it lists all of the hardware that is installed on your computer, and it allows for the manipulation and configuration of the hardware.

Dial-up Connection—The most popular way of accessing the Internet at present day. A dial-up uses an analog modem over POTS (plain old telephone lines) to connect to your ISP or the Internet.

Dial-up Networking—DUN—A built in feature of Windows that lets a computer connect to a network via a modem. It usually uses either the PPP (Point-to-Point Protocol) or SLP (Serial Line Internet protocol) to control the traffic between the computer and remote network. Windows 3.1 did not offer built-in DUN support. Instead, users had to obtain dial-up software such as Trumpet Winsock. Dial-up networking is almost exclusively used for connecting PCs to the Internet.

Digital Subscriber Line—Technology used to transmit digital data on regular copper phone lines. DSLs can be used to provide connections to the Internet or local-area networks (LANs) or for videoconferencing. The technology differs from Integrated Services Digital Network (ISDN) lines in that it can send analog and digital signals over the phone line. ISDN is digital only and has to convert analog voice phone calls to digital signals. With DSL, the analog voice phone calls and digital signals can coexist on the same wires. This works because analog signals require only a fraction of the capacity of the copper wires that make up a phone line. The limitation of the analog signal carried on those wires, not the wires, has kept phone lines from delivering greater data transfer speeds. Sending digital signals over copper wires breaks that barrier.

DIMM—See Dual In-Line Memory Module

Dip Switches—Tiny switches that allow for the adjustment of the IRQ and I/O port address of legacy equipment that are necessary for the manual configuration of hardware. Jumpers serve the same purpose; some hardware has jumpers and some may have dip switches. Generally, only very old hardware will have dip switches these days. You will still find jumpers on certain devices such as hard drives even in the plug & play environment.

Directory—A folder on a computer that can contain files. Microsoft dubbed a directory a folder to be less confusing to the consumer. Compare Root Directory definition.

Direct Memory Access—Addressing used by some hardware. Your system should have 6 available addresses 00 to 05. No two pieces of hardware can share a DMA channel. Most new hardware no longer uses a DMA.

Directory Path—SEE PATH

Disk Defragmenter—A diagnostic utility that is built into the Windows operating system. It rearranges files on the drive to put them in some semblance of order and to make them more quickly accessible to the CPU. Due to normal wear and tear, the hard drive can become fragmented over time. This means that files can be spread around the hard drive in pieces when they should be in one place. i.e. One program may be spread around the hard drive in several or more places. Disk Defragmenter puts all of the respective files that belong to each program back in one place, meaning that they can be accessed faster because the hard drive doesn't have to search around in many places to bring one file together.

Disk Drive—A device that accesses a disk for information.

Diskette—A magnetic object used to store files from a computer.

Disk Operating System—See DOS

DMA—See Direct Memory Access

DNS—Domain Name Servers—Computers that translate universal resource locators (URLs) to numeric IP addresses in order to facilitate Web browsing.

Domain Name—The unique name of a collection of computers connected to a network. On the Internet, domain names typically end with a suffix denoting the type or location of a site. For example, ".com" usually denotes a for-profit company; ".edu" an educational institution, ".gov" a government agency, and ".org" a not-for-profit organization. Country domains include ".jp" (Japan), ".cn" (China), and ".uk" (England).

Domain Name Servers—See DNS

DOS—Disk Operating System—Text only Operating System

(OS) for a PC that requires DOS commands, or text-based commands, to operate the computer. DOS is the Operating System that

preceded **Windows. Windows greatest technological advancement over DOS is the GUI (Graphical User Interface).**

DOS Prompt—This is a signal to the user that the operating system is ready to be given a command. You will see the DOS prompt as a letter followed by a colon, a backslash, and a greater than sign. (c:\>)

Download—To receive a file sent from another computer via modem.

Drive—A storage device that can be removable or fixed. A removable drive is something like a floppy or CD-ROM drive. A fixed disk is one that cannot be easily removed such as the C drive that holds all of the operating system files. Compare Hard Disk definition.

Driver—Also know as a device driver; it is a little program that allows for communication between the computer processor and a peripheral.

Drop-Down Menu—Menu on the computer where you select a choice instead of having to type something in. A drop-down can be characterized by a little down arrow (?) that you can click on to drop down several or more choices from which you can click on and select.

DSL—See Digital Subscriber Line

Dual In-Line Memory Module—A small circuit board containing memory chips. These boards are inserted into memory expansion slots to increase the amount of a computer's random-access memory (RAM). DIMMs differ from single in-line memory modules (SIMMs) in the width of memory bus supported.

DUN—See Dial-Up Networking

Dynamic Data Exchange—(DDE)—A two-way connection between multiple programs that let the programs actively exchange data while both programs are running. This exchange of data without user intervention is known as a conversation. Available with Windows and OS/2, this feature lets users use one program to manipulate data in another program. For example, if you use a communications program and a modem to connect to an information bulletin board, you can use a DDE to connect the incoming information to a word processing template for viewing. The incoming information may change, but the template will remain the same.

Dynamic-Link Library—An executable subroutine stored as a file separate from the programs that may use it. Dynamic-link libraries allow for the efficient use of memory because they are loaded into memory only when needed.

ECP Port—Extended Capabilities Port—Card that can be installed in a computer to expand its functionality. One example is a card that will add an extra parallel port to your computer. In that example, you could call the card a parallel port, but generally speaking, that card would be an ECP port also since it expands your computer by adding an extra parallel port.

EIDE—Enhanced Integrated Drive Electronics—Also known as Fast ATA (Fast AT Attachment), this is an updated version of the IDE (Integrated Drive Electronics) storage interface that works with hard drives and CD-ROM drives. It can shuttle data to and from the drive three to four times faster than the IDE standard (transferring data between 11MB and 16.6MB per second) and can support data storage devices that store up to 8GB more than IDE drives.

E-mail—Electronic Mail—Text messages sent through a network to a specified individual or group. Received messages are stashed in an inbox, and can be kept, deleted, replied to, or forwarded to another recipient, depending upon your E-mail program. Besides a message, E-mail can carry attached files so you can send word processing files or graphics.

E-mail address—Address used to send e-mail on the Internet. Normally, all e-mail addresses should be in lowercase with no spaces unless otherwise specified by the intended recipient. E-mail addresses are made up of essentially 3 parts: The first part is known as the username, screenname, or membername. After the name is an **@** (pronounced at), and then the ending that is called the domain name. An example e-mail address is *orion2400@aol.com.* The domain name in that example is aol.com. Some large servers, such as those that may be found at universities or large corporations, contain another part after the domain name called a subdomain. An example e-mail address with a subdomain is *metcalf@mit.edu.ras;* ras is the subdomain in that example.

Embedded Graphics—Pictures that are inserted directly into programs such as an e-mail program. When a picture is embedded, it is opposed to a file attachment. Embedded graphics can be seen directly in a program such as e-mail; an attachment must be downloaded in order to view it.

Emoticons—Punctuation marks that are used in combination with one another to make symbolic representations of moods or thoughts. Usually an emoticon is some variation of a smiley, such as >:-(is an angry smiley; this is not necessarily true because punctuation marks can be used to create all sorts of imaginative designs. **Also see Smiley**

End User—You, the person that runs the computer.

Enhanced Integrated Drive Electronics—See EIDE

Expanded Memory—A type of memory that allows programs to use memory above one megabyte. This is for programs that are not capable of using extended memory by themselves.

Expansion Card—An expansion card is a device that is plugged into the motherboard to give the computer extra features. Examples of these are sound cards, modems, and video capture cards.

Expansion Slot—The connector that connects internal devices to the computer bus.

Explorer—This could be Windows Explorer or Microsoft Internet Explorer. The first one is a part of Windows that show you all of the files on the computer; it is accessed by clicking Start, Programs, and Windows Explorer. The latter is the Microsoft Internet Explorer Web browser.

Export/Import—A means of taking information out of the Registry and saving it as a text file in a format that can be put back in the Registry. Inputting this information is called Importing. This procedure is done by opening RegEdit clicking on the key you want to Export, then the clicking on *Registry* in the menu bar and then *Export*. It needs to be saved as a file without an extension. It should be saved within the Windows Directory so that you can Import it back if need be. To save the entire Registry, you click on *Computer* then *Export*. In general terms, Importing and Exporting can be done with many files among applications. For example, you may Import a picture into a graphics-editing program such as PaintShop Pro in order to manipulate the picture.

Extended Capabilities Port—SEE ECP PORT

Extended Memory—Additional memory above one megabyte.

External Modem—Unlike an internal modem, this is a self-contained device that sometimes resembles a cable box in looks and size. It performs the same function as an internal modem; because it is a separate unit from the computer itself, there is room for status lights that inform you of such things as whether the modem is transmitting data from the computer or receiving data from the telephone line.

Eudora—A popular e-mail program

FAQ—Frequently Asked Questions—Found on most Web pages, they are intended to answer the more obvious questions that may be asked about the content of a particular Web site. For example, if you go to *www.winzip.com* to download the WinZip program, you will find an extensive array of FAQs that will address all of the potential problems or concerns you may have about using WinZip except the most unusual circumstances.

FAT— See File Allocation Table

Fatal OE—Known as the Blue Screen of Death, it is when Windows becomes unstable and a blue screen appears on the monitor that tells you that a fatal error has occurred; it usually tells you to press a key to continue or in many cases you have to reset or shut down the system in order to clear the error.

FDISK—A Dos command and a utility in Windows that allows you to partition drives. Fdisk is cruder and a lot harder to use than commercial software that lets you do the same thing as fdisk but with a graphical interface. One such application is Partition Magic by PowerQuest that allows something as complex as partitioning drives to be a relatively easy task.

File—A collection of data that is stored as one unit.

File Allocation Table—Table information that is stored in the Data section of a bootable disk (floppy or hard). It normally consists of the first 63 sectors. Information about each file, size, location, and number of sectors used to store the file are kept there. If the table (Table 1) becomes corrupted, there is a backup table (Table 2). Windows uses Table 1 to read files, Scandisk for Windows can also read Table 2 if needed. Fdisk can read Table 2 also, if you use the MBR switch (fdisk/mbr) to repair the boot sector. If the Table becomes corrupted this is known as losing the FAT.

File Attachments—SEE ATTACHMENTS

File Format—All Windows files have a 3-letter extension that determines what format they are in. Some common file formats that are widely used across the Internet are GIF, JPG, and BMP. The format of a file determines what application is needed to open that file. Sometimes, it is necessary to have a particular program installed on your computer to read a proprietary file format or a file that is not widely accepted across the Internet.

File Transfer Protocol—FTP—A standardized, text-based method of transferring files over telephone lines from one computer to another. FTP often refers to a standard way of transferring many types of files over the Internet.

Firewall—A software and hardware implementation that protects an internal network from penetration and damage originating from an outside network. Also, a security model that allows a company to connect its internal network to the Internet—Allows for PUBLIC ("Sacrificial") and PRIVATE servers.

Fixed Disk—A disk such as a hard drive (C drive) that is permanent and cannot be easily removed. A fixed disk is in contrast to a removable disk. Compare fixed disk and removable storage media definitions.

Folder—A directory on a computer that can contain files. A folder will normally appear on a computer as a tiny folder icon that looks like a manila folder that you would use to store papers in a filing cabinet.

Font—The styles in which text appears. Some examples of fonts include, Times New Roman, Ariel, and Courier New.

Foreground Task—An operation or program that is being performed while another task is working in the background.

Formatting—This is the preparation of a diskette to be used for storage.

FTP—See File Transfer Protocol

Function Keys—The row of keys on top or on the side of the keyboard that are used for doing special tasks. (F1-F12)

General Protection Fault—When the operating system cannot process a command generated by a program it falters and cannot continue without dropping the command from memory. GPFs are displayed as an Illegal Operation something like Explorer caused an invalid page fault in module Kernel32.dll@01104:44455. This could be compared to a Fatal OE known as the Blue Screen of Death.

GIF—Graphics Interface Format—(Pronounced "jiff"). A method used to compress and transfer graphics images into digital information; it is commonly used to transfer graphics files on the Internet because of its excellent display of solid colors on all Web browsers.

Gigabyte—A unit of memory measurement that is equal to one billion bytes.

Gopher—Grouping of information servers throughout the Internet. Displays Internet documents and services as lists of menu options. If you select a menu choice, Gopher either displays a document (usually text only) or transfers you to a different Gopher system.

GPF—See General Protection Fault

Graphical User Interface—See GUI

Graphics Interface Format—See GIF

GUI—Graphical User Interface—The icons, graphics, toolbars and menu items that can be clicked on to perform functions on a computer. As far as an IBM-based machine, GUI first appeared in Windows 3.x; prior to that, computers were text-based. It was necessary to type cryptic-looking commands in DOS to operate an IBM machine before the graphical user interface.

Handshake—Noise that you will hear if your modem speaker is not turned off that represents the modem negotiation with a remote computer. A handshake sounds like a screeching noise that comes from data bits being shoved through the copper telephone wire as well as modulation and demodulation.

Hard Disk—A "hard" platter that stores mass amounts of information for extended periods of time.

Hardmodem—Modem that does not require software to be running all of the time in the background to function. They usually have their own processor or power and are not dependent on the power of the computer's Central Processing Unit (CPU). Compare a softmodem.

Hardware—Any peripheral of the computer that are tangible. Examples of hardware include the keyboard, modem, sound card, video card, mouse, and hard drive.

Hashed Password—A password encrypted with a very simple cipher that is easily broken if the password is picked up in transmission.

Helper Applications—Essentially browser plug-ins. Plug-ins were called helper applications in older versions of Web browsers.

History—A folder in the Windows directory that contains a trail of where you have been on the Web. Hence, you will usually find that there is a list of WWW addresses in the History folder.

Home Page—Document intended to serve as an initial point of entry to a web of related documents. It is also called a Welcome page. Contains general introductory information, as well as hyperlinks to related resources. A well-designed home page contains internal navigation buttons, which help users find their way among the various documents that the home page makes available.

HTML—Hypertext Markup Language—A language used to create electronic documents, especially pages on the World Wide Web, that contain connections called hyperlinks. Hyperlinks allow users to jump from one document to a related document by clicking an icon or a hypertext phrase. For instance, you might jump from a company logo or name on a Web page to the company's home page on the Internet.

HTTP—Hypertext Transfer Protocol—The set of standards that lets users of the World Wide Web exchange information found in Web pages. Web browser software is used to read documents formatted and delivered according to HTTP. The beginning of every Web address, "http://", tells the browser that the address' document is HTTP-compatible.

Hyperlink—An icon, graphic, or word in a file that, when clicked with the mouse, automatically opens another file for viewing. World Wide Web pages often include hyperlinks that display other Web pages when selected. Usually these hyperlinked pages are related in some way to the first page. Hyperlinks include the address or names of the files to which they point, but typically this code is hidden from the user.

Hypermedia—Combination of hypertext and multimedia on a Web page.

Hypertext—Also know as HTML, it is a type of text that allows embedded links to other documents. Clicking on or selecting a hypertext link (hyperlink) summons another document or section of a document to appear.

Hypertext Markup Language—See HTML

Hypertext Transfer Protocol—See HTTP

IDE—Integrated Drive Electronics—A standard in computer engineering that has since turned into Enhanced IDE. IDE has one channel on which 2 drives can be installed. EIDE added another channel so that a total of 4 drives could be installed on a computer. IDE can't move data as fast as its enhanced counterpart and it can't support as large of drives either.

I/O Port—An address given to a computer component. This address is specific to only that one component and no other. It is kind of like a street address. Your neighbor and you do not have the same address just as computer components don't have the same I/O port.

Illegal Operation—Error message that may be seen on a Windows-based computer. It does not mean that you have done anything wrong, but it is the way that Microsoft worded the message in the programming code that makes it sound somewhat intimidating.

IMAP—Interactive Mail Access Protocol—A standard Internet e-mail protocol that has superceded POP protocols. The POP (Post Office Protocol) is still widely used, although a lot of newer mail clients support IMAP as well.

Integrated Drive Electronics—SEE IDE

Interrupt Request Line—(or IRQ or Interrupt)—An interrupt is an address given to computer components like an I/O address. Unlike the I/O port, not every computer component has an interrupt.

Internet—The global Transmission Control Protocol/Internet Protocol (TCP/IP) network linking millions of computers for communications purposes. The Internet originally was developed in 1969 for the U.S. military and gradually grew to include educational and research institutions. Today, commercial industries, corporations, and home users all communicate over the Internet, sharing software, messages, and information. The most famous aspect of the Internet is the World Wide Web, a system of files saved in Hypertext Markup Language (HTML) format.

Internet Backbone—Communications networks that tie together the various infrastructural components that make the Internet work. These high-speed data lines are the fastest and most direct routes for Internet data to travel, and they carry the most Internet traffic.

Internet Options—Applet in the control panel where you can adjust all of the possible settings for the Microsoft Internet Explorer Web browser.

Internet Connection Wizard—A component of Internet Explorer that walks you through setting up your Internet connection.

Internet Protocol—See IP

Internet Relay Chat—See IRC

Internet Service Provider—See ISP

Integrated Services Digital Network—See ISDN

InterNIC—Internet Network Information Center—A private agency responsible for registering World Wide Web site domain names.

Interrupt Request Lines—Hardware lines over which devices can send signals to get the attention of the processor when the device is ready to accept or send information. Typically, each device connected to the computer uses a separate IRQ. There are 15 IRQs available. No two pieces of hardware can share the same IRQ, with the exception of your IDE controllers. These are usually 14 and 15. A special card can be installed in your machine to make more IRQs available.

IP—Internet Protocol—The address of a computer on a Transmission Control Protocol/Internet Protocol (TCP/IP) network. IP addresses are written as four groups of numbers (each group may consist of as many as three numbers) separated by periods. An example of an IP address is 118.173.113.13.

IRC—Internet Relay Chat—A type of interactive communication on the Internet in which computer users engage in real-time communication.

IRQ—See Interrupt Request Lines

ISDN—Integrated Services Digital Network—A telecommunications network that allows digital voice, video and data transmissions. ISDN replaces the slow and inefficient analog telephone system with a fast digital network. ISDN lines can transmit data at 128Kbps. Special equipment is required to connect to ISDN lines, which may soon become as affordable as other communications services.

ISP—Internet Service Provider—An organization that lets users dial into it's computers to connect to its Internet link for a fee. ISPs generally provide only an Internet connection, an e-mail address, and maybe World Wide Web browsing software. You can use an ISP based in your town that offers an access number in your local calling area or a national ISP that provides local-access numbers across the country. You also can connect to the Internet through a commercial online service, such as America Online or CompuServe. With this kind of connection, you get Internet access and the proprietary features offered by the online service, such as chat rooms and searchable databases.

Jazz Drive—A removable storage device medium that has a high-storage capacity. Disks available for a Jazz drive hold either 1GB or 2GB, respectively. It is not industry standard, meaning that a Jazz drive must be installed on a particular system to be able to read the removable disks.

Joint Photographic Experts Group—See JPEG

JPEG—Joint Photographic Experts Group—(Pronounced "jay-peg") A color image graphics compression format in which a lossy compression method is used and some data is sacrificed to achieve greater compression.

Jumpers—Little electrical prongs that allow for manual configuration of a legacy device. Little plastic caps can be positioned over metal prongs in various combinations that determine the interrupt request and the I/O address of a device. These were mainly in use before plug & play prior to Windows 95. They are still on some hardware such as hard disks where you position the jumpers one way to make the drive a primary and another way to make it a slave drive.

Juno—A fully-featured Internet Service Provider. They once had a free e-mail program that is still in use today. The free e-mail service is somewhat antiquated compared to today's standards, however; it offers nothing but e-mail at a 9600 baud connection.

Keyboard—The typewriter-like input device that is used with a computer. A standard keyboard has 101 keys, and there is a number pad on the far right-hand side that resembles a calculator.

Keyboard Commands—A series of either 2 or 3 keys that can be pressed simultaneously on the keyboard to invoke a particular function. For example, the CTRL+ESC keys pressed simultaneously will bring up the Start menu, and pressing the CTRL+ALT+DEL keys twice in rapid succession will warm boot the computer.

Kilobyte—1024 bytes of data

LAN—Local Area Network—A group of computers that are joined in some way, usually by a physical cable, in order to share resources such as printers, scanners, and files.

Laptop—A portable computer that can either be plugged into an electrical source or it can run off of a battery for a limited amount of time before the battery needs to be recharged.

Legacy—The way that hardware was classified before plug and play. Legacy devices needed to be manually configured by adjusting jumpers or dip switches in contrast to plug and play whereby the computer generally detects the device itself and an installation wizard walks you through the process of setting up the hardware.

Local Area Network—See LAN

Lynx—A Web browser like Microsoft Internet Explorer or Netscape, but Lynx is not that widely used. Like the Opera browser, it tends to have a niche group of users.

Macintosh—Type of computer and operating system that rivals Microsoft Windows. It is not nearly as widely used as Windows, but it has grown in popularity to the point where it has a major foot hold in the computer industry. The Mac OS is more widely used in end user environments than any other operating system save Microsoft Windows.

Macros—A series of keyboard and mouse actions recorded to a single key, symbol, or name. Macros are helpful when you perform a task often.

Mailer Daemon—An automated response that is sent out via e-mail from a mail server; it does not come from a human being, but it is a computer-generated response that you will usually receive if your e-mail was undeliverable.

Mail Header—In e-mail, a header lists what mail server or servers the mail has passed through from point A to point B. In other words, it tells you where the e-mail originated from and where it was sent to and everywhere in between.

Mainboard—SEE MOTHERBOARD

Manufacturer—Companies that actually make computers. Some examples of large well-known manufacturers include Hewlett Packard, Gateway, Compaq, and Dell.

Math Co-Processor—A chip that is used to increase the speed of math functions. It is designed to handle the majority of math computations so the CPU can handle all the rest of the processing.

Megabyte (MB)—A measure of information totaling one million bytes (technically 1,048,576 bytes). This is commonly used to show size of hard disks, amount of memory, and the size of files.

Memory Address—A space that is allocated to processes on your computer. Each process is allocated its own address; when you get a message that a program has performed an Illegal Operation, two processes tried to occupy the same space at the same time and thus bumped heads. An analogy to memory addressing would be a parking lot. Each car has its own space where it can park; when two cars try to pull into the same space at the same time, it would be equivalent to a GPF (Illegal Operation) on a computer.

Memory Allocation—Windows uses the random access memory (RAM) and a virtual memory address (Swap File). Windows places information into RAM and then moves it to the Swap File when it needs to make more room in RAM; it moves the information into the Swap File that is not needed immediately.

Memory Manager—A program that tries to maximize the utilization of memory by the computer.

Memory Resident—A program that is loaded but not currently functioning. You can usually access this program by pressing a combination of keys like ALT-TAB.

Menu Bar Item—The words that are printed across the top of a window above the Toolbar. These usually include at least *File Edit View* and *Help*.

Metacrawler—Popular search engine that is technically a multi-search engine meaning that it has the ability to search many search engines at once.

Microprocessor—Also called the CPU or Central Processing Unit; it is essentially the brain of the computer that controls all of the hardware, and how fast the computer can perform operations depends on the speed of the Microprocessor. The speed is expressed in Megahertz (Mz) such as 800Mz.

Microsoft Internet Explorer—Microsoft's popular Web browser that is integrated into Windows 98. Windows 95 could function without Internet Explorer, but for all practical purposes Explorer has to be included in Windows 98 in order for Windows to work properly. Therefore, it can't be easily removed from Windows 98 like it could with Windows 95. The only other browser that comes close to Explorer's popularity is the Netscape browser, running a distance second to Explorer.

Microsoft Network—See MSN

Microsoft Outlook—Popular e-mail program; a condensed version, called Outlook Express, comes integrated with the Microsoft Internet Explorer Web browser.

MIDI—Musical Instrument Digital Interface—Device that bridges the gap between a musical instrument and a computer. With a MIDI and the right software, you can perform such tasks as automatically making sheet music that reflects the notes that you play on an instrument.

Mime—Multi-Part Internet Mail Extensions—Because there is no Internet standard for e-mail yet, sometimes when you attach several files at one time to e-mail, the Internet e-mail system may encode the file attachment in MIME format to facilitate its transfer across the Internet. Essentially, the Internet may compress all of the files into one MIME file (.mim extension), and it is necessary to have an application that is capable of decoding or decompressing the file in order to be able to view it.

Minimize—You can minimize any Windows on a Windows operating system by clicking the – sign in the upper-right hand corner of a window. This shrinks it down to the Taskbar, usually located at the bottom of the screen, and you can maximize the window again simply by clicking on its icon on the Taskbar.

Modem—Acronym for *mo*dulator/*de*modulator. The device that lets a computer transmit and receive information over the telephone lines by converting digital data from computers into analog data that can be transmitted over phone lines. The opposite process takes place on the receiving end. Modems are the primary way computer users connect to outside networks, such as the Internet.

Modulate—A modem modulates information so that it can be sent over a standard telephone line. In other words, a modem converts digital data to an analog signal so that the data can be transferred via a phone line.

Monitor—Also called the screen or CRT, this is the output device that allows you to view what your computer is doing. (Hint: It looks like a TV)

Motherboard—This is the foundation of your computer. Everything in the computer is attached in some way to the motherboard by a cable or connector. The motherboard also houses the CPU and memory.

Mouse—A device that can be rolled across a flat surface to position the cursor on the computer screen. A mouse normally has 2 buttons—the left one controls all of the elementary functions that can be performed by either a single-click or a double-click. The right mouse button will produce a drop-down list where some specialized functions can be performed. A mouse may have 3 buttons; the 3rd button can perform even more specialized functions. There are other special features that you can find on some mice such as a wheel on the top that can be used to scroll documents or a track ball, a ball that you roll on top of the mouse to position the cursor instead of pushing the mouse around on a flat surface.

Mouse Pad—A place mat that you roll a mouse on to improve the traction of the ball on the bottom of a mouse that controls the cursor movement. A mouse pad generally has a rubber-like surface to maximize the traction.

MSN—Microsoft Network—An Internet Service Provider that is owned and operated by the Microsoft Corporation.

Multimedia—Multimedia is a description of anything that uses more than one media to achieve a desired effect. In the real word, an example of multimedia is a movie theater that uses picture and sound to achieve its desired affect. In the world of computers, multimedia would be the use of sound, pictures, video, and voice to achieve a desired affect of entertainment or education.

Multitasking—Running two or more programs at the same time.

Musical Instrument Digital Interface—SEE MIDI

National Science Foundation Network—See NSFNet

Netiquette—Slang for the unwritten rules of Internet courtesy.

Netscape Navigator—Popular Web browser that is still a distance second to Microsoft Internet Explorer, however many people use both Netscape and Explorer.

Network—A set of conjoined computers that can share storage devices, peripherals, and applications. Networks may be connected directly by cable connection or indirectly by telephone lines or satellites and can be part of a small-office system or a global web of numerous other networks.

Network News Transfer Protocol—See NNTP

Newsgroup—A group of messages about a single topic. On the Internet, newsgroups bring together people around the world for discussion of shared interests.

Notepad—A simple word processor and text editor that is included with the Windows program. It is very rudimentary, but it is effective to do simple tasks, like type a letter, when you don't need to do a lot of fancy text formatting.

NNTP—Network News Transfer Protocol—Industry standard protocol for the distribution, inquiry, retrieval, and posting of news articles to newsgroups on the Internet.

NSFNet—National Science Foundation Network—A network that was originated circa 1980 that consisted of mainly academics and scientists. This network joined with ARPANet, beginning the Internet as we know it today.

OCR—See Optical Character Recognition

Online Services—Any number of electronic forums that can be accessed via a modem. Examples of these are Prodigy, America Online, and CompuServe. On them you can receive a variety of information and can chat with people all over the world.

Opera—A Web browser that sort of has a niche user group.

Operating System—A complex set of instructions that tell a computer and its hardware how to function. Operating systems include Windows, MAC OS, Linux, Unix, and OS/2 as well as many others.

Optical Character Recognition—The process in which the images of letters, entered into a computer with a scanner, are translated into characters that are worked with in the computer as text, not as an image. OCR is far from perfect, but it is a fast method for digitizing typed pages of text. Some computer fax applications also use OCR to transform incoming faxes from graphics files to word processing documents.

Outlook—Popular e-mail program made by Microsoft.

Parallel—Type of port to which most printers and some external components are connected. Parallel ports transmit data 8 bits at a time.

Parallel Port—A card that fits into a slot on the motherboard that houses a parallel cable that might come from a printer or scanner. In other words, where the other end of your cable from a printer plugs into is going to be the parallel port.

Partition—A portion of the hard drive that is formatted to hold data. A hard drive may just have one partition or more; partitions can be formatted using several different drive structures such as FAT, FAT32, or NTFS.

Patch—A piece of code inserted into software to temporarily fix a defect. While most users do not consider a patch as a shortcut or a shabby way to fix a problem, adding too many can make a program difficult to maintain. Programmers often create patches to fix problems and add features to a program during the timeframe when users are awaiting the release of a new version of the program that already includes the "patched" corrections and new features.

Path—This defines exactly where a file, folder, or directory is located on a drive of the computer. For example, if there were a text document called letter.txt on the hard drive in a folder called Mytextfiles, the path to the text file would be C:\Mytextfiles\letter.txt.

Pegasus—An e-mail program, like Outlook, but it is not that widely used.

Peripheral—Any physical device connected to the computer.

Physical Memory—This is the Random Access Memory (RAM) on a computer. You can view the physical memory by clicking on Help then About Windows in the My Computer window.

PIM—Personal Information Manager—Program that helps users get more organized. PIMs often include calendars, telephone lists, and programmable reminders that are easy to use. Some PIMs included in operating systems or office suites also can be purchased separately. Some of the best-known PIMs include Microsoft Schedule+ and Starfish Software's Sidekick.

Ping—DOS command that will tell you how long it takes for a signal to pass from point A to point B on the Internet.

Pitch—Number of dots per inch used as a measure of typed characters.

Pixel—The smallest part of an image that a computer printer or display can control. An image on a computer monitor consists of hundreds of thousands of pixels, arranged in such a manner that they appear to each be connected. Each pixel on a color monitor comprises three colored (blue, red, and green) dots. The term comes from the words picture element and also is abbreviated PEL (Pronounced *pell*).

Plain-Vanilla ISP—An ISP that offers a connection to the Internet and that's it. A no frills ISP that may include an e-mail account and but no more. These are generally harder to use than an online service because they don't offer the handholding that a lot of the online services have.

Plug & Play—The user-friendly hardware installation that came about with Windows 95. Prior to that time, hardware was known as legacy; it was necessary to manually configure legacy hardware with jumpers or dip switches to make them work on a system. Plug & play means that you can usually just plug hardware in, boot the computer, and the installation is automated by the operating system.

Plug-Ins—Software that expands the features of main programs and adds multimedia capabilities to Web browsers. A plug-in is a small program that "plugs into" a large application and runs as a part of that application.

Point-To-Point Protocol—See PPP

POP—Post Office Protocol—A protocol that manages your Internet mail until you pick it up from your ISP.

POTS—Plain Old Telephone Service—Acronym that defines an analog connection as opposed to a high-speed connection such as a cable modem.

PPP—Point-To-Point Protocol—A communications language that lets users connect their PCs directly to the Internet through their telephone lines. Considered more advanced than the Serial Line Internet Protocol (SLIP) connection it is quickly replacing, PPP offers more error-checking capabilities as well as several forms of password protection.

Port—A connector that allows peripherals to be connected to the computer.

Portal—A site on the Web that offers a wide variety of resources, such as new articles, and services, such as e-mail, Web site hosting, and online shopping. Online services such as America Online were the first portals. Traditional search engines and computer giants such as Netscape and Microsoft are currently positioning themselves to take advantage of the interest in portals.

Postmaster—In the Internet world, the person that is responsible for handing the flow of mail for a domain. A Postmaster is an actual human being whereas Mailer Daemon is a computer-generated response from a mail server that is generated when e-mail is undeliverable.

Private Key—The secret half of a two-part public key encryption system. The private key is kept secret and never transmitted over an open network. The private key is used to decode data that has been encrypted with a user's public key, which is available to everyone over a network. In this way, a person can send information encrypted with Ron's public key, safe in the knowledge that only the holder of Ron's private key will be able to read it.

Prompt—On screen symbol that tells the user that the computer is ready to accept information or requests.

Proprietary—In general, something that is not used by everybody or that is specific to a certain company or agency. In the computer world, you may frequently hear programs or applets referred to as proprietary. i.e. proprietary e-mail, proprietary dialer.

Proprietary Dialer—A dialer that is used by a specific Internet provider or online service to connect to their system. Since it is proprietary, it will not work to connect any other ISP to the Internet besides the one that it is specifically designed for. Dial-up Networking is known as a standard dialer because it comes installed on all Windows machines (called Remote Access Service on Windows NT but virtually the same thing) and it is used by most standard ISPs. America Online is one service that has a proprietary dialer and does not use Dial-up Networking.

Public Key—The public part of a two-part encryption system. Users can encrypt information using someone's public key with the knowledge that only the owner of the corresponding private key will be able to open it. Conversely, users can encrypt information with their private keys so that the only way to read it is to decode it with the commonly available public key. This way, other users know for sure who sent data because only the correct public key will decode the information.

Push Technology—Personalized news and information from the Internet that can be delivered to you on a timely basis. One of the biggest buzzwords in the computer industry, a big advantage of push is that you can customize the news content that you receive to your liking. Whereas with newspaper technology, you get the whole thing—like it or not. The big names in push technology are PointCast, Marimba Castanet, and AirMedia Live. A lot of push client software displays information in a small window at the bottom of your screen. This small window is called a ticker. Some of these tickers include IBM News Ticker and My Yahoo! News Ticker. Sometimes, push takes the form of a screensaver that displays the latest news of your choice when the computer is idle. AfterDark Online and PointCast take the screensaver form of push.

Quick Launch Toolbar—**The little set of icons that are located between the Start button and the Taskbar. You can add things to this toolbar to make them easily accessible thus making it convenient to launch a program.**

Radio dials—The little hollow circles that you will find on some screens on the computer where a choice is required. You click inside the circle of the choice that you want, and it will put a little black dot inside the circle indicating your selection. They are called radio dials after the antiquated car radios that were around when 8-tracks were prevalent. The little knobs that had to be turned to change radio stations were called radio dials.

Random Access Memory—See RAM

RAM—Random Access Memory—Memory that is available to programs when the computer is running. When the computer is off, all information stored in the memory is lost.

Read Only Memory—See ROM

Read The Freaking Manual—See RTFM

Refresh Rate—The number of times per minute that a computer screen image is renewed.

Registry—The hierarchical program that controls the most rudimentary functions of Windows. It has the look of the Windows Explorer, but it essentially consists of 6 keys that control different functions of the system. The registry is composed of 2 files: user.dat and system.dat.

Removable Storage Media—Any drive that has a disk that can be removed easily. Essentially any drive that is not a fixed disk. Removable drives include floppy drives, Zip drives, CD-ROM drives, and Jazz drives.

Resolution—The amount of definition and clarity in an image on a monitor or from a printer. In monitors, resolution is measured by the number of pixels the device can display. In printers, resolution is measured in dots per inch (dpi) that can be printed on paper. Generally a user can dictate the number of pixels on a monitor, up to its capacity, by changing the display standards. In Windows, this capability is found in the Control Panel Display applet.

Restore Disk—A lot of computer manufacturers will include one of these in their software package. It provides an easy way to restore the computer back to the way it was when it was new. In other words, a restore disk will reinstall Windows and set all of the hardware configurations to factory default.

Ribbon Cable—Wide gray cable that attaches the internal drives of the computer to their controller cards.

ROM—Read Only Memory—Memory that is available to the computer only. Programs can not use it. ROM does not lose its information when the machine is turned off.

Root Directory—The mother of all directories. The root directory is the one from which all the other directories branch out; it has no parent directory. The root directory of a drive is the letter name of that drive followed by a backslash; for example, the root directory of the C: drive is the C:\DIRECTORY.

RTFM—Read The Freaking Manual—A techie acronym that is often used to allude to novice computer users that have a question that is answered in the computer manual.

Safe Mode—A diagnostic mode that a computer can sometimes be started in if it will not start normally. Safe Mode doesn't load any of the specific device drivers or anything that's not absolutely essential for Windows to boot. Frequently, when a computer won't start, it is due to a corrupt or conflicting driver and that is why Safe Mode is likely to start; it will not load that troublesome driver that is preventing the system from starting normally. Therefore, you can uninstall or change the driver that is keeping the computer from booting and then reboot in Normal Mode.

Scandisk—A Windows diagnostic program that is built into the operating system that scans the drive for errors and usually has the ability to self-fix them.

Screensaver—An animated picture or graphic that can be programmed through the Display control panel to come on the computer screen after so much inactivity time has elapsed. The main reason for a screensaver is to reduce wear and tear on the CRT (Cathode Ray Tube) inside the monitor that can burn out or become etched if the same window is left on for extended periods of time.

SCSI—Small Computer System Interface (Pronounced scuz-zee)—A standard for parallel interfaces that transfers information at a rate of up to 80MBps (megabytes per second). Up to seven peripheral devices, such as a hard drive and CD-ROM drive, can attach to a single SCSI port on the system's bus. SCSI ports were designed for Apple Macintosh and Unix Computers, but also can be used with properly equipped PCs.

SCSI ID—Number assigned to a SCSI device to set it apart from the other SCSI devices in the computer. The SCSI controller is usually seven and the boot hard drive is usually zero.

Search Engine—Software that searches through a database (a large cache of information) located on your computer. At Web-based search engines, users type a keyword query (descriptor words), and the search engine responds with a list of all sites in its database fitting the query description.

Secure Socket Layer—See SSL

Serial—A type of port that is usually used for the mouse and other external components such as a scanner. Serial ports transmit data one bit at a time.

Serial Line Internet Protocol—See SLIP

Server—A computer that is dedicated to a specific purpose such as a mail server or Web server. A server can actually be dedicated or non-dedicated. The latter is when a computer is used as a server of some sort and used for basic personal computing.

Shareware—Copyrighted software distributed on a time-restricted trial basis either via the Internet or by being passed along by satisfied customers.

Shorthand—In Internet lingo, these are really acronyms that are used in chat rooms and in newsgroups frequently to help abbreviate the conversation or message. An example of Internet shorthand is IIRC—If I remember correctly.

Signature File—A block signature that you can program your e-mail client to insert into every e-mail that you send out. It may include your real name or even a graphic of some sort that represents you or your company; these things will normally appear at the bottom of all of the e-mail that you send out once it is programmed into your mail program.

SIMM—See Single In-Line Memory Module

Simple Mail Transfer Protocol—See SMTP

Single In-Line Memory Module—A slender circuit board dedicated to storing memory chips. The chips are random access memory (RAM) upgrade chips used to expand the system's RAM capacity.

SLIP—Serial Line Internet Protocol—An Internet protocol that lets users gain 'Net access with a modem and a phone line. SLIP lets users link directly to the 'Net through an Internet service provider (ISP). It is slowly being replaced with its successor, Point-To-Point Protocol (PPP).

Small Computer System Interface—See SCSI

SMTP—Simple Mail Transfer Protocol—A mail server that handles the flow of all outgoing mail.

Smiley—Also referred to as emoticons. These are symbols that are used to portray moods or emotions. For example, ;-) is a winking smiley face. You may have to tilt your head sideways to recognize it. Smileys are usually used in chat rooms, e-mail, or instant messages to portray an entire mood or idea in just a symbol or combination of symbols. The stock smiley (J) can denote humor or sarcasm depending on the context in which it is used. See the long list of emoticons in the Appendix.

Snail Mail—Conventional mail handled by the United States Post Office. Snail mail was dubbed after e-mail was invented since electronic mail is so much faster.

Soft Modem—A modem that requires software to operate; usually these modems do not have their own processor, requiring the processing power of the CPU. As a result, soft modems use more computer resources than hard modems, but they are less expensive.

Soft Power Button—A power button to shut down or start a computer that can be programmed to have a delay of so many seconds. For instance, you can program the computer to require that the power button be held in for 5 seconds for the computer to be started or shut down.

Software—A set of instructions that can be executed on a computer to perform a specific function or functions.

***Sound Card**—An expansion card that adds audio capability beyond basic beeps.*

SSL—Secure Socket Layer—A method of securing the transmission of confidential data through the Internet.

Standalone Computer—A computer that is not networked or directly linked with other computers.

Start Menu—The menu that ensues after clicking on the Start button; it can be invoked by pressing CTRL+ESC simultaneously.

Start Up Group—Applications that are programmed to load up and run in the background as soon as the computer is started. They are contained in a folder called Start Menu that is in the Windows directory; you can view all of these start up programs by looking at the list in the Close Program window.

Streaming Audio—An audio format experienced in real-time—users hear the audio file as it is downloaded without waiting for it to be completely downloaded.

Streaming Video—Technology that allows a user to see the contents of a video file as it is downloaded without waiting for the entire content of the file to be downloaded.

SuperDisk—A removable storage medium that resembles a floppy drive, but it has a much higher capacity or 120MB.

SVGA—Super Video Graphics Array—

Switch—A parameter added to a DOS command to modify or specialize it. This is done by adding a forward slash after the command and proceeded by the switch. For example, a "/h" switch will usually give help on how to use the command.

System—**1** Applet in the control panel where you can access the Device Manager where all of the installed hardware is listed. **2** The computer itself as a whole.

System Administrator—Someone that is responsible for the configuration, maintenance, and security of a network. A Sys Admin Usually works in a corporate LAN environment.

System Resources—Defines how efficiently the computer is using the memory that it has available. The resources are expressed as a percentage and can be seen in My Computer by clicking Help then About Windows.

Systray—System Tray—The little section where the system clock sits usually in the lower-right corner of the Desktop. Sometimes, there will be a little megaphone on the Systray that you can use to adjust the speaker volume.

T1—A type of data connection able to transmit a digital signal at 1.544 megabits per second. T1 lines often are used to link large computer networks together, such as those that make up the Internet.

T3—A type of data connection able to transmit a digital signal at 44.746 megabits per second. Since this is about 40 times faster than T1 lines, large corporations, particularly computer or communications-type companies, will typically be networked with a T3 connection.

Tagram—The Tagram is what controls the speed enhancing feature of the computer, the cache memory.

TAPI—Telephone Application Programmers Interface—

Taskbar—Located between the Start button and the System Tray, the Taskbar will contain a rectangular icon for each program that is currently running at the time. If there are a lot of programs on the Taskbar, the icons will look more square and almost like they are stacked on top of one another.

TCP/IP—Transmission Control Protocol/Internet Protocol—A protocol governing communication among all computers on the Internet. It dictates how packets of information are sent over networks and ensures the reliability of data transmissions across Internet-connected networks.

TCP/IP Stack—Needed to properly use the TCP/IP protocol. A stack consists of TCP/IP software, sockets software (wsock.dll in Windows machines), and hardware drivers called packet drivers. Windows operating systems come with a TCP/IP stack built in including the wsock32.dll file.

Telephony—Technology that lets users use a PC to make and receive telephone calls. Telephony software often includes features such as voice mail, fax, auto dialing, and on-screen messaging.

Template—A ready-to-use, permanent document setup with basic layout, formatting commands, and formulas. Users can enter information to create individualized reports, letters and other documents.

Temporary Internet Files—A folder in the Windows directory that contains the text and graphics of every Web site that you have visited with Microsoft Internet Explorer.

Terabyte—1000 gigabytes or 1 trillion bytes.

Third-Party Programs—So called because these are applications that are not manufactured by your ISP or computer manufacturer, thus they belong to a 3rd party software maker. It could refer to an application that is not made by your company or the computer manufacturer or any similar circumstance.

Thumbnail—This is a miniature icon that represents a graphic and the icon is the graphic itself. In Windows Explorer, you can set the icons to be displayed as thumbnails by clicking View then Thumbnails.

TIFF—Tagged Image File Format (Pronounced *tiff*)—A common way to store bit-mapped graphic images on both PCs and Macintosh computers. TIFF is a platform-independent format, which means a TIFF image created on a PC can be viewed on a Macintosh, and vice versa. Bit-map files, on the other hand, are a graphic format for the Windows environment. This format was specifically designed for scanned images and is commonly used for that purpose. It can also be used in some applications to save images created on a computer. TIFF graphics can be color, grayscale, or black and white. The file extension for TIFF images is .tif.

Toolbar—Bar that is at the top of many windows on your computer. It lies beneath the Menu Bar and usually consists of a series of icons each offering different options or functions when clicked on.

Tower Unit—The box that houses all of the computer components.

Trace Route—A helpful Windows DOS command that will tell you the hops that a signal takes between server A and server B on the Internet and every server in between the 2 points that the signal may pass through.

Transmission Control Protocol/Internet Protocol—See TCP/IP

Trojan Horse—A program that is usually disguised as something fun or attractive like a graphic or screensaver, but that is really similar to a virus. Typically, A trojan horse program will not do any severe damage to your computer, unlike a virus, but it will do annoying things that are similar to a practical joke. For example, a trojan may make your computer not shut down when you choose to do so, or it may make your screen freeze when you sign onto your ISP. When the trojan is abolished, your computer will usually go back to working normally without having to reinstall Windows or something of that nature. A trojan carries within itself a means to allow the program's creator access to the system using it.

Universal Resource Locator—See URL

UNIX—Computer operating system that is designed to be used by many people at the same time. It is the most common operating system for servers on the Internet and it has TCP/IP integrated into it.

Update—To replace older versions of software or files with a newer version. Also refers to when a company releases a new version of software that's already on the market. This is usually indicated by a change in the version number, such as changing from 6.2 to 6.21. These software updates usually fix minor problems, or bugs, the older version contained.

Upload—To send or transmit a file from one computer to another via modem.

URL—Universal Resource Locator—In short, an Internet address. A standardized naming or addressing system for documents and media accessible over the Internet. For example, *http://www.microsoft.com* includes the type of document {a Hypertext Transfer Protocol [HTTP] document}, and the address of the computer on which it can be found {www.microsoft.com}.

Usenet—More commonly known as newsgroups. There are thousands of groups hosted on hundreds of servers around the world, dealing with nearly any topic imaginable. Newsreader software is required to download and view articles in the groups; the software generally uses the NNTP protocol. However, you can normally post an article to a group via e-mail.

UUencoding—Unix to Unix Encoding—A method for converting files from Binary to ASCII (text) so that they can be sent across the Internet via e-mail.

UUNET—The "Bulletin board of the Internet." Contains a collection of more than 20,000 discussion forums called newsgroups.

Veronica—Searches Gopher sites for file names and directories and consists of index server and search tool.

VESA—Video Electronics Standard Association—Newer protocol that supercedes VGA (Video Graphics Array) and SVGA (Super Video Graphics Array). It offers more support for new video cards available today that have a lot of RAM memory and can offer close to true-to-life 3d-rendering.

VGA—Video Graphics Array—

Video Capture Card—A special type of video card that is needed to perform certain functions such as to transfer an image from a video camera to your computer screen. There are All-In-Wonder video cards that serve as a video card, video capture card, and they can do such things as enable you to have your TV programs on the computer screen as a picture-in-picture.

Video Card—Hardware that controls how graphics are rendered on your computer monitor screen.

Virtual Memory—A type of hard drive space that mimics actual memory (RAM). When actual memory space is limited, the use of virtual memory can let users work with larger documents and run more software at once.

Virtual Private Networking—VPN—A protocol that can be installed in the Add/Remove Programs applet in the Control Panel (Add/Remove>Windows Setup>Communications). It enables a user to connect directory to another computer via the Dial-up Networking program and the data transmission is encrypted thus making it private.

Virus—A nasty program that is designed to harm your computer in some way. Some are nothing more than annoying pranks, and others can destroy the information on the hard drive or permanently damage internal components. Watch out and protect yourself from them using Anti-Virus software.

W3—World Wide Web Consortium—Organization that is responsible for establishing standard protocols on the WWW. More can be learned about the W3 by visiting their Web site at www.w3.org.

WAIS—Wide Area Information Server—A Unix-based system linked to the Internet or a program that allows users to search worldwide archives for resources based on a series of key words. Also called a Search Engine and it often times generates a list of documents that contain many "false drops" (irrelevant documents that don't really pertain to the search subject).

Warm Boot—The process of resetting the system by pressing Ctrl+Alt+Del at the same time.

Watermark—A feature in some digital cameras that automatically adds the date, time, text, graphics, borders, or other information to images.

Web—SEE WORLD WIDE WEB

Web Browser—Software that gives access to and navigation of the World Wide Web. Using a graphical interface that lets users click buttons, icons, and menu options to access commands, browsers show Web pages as graphical or text-based documents. Browsers allow users to download pages at different sites either by clicking hyperlinks (graphics or text presented in a different color than the rest of a document, which contains a programming code that connects to another page), or by entering a Web page's address, called a universal resource locator (URL).

Web Client—Synonym for Web browser.

Web Page—A document written in Hypertext Markup Language (HTML) that can be accessed on the Internet. Web pages are found by addresses called universal resource locators (URLs). Web pages can contain information, graphics, and hyperlinks to other Web pages and files.

Web Server—A computer on which a Web page resides. A server may be dedicated, meaning its sole purpose is to be the server, or non-dedicated, meaning it can be used for basic computing in addition to acting as the server. Good performance from a Web server, especially for busy sites, is crucial.

Wide Area Information Server—See WAIS

Windows Explorer—Screen that can be accessed in Windows 95 and above where you can view all of the files installed on the hard drive, or any drive for that matter, in a convenient hierarchical view. This is not to be confused with Internet Explorer, a Web browser made by Microsoft.

Wingdings—A type of font where each letter and number that you press on the keyboard will produce a symbol of some sort such as with the Wingdings2 font, typing the number 4 will produce a ?. There are different versions of the Wingdings font such as Wingdings1, Wingdings2, and Wingdings3; each version will have a different set of symbols associated with it.

WinZip—Application that is available on the Web site *www.winzip.com*. It is capable of unzipping (decompressing) or zipping (compressing) files.

Windows 3.x—Version of Windows that preceded Windows 95. Windows 3.x stands for Windows 3.1 and Windows 3.1.1—Windows for Workgroups—which contained support for networking that Windows 3.1 lacked. While Windows 3.x did have a GUI, it isn't, by definition, an operating system; it is really a Graphical User Interface that overlays DOS (Disk Operating System).

Windows 95—Major upgrade from Windows 3.x and the first genuine operating system for an IBM based machine. The entire look and feel was changed in this Window version over Windows 3.x, and the navigational menus and screens were almost completely different. The Program Manager in 3.x became the Desktop; the File Manager became the Windows Explorer, for example.

Windows NT 4.0—Similar on the surface to Window 95. The bare bones of NT is much different than Windows 95, however. Not actually an upgrade to Window 95, but it is sometimes considered one. It is geared towards a network environment such as a corporate LAN. Windows NT is not as user-friendly as Windows 95, and the 2 operating systems are really best used for their intended purposes. Windows 95 is a better choice for a computer novice or someone that mainly just uses the PC to send e-mail, go to the Web, and do basic tasks such as Word Processing.

Windows NT is the best choice for a computer professional or someone that is very computer literate; it is known for it's increased security over Windows 95 meaning that it would be the best choice for a network—especially where security is a concern.

Windows 98—Direct upgrade from Window 95. Although it is considered a major upgrade, it is not nearly as drastic of a change as from Windows 3.x to Windows 95. Windows 98 appears a lot like Windows 95, but it has many enhancements hidden under its skin. Windows 98 has increased driver support for a lot more hardware than Windows 95 offers; it has increased networking support over Windows 95 as well. Windows 98 has an incremental upgrade called Windows 98 Second Edition; it is a minor upgrade in comparison to the other Windows upgrades, but it has Microsoft Internet Explorer 5.0 integrated into the operating system and it has even more networking support than Windows 98 as well as more multimedia capabilities.

Windows Millennium Edition—Major upgrade from Windows 98 that is the biggest technological advancement to the Windows operating system since the jump from Windows 3.x to Windows 95. It is much more stable than Windows 98, and it has very good unprecedented multimedia capabilities. It does appear similar to Windows 98, but many of the menus, icons, and drop-down lists changed in Windows Millenium. In short, it is a good fully featured stable OS that has many improvements over Windows 98. It's user-friendliness and networking capabilities makes it a wise choice for a computer novice and an expert alike.

Windows 2000 Professional—Windows NT based operating system that is really a direct upgrade path from Windows NT 4.0 Workstation. Like Windows NT, this operating system is best suited to a computer expert or system administrator and computer novices should shy away from this OS unless they have a specific reason for using it.

Winsocks—1 Stands for Windows Sockets. Winsocks is a set of protocols that programmers use for creating TCP/IP applications for use with Windows. **2** Part of the TCP/IP stack that is necessary to use the TCP/IP protocol. In laymen's terms, a file called wsock32.dll is necessary on a Windows machine to make a connection to the Internet. The wsock32.dll file should be located in the C:\Windows\System directory; it should be 65kb in Windows 95, 40kb in Windows 98, and 36kb in Windows Me.

Wordpad—Word processor that is built into Windows 95 and every subsequent version of Windows. Prior to Windows 95, the rudimentary version of the Wordpad program was called Write. It is a rather simple word processor that is more sophisticated than Notepad but simpler than a full-fledged word processor such as Microsoft Word.

World Wide Web—The portion of the Internet that has become the most popular and consists of millions of Web pages that are joined together by hyperlinks.

World Wide Web Consortium—SEE W3

Worm—A computer program that replicates itself and is self-propagating. The main difference between a worm and a virus is that viruses are intended to cause problems on standalone machines and attack boot sectors and files on the hard disk. Worms are specifically designed to permeate network environments. The most notorious worm was the Internet Worm of November 1988. It propagated itself on over 6,000 systems across the Internet.

Zip Drive—A removable storage media kind of like a Jazz drive, but its disks don't hold as much information. However, Zip drives are in much greater use than Jazz drives probably due to the higher cost of Jazz drives and the disks that are needed for them.

Zip File—A file that has been compressed usually to expedite its transfer over the Internet in e-mail. It is necessary to have software that is capable of unzipping or decompressing a zip file. The most popular program that will unzip files is WinZip.

Bibliography

5 Anderson, Heidi V. *Windows Tips & Tricks Superguide To Troubleshoot, Customize & Tweak Windows 98, NT, 95, and 2000* "**Windows File Management**—Organizing Your Files & Folders Into A Logical Sequence," Volume 6 Issue 6 pgs 56-59.

(chapter 16)

Excerpts:

6 Jerome, Marty *PC Computing* Magazine

"The Internet is Crushing Whole Industries...Is Your Company Next?" Golden Opportunity—

February 2000 edition   pgs. 102-104

(chapter 17)

7 Jerome, Marty *PC Computing* Magazine

"The Internet is Crushing Whole Industries...Is Your Company Next?"

February 2000 edition   pg 100

(chapter 17)

8 Jerome, Marty *PC Computing* Magazine

"The Internet is Crushing Whole Industries...Is Your Company Next?"

February 2000 edition pg 98

(chapter 17)

9 Jerome, Marty *PC Computing* Magazine

"The Internet is Crushing Whole Industries...Is Your Company Next?" Golden Opportunity—

February 2000 edition pg 103

(chapter 17)

10 Katz, Jon *Yahoo Internet Life: How America Uses the Net* (Special Anniversary Issue

magazine) "How the Net changed America," pg 97

www.yuk.com * September 1999

(chapter 21)

11 Phelps, Alan *PC Novice Guide to Internet Basics* (Quick Answers to all your Internet

Questions) *special reprint Guide to Series* "Understanding The Internet," Volume 6 Issue 10 p.6

* September 1998

(chapter 21)

12 Phelps, Alan *PC Novice Guide to Internet Basics* (Quick Answers to all your Internet

Questions) *special reprint Guide to Series* "Understanding The Internet," Volume 6 Issue 10 p. 5

* September 1998

(chapter 21)

13 Burns, Joe Phd. "E-mail Netiquette" (newsletter sent via e-mail)

(chapter 22)

14 Phelps, Alan *PC Novice Guide to Internet Basics* (special reprint) "The Life of E-mail," Volume 6 Issue 10 p. 7

(chapter 22)

15 Meers, Trevor *PC Novice Guide to Internet Basics* (special reprint) "No Stamp Required," Volume 6 Issue 10 pg 64-65

(chapter 22)

16 **What if people bought cars like they buy computers?* unknown source. The piece was circulating via e-mail around the Internet.

(chapter 25)

17 Collins, Steve *.net magazine* "**Place Your Bets**—How to win at Net roulette" *Words For The Wise* (The real life and on the Net), issue 48, August 1998, page 78.

(**Appendix R**- Internet Terms Glossary)

18 Lichty, Tom *The Official America Online Tour Guide* version 3 pg 95-96

(**Appendix T-MIME**-Attaching Files to Internet Messages)

Index

_____I_____

www.ingramcontent.com/pod-product-compliance
Lightning Source LLC
Chambersburg PA
CBHW051220050326
40689CB00007B/741